Contents

Preface   v

1   New Rome, New Theories on Inter-Regional Exchange.   1
An Introduction to the East Mediterranean Economy in Late Antiquity
(Sean Kingsley and Michael Decker)

2   Urban Economies of Late Antique Cyrenaica *(Andrew Wilson)*   28

3   The Economic Impact of the Palestinian Wine Trade in Late Antiquity   44
(Sean Kingsley)

4   Food for an Empire: Wine and Oil Production in North Syria   69
(Michael Decker)

5   Beyond the Amphora: Non-Ceramic Evidence for   87
Late Antique Industry and Trade *(Marlia Mundell Mango)*

6   The Economy of Late Antique Cyprus *(Tassos Papacostas)*   107

7   LR2: a Container for the Military *annona* on the Danubian Border?   129
(Olga Karagiorgou)

8   Specialisation, Trade, and Prosperity: an Overview of the Economy   167
of the Late Antique Eastern Mediterranean *(Bryan Ward-Perkins)*

Preface

This collection of papers is based on a one-day conference held at Somerville College, Oxford on 29th May 1999. Around that time, a number of Fellows and doctoral students at the University of Oxford were conducting (or had recently completed) various research into topics both directly and tangentially related to the late antique economy and long-distance exchange in the East Mediterranean (fourth to seventh centuries A.D. in Greece, Cyprus, Syria, Palestine, Egypt, and Libya).[1] This seemed an opportune moment to bring various scholars 'out from the cold' to discuss and compare fresh and unpublished results. We would like to extend our sincere gratitude to all the speakers for their hard work in preparing their presentations, and for finding the time in their busy schedules to transform them into publishable form.[2]

This project was supported morally and academically by several scholars: Bryan Ward-Perkins and Marlia Mango encouraged some of their doctoral students to present new work at the conference, and subsequently 'endorsed' its publication. Bryan Ward-Perkins also made invaluable comments about the text, graciously permitted us to coerce him into penning a summary, and generally supported all stages of the conference and publication unreservedly and with humour; our great appreciation is extended to him. James Howard-Johnston chaired the afternoon session of the conference with his usual aplomb and charm; everyone at the event was extremely pleased that he managed to fly back from Jerusalem in time to attend. The day would simply not have been the same without him.

It is a great regret that illness deprived the conference of the sharp mind, energy, and depth of knowledge of John Lloyd (Lecturer in Roman Archaeology at the Institute of Archaeology, Oxford, and doctoral supervisor to A. Wilson and S. Kingsley), who passed away the day after the conference. Dr. Lloyd's spirit did, however, affect the proceedings deeply: amphorae, quantification techniques, landscape archaeology, and urban economies were all themes which he was fascinated by and passionate about. As unassuming as he was, we would like to think that he would have been proud of how his legacy has been received by a younger generation. Thus, it is wholly appropriate that Andrew Wilson's paper is dedicated to John Lloyd (Dr. Wilson continues his work as the new Lecturer in Roman Archaeology at Oxford, and through the on-going excavations at Euesperides/Benghazi in Libya).

The conference was enthusiastically sponsored by Somerville College. Resources were generously made available from the Katharine and Leonard Woolley Fellowship Fund at Somerville, and we would like to sincerely thank Dame Fiona Caldicott (College Principal), Miriam Griffin, and all the committee for their support and interest. Somerville has an interesting tradition in Near Eastern archaeology, having educated the Biblical Archaeologist Kathleen Kenyon, and bestowed a Fellowship on Prof. Claudine Dauphin (the renowned Byzantinist specialising in demography, society, and mosaics in late antique Palestine). It is fitting that the conference should have been sponsored through the Woolley Fund because Leonard Woolley was a pioneer of late antique archaeology in the East Mediterranean in his own right: at the turn of the twentieth century, along with one T.E. Lawrence (subsequently 'of Arabia'), he surveyed the standing Byzantine ruins in the Negev Desert of southern Palestine on behalf of the Palestine Exploration Fund. Our continued awe at these impressive remains, and on-going endeavours to understand how such an arid landscape was made to blossom, derives directly from their fieldwork and published results (*The Wilderness of Zin*, by C.L. Woolley and T.E. Lawrence 1914–1915 – PEF Annual, 3rd. Volume).

Thanks are also offered to Sandy Hellig for helping arrange the conference logistics; to Phillip Munday and the catering staff for their hard work organising lunch and refreshments; to Mark Merrony for the loan of his precious laptop; to Eric Cooper for assistance proof-reading.

As ever, thanks to our families for trying to understand the personal sacrifices which assembling such a volume requires. Finally, a word of appreciation to Classic FM for late night moments of sanity.

S.A. Kingsley and M.J. Decker
Oxford, 2000

Notes

1   For the purpose of this paper Late Antiquity is defined as extending from the foundation of Constantinople in A.D. 330 to the completion of the Arab conquest *c.* A.D. 640. It should be emphasised that this period is termed 'Byzantine' by archaeologists and historians working in countries located between North Africa and Syria. Where this term appears within the following text, a comparable time-scale is applicable.

2   It is a real regret that we were unable to tempt our eminent 'Egyptian' speaker to submit his paper for publication in our humble volume; we greatly hope he manages to find the time to make his results accessible to the wider scientific community. However, of great importance to the subject of this book is the recent work of Jairus Banaji, to whom we would direct all parties interested in late antique Egypt (see the bibliography in Chapter 1).

New Rome, New Theories on Inter-Regional Exchange. An Introduction to the East Mediterranean Economy in Late Antiquity[1]

Sean Kingsley and Michael Decker

The Later Roman Empire's exchange patterns have long held a fascination for scholars working on the history and archaeology of the western Mediterranean. The wide variety of tools which serve as an interface to examine the economy – historical texts, industrial and agricultural installations, inscriptions, *papyri*, pottery sherds, shipwrecks, and comparative sources – have been integrated in recent decades to forge a remarkably stimulating field, where even the most phlegmatic individual can be caught expressing flashes of passion. The inclusion of a section discussing the economy in a recent summary of the most pivotal topics of contemporary research into Roman society further reflects its ever-increasing centrality to understanding antiquity.[2]

The situation in the East Mediterranean, by contrast, is conspicuously different to that in the West. Although the quantity of archaeological data available continues to increase rapidly, syntheses of the economic landscape of Late Antiquity in this half of the Mediterranean basin are few. Why this is the case is not immediately apparent. Certainly interest in the social and economic life of town and country in ancient times has a long tradition stretching back to the turn of the twentieth century, and even earlier. Travelogues dating between the eighteenth and early twentieth century often described the perceived wonders of ancient agricultural and industrial installations, which were dutifully recorded by representative of the clergy and military, by school teachers, and learned individuals attached to other entourages. Among the early travellers to Syria was the Marquis Melchior de Vogüé, whose *Syrie Centrale* remains a reminder of the wonders and prosperity of late antique Syria, and inspired Howard Crosby Butler's work. Butler himself recognised that Greater Syria's past was based on an agricultural wealth that had disappeared by his day of Ottoman domination. Like Butler, Ernest Rénan's *Mission de Phénicie* depicts landscapes full of terraces, cisterns, silos, wine and oil presses, testimony to how highly developed ancient agriculture had been.[3] In addition to these silent standing stones, artifacts of late antique date were also amongst the earliest materials scientifically excavated in the region. A variety of sixth and seventh century A.D. imported and local amphorae and fine-wares were uncovered in the Tyropoeon Valley in Jerusalem in 1927.[4] Who can turn the pages of the final report on the royal tombs of Ballana, excavated in lower Egypt in the 1930s, where each tomb was carefully stocked with between 200 and 300 LR1, LR3 and LR4 amphorae from Syria/Cilicia, the Aegean, and southern Palestine, without wondering about the economic mechanisms which underlay their import (market forces or political gift exchange)?[5]

Despite the importance of this early pioneering fieldwork, the East Mediterranean has failed to keep abreast of methodological and theoretical developments which have evolved subsequently in the West, particularly regarding quantitative analysis.[6] Remote sensing techniques, soil flotation, quantitative pottery studies, and even landscape archaeology were all adopted relatively late on Eastern shores, where some of these archaeological tools remain remarkably undeveloped and simplistic even today.[7] Although specialised agricultural and industrial production has been examined in detail in some regions – Syria, Israel, Jordan and Egypt, in particular[8] – little attempt has been initiated to relate localised patterns to broader macro-economic structures. Other than very recent scholarship, Abadie-Reynal's work on amphorae and fine-wares imported to Argos, and Watson's work at Pella, are the only published studies which have addressed aspects of the character and structure of inter-regional exchange in the East Mediterranean.[9]

In view of this rather stagnant situation, in the following pages we have briefly discussed the economic rhythms of life and the structure of long-distance exchange in the late antique East Mediterranean. We hope that this initiative will help stimulate greater informed debate about the mechanisms that underlay production and exchange, but appreciate that due to the sheer geographical size of the area under discussion these observations are necessarily selective and not equally relevant to all provinces.

Capital Demands: Rome, Constantinople and the annona civica

In her pottery based discussion of exchange at Argos, Abadie-Reynal adopted a model originally formulated in the West to explain the apparently abrupt decline in N. African imports entering the city in the fifth century and their replacement by Eastern amphorae (the Syrian/Cypriot or Cilician LR1, and the Palestinian LR4 and LR5). She interpreted this transformation in the provenance of incoming wines and olive oil as a result of state intervention and, more directly, to the foundation of Constantinople, which "a tendânce à drainer vers elle toutes les richesses du Moyen-Orient".[10] Without labouring the point, Abadie-Reynal implied that much of the imported foodstuffs packaged in Eastern amphora which arrived at Argos were embedded within a tied economy based on provincial taxation.

With a population of perhaps between 300–400,000 in *c.* A.D. 450, like the mother city in the West New Rome was a consumer of enormous magnitude.[11] Between A.D. 332 and 610, an estimated 80,000 beneficiaries were entitled to free distributions of *panis aedium* and olive oil.[12] If the quantity of wheat provided by the State was comparable to that distributed in Rome (which is very likely given that it is logical to assume Constantinople adopted a system tried and tested in the western capital) then 31,200 tons of wheat alone would have been required. This is the equivalent of 624 annual shipments in a merchant vessel capable of accommodating 50 tons (such as the seventh century Yassi Ada A ship).[13]

The role that Abadie-Reynal seems to propose for LR1, LR4 and LR5 was very similar to that of N. African amphorae in the West. Both were manufactured in enormous quantities in restricted geographical areas and exported in mass, with a strong gravitational pull toward the capitals. This idea is important in demonstrating how the theory of exchange in the West has had a direct bearing on the East Mediterranean. Just as imperial Rome is envisaged as the principal manipulator of inter-regional exchange in the West, importing wheat and oil as *annona civica* and selling-on surpluses commercially to Spain, Gaul and other regions,[14] so Constantinople is often assumed to be the exchange magnet of the East. This theory, of course, is entrenched in the traditional Finley/Jones historocentric view of the Roman economy as primitivistic and dominated by a central authority. And in all fairness, without access to archaeological data it is easy to realise how some primary historical sources, such as the influential Theodosian Code,[15] could be interpreted as accurate reflections of a harsh regime strictly structured toward the containment of merchants and sea-captains within a tied economy, where the obligatory *annona* transport of foodstuffs to the civil population in Constantinople, and to military garrisons elsewhere, was of paramount importance within long-distance exchange. If the Code is accepted as the simple truth, then the State economy rigorously suppressed private commerce between the fourth and fifth centuries. But to what extent are such historical texts accurate portrayals of reality? Just how much importance should be attached to the word of Libanius, for example, who referred to Constantinople in A.D. 390 as "that city which grows fat on the sweat of the others"?[16]

The Rome/Constantinople analogy provides an interesting means of appreciating the level of demand an imperial capital might generate, and for demonstrating how various forms of exchange might have been structured. However, such a comparison also vividly clarifies how *different* exchange patterns were in the two halves of the Mediterranean. The argument that N. Africa – modern Tunisia in particular – dominated exchange in the West is uncontroversial. Exported amphorae occur in huge quantities in deposits excavated in cities throughout Italy, southern Spain and southern France. Thus, at the Crypta Balbi, Porticus Liviae and Temple of Magna Mater in Rome, N. African products account for 52–60% of all amphorae between A.D. 350 and 420.[17] At Tarraco and Alicante in Spain, N. African imports represent about 75% of amphora assemblages between the end of the fifth and first half of the sixth century.[18] The same type of wares can also comprise up to 68% of deposits in fifth and sixth century Marseille.[19] Not only have surveys of olive oil presses around Lepcis Magna identified impressive evidence of the olive cultivation that was developed deliberately to produce a massive surplus, but the discovery of pottery workshops and inscriptions on vessels has helped identify the social context of some producers and distributors.[20]

Not surprisingly, N. African amphorae are by far the most common cargo type discovered on shipwrecks between Carthage and southern France.[21] The extremely wide and dense diffusion of African red-slip (ARS) fine wares throughout the West evidently indicates that other manufactured goods (not preserved archaeologically) frequently accompanied the large-scale shipment of state-procured wheat and olive oil as secondary consignments of commercial value. ARS fine wares were manufactured on numerous estates south of Carthage, and cargo consignments such as the fifty plates

on the Dramont E shipwreck, and the 250 lamps on the wreck La Luque B (of A.D 425–
455, and of the early fourth century respectively) confirm that these products were
indeed exported as minor consignments, almost certainly stowed in convenient spaces
between primary cargoes.[22]

By contrast, in the East Mediterranean no single region or province served a
comparable dominant role as N. Africa. Following the foundation of Constantinople,
Egypt was exploited as the capital's granary up to at least A.D. 534.[23] The province's
general prosperity is reflected in the 2.5 million *solidi* obtained annually through the
taxation of her approximately 4.75 million inhabitants, which is thought to have
accounted for an impressive 35% of the total revenue of the Empire in Late Antiquity.[24]
However, despite the State's great dependence on Egypt, there is neither substantial
historical, nor archaeological evidence that as close an economic relationship was
fostered between capital and province as had linked N. Africa and Rome. Egyptian
wine was, of course, consumed throughout the Mediterranean, but only in extremely
limited quantities. Although common in Carthage, LR7 (the main wine amphora
produced in late antique Egypt) is rare in Italy and France, unattested in Spain, and
was evidently not exported as primary cargo. LR7 is equally rare along the sea-lanes
leading to Constantinople, and has not been identified at Anemurium or Thasos, for
example. The type only occurred at Saraçhane in Istanbul in small quantities in sixth
and seventh century deposits, and has been identified in only four of 340 published
pottery assemblages in Israel. At Caesarea, LR7 accounts for less than half a percent of
all amphorae.[25] Furthermore, although Egyptian red slip (ERS) bowls and plates are
prevalent throughout Egypt, their circulation north of Alexandria is extremely
restricted.[26] No attempt seems to have been initiated to imitate established and
presumably lucrative N. African trade patterns, by loading state-commandeered corn
ships with crates of quality ERS destined for the open market. It is not until after the
Umayyad conquest that these products found a receptive market outside Egypt,[27]
presumably mainly to meet the new demand created by the economic dislocation
between the Byzantine Empire and Umayyad provinces in the second half of the
seventh and in the eighth century. But even then, the diffusion of ERS seems to have
been limited mainly to early Islamic Jordan and Palestine.

In addition to this dissimilarity between the pattern of Egyptian agricultural and
manufactured exports and N. Africa's economic relationship to Rome, recent
archaeological research is demonstrating another considerable difference: early
Byzantine Egypt was a massive market for a cosmopolitan range of East Mediterranean
staple foodstuffs and other products. Wines from Gaza and Ashkelon in Palestine seem
to have almost monopolised those imported in amphorae through the port of
Alexandria, where they comprised 76% of all deposits in Sector G, Building 12. LR1
were also extremely popular throughout Egypt (representing 14% of amphorae in
some deposits at Alexandria), and were even imitated on a limited scale at pottery
workshops located in the monastery of St. Jeramia at Saqqara and at Margham in the
Mareotis region.[28] An estimated 80% of LR1 amphorae from Alexandria, Middle Egypt
and the Fayum are of Cypriot origin and 15% derive from Cilicia.[29] Manufactured
commodities, represented in the archaeological record by Phocaean, Cypriot and
African red slip wares, are also common within the province.[30] Bearing in mind that

exported wheat seems to have been shipped from Egypt apparently exclusively as tax procured for the *annona civica*, on the basis of currently available archaeological evidence the foreign produce which arrived on the docks of Alexandria in Late Antiquity must be defined largely as one-way traffic. This picture of imbalanced trade could not be more different to the documented situation in N. Africa, which exported great quantities of ARS as commodities, but seems to have imported few Mediterranean goods in return.

The theory of supply and demand make this pattern difficult to explain, and it seems probable that a crucial link is presently missing from our understanding of Egypt's exchange equation. What was the source of the purchasing power underlying these transactions? Egypt had always been poor in olive oil resources, and a logical explanation for at least a significant part of the amphorae imported into the province in Late Antiquity may well have been economic dependency on non-local olive oil for daily sustenance (and this may partly explain the prevalence of Cypriot LR1 vessels amongst amphora imports).[31] One suspects that in the cities the large-scale specialised manufacture of cloth, ivory carving, and perhaps papyrus processing, created broad-based purchasing potential.[32] Evidence from *papyri* also suggests that the economy of the rural sector was partly monetised and that workers on estates and villages were paid in coin;[33] the extent of the spending potential can hardly have been especially great, but probably enabled rural workers to splash out on the occasional 'exotic' import. The daily economics which underlay commercial forces in late antique Egypt are complex and deserve detailed future analysis. Recent studies of *papyri*, coin hoards, and the increased interest in archaeological sites of late antique date, promise to make Egypt one of the most important provinces in coming years for studying inter-regional exchange in the East Mediterranean.

While Egypt is widely perceived to be the bread basket of Constantinople, it is often assumed that the capital imported most of its oil from Syria.[34] However, Empereur and Picon's survey of LR1 amphora workshops in Cilicia, Cyprus and Rhodes has not only become a watershed in the realisation that in some instances equating a single amphora type to a single region and agricultural product is simplistic and incorrect, but it has also created awareness that oil production was common within a far broader expanse of the north-east Mediterranean. The likelihood that a significant proportion of LR1 amphorae – once considered a specific Syrian oil amphora – also contained wine (see Decker, Chapter 4) complicates and weakens our understanding of Syria's relationship with Constantinople further. The combination of the above evidence indicates that although scholars working in the East Mediterranean can benefit from theoretical models formulated, tried and tested in the West, in many ways they simply serve to accentuate the different exchange structures existing at different ends of the Mediterranean basin.

The Army and annona militaris

The behemoth of the Roman army struggles to emerge from its lair of the past. Despite the vast literature on the subject, we have comparatively little reliable information about its size and disposition, key elements if we are to understand its economic impact in Late Antiquity. In war and in peace the army was a fixture in the eastern provinces, a boon and burden, which Lydus (*De Mens.* I.27) numbered at 389,704. Based on these figures, the proposed estimate of 301,300 for the army of A.D. 518, increasing to 379,300 by A.D. 565, seems perfectly reasonable.[35] Such figures are obviously vital should one wish to grasp any notion of State military expenditure and the subsequent burden on provincial production. Equally vital is the disposition of the army throughout the Empire. The eastern armies, between the reigns of Constantine and Justinian, were divided into mobile (*comitatenses*) and frontier soldiers (*limitanei*), and their distribution varied across time. Based in forts and fortress cities from the upper Euphrates to the Red Sea, the army formed a tourniqet against the aggression of Sasanid Persia, one which often proved incapable of staunching enemy incursions. Sasanian armies wreaked havoc from 540–544 and between 572 and 591 despite the impressive array of installations built to contain them noted in detail in the *Notitia Dignitatum* and confirmed on the ground by archaeologists.[36] The tendency for the field army to be billeted in cities, especially during campaign preparations in order to ease access to supplies, often backfired with serious political and economic consequences, as during Julian's preparations for war at Antioch in A.D. 363, and at Edessa during 505–506.[37]

In order to maintain their forces, the late Roman State formalised army coemption of resources by legalising and regulating the *annona militaris*. This military tax was a major component of the 'state economy', in which the central government oversaw the collection, transportation and distribution of essential rations and manufactured products, a subject that has framed discussion of the ancient economy for decades. The negative impact of the *annona militaris*, which remained a fixed institution until the Arab conquest, should neither be exaggerated nor belittled.[38] A number of factors complicate efforts to fully understand the methods and implications of provisioning soldiers. Both the value of the individual *annona militaris* and the total salary soldiers received are disputed.[39] Further, it is clear that from the late fourth century onward the soldier's *annona* was paid increasingly in coin, until cash allowances became predominant under Anastasius.[40] Additional complications arise when one considers that the *limitanei* exploited land in the vicinity of their postings, and were the victims of imperial economies that undermined their position (until such soldiers probably ceased to exist by Heraclius' reign).[41] By the mid-sixth century, many of these units may well have been replaced by *foederati*, the allied forces of client rulers: this feature is especially clear in the case of the Ghassanid phylarchs located along the eastern frontier, from Bostra to Resafa. The Ghassanids themselves drew the *annona*, probably primarily in cash. Such shifts across time make the overall number, posture, and impact of the military on the eastern provinces extremely difficult to gauge.

From the reign of Constantine the eastern provinces were increasingly the domain of *limitanei*, who, under normal circumstances, provided at least a portion of their food from their own land and resources. Military territory assigned to soldiers for their own upkeep is known from the time of Septimius Severus.[42] Agricultural activity around eastern forts has left its impression in the Syrian steppe, around sites such as Acadma (Qdeym) and 'Amsareddi, where Roman and Byzantine forts are surrounded by *qanat-*

fed irrigation systems that presumably were exploited by the garrison to supply themselves and their mounts.[43] It is also possible that at least a portion of the produce from imperial domains was used to feed the army in the East. Nevertheless, the burdensome task of supplying the soldiery fell primarily on the shoulders of the general populace.

Throughout the East, as evidence from Egypt demonstrates, the actual soldiers collected the *annona* from civilian lands near their postings.[44] Abuse was common, and the task of transporting the *annona* could be ruinous, as was the case for Antiochenes forced to haul grain from their home city to the Euphrates during Constantius' Persian War.[45] This example of long-distance military exchange is one of several that probably reflect extraordinary wartime circumstances, probably undertaken no more than once or twice in a well-off councillor's lifetime. For a small-scale cultivator, army requisition of his draught animal for military transport often resulted in a permanent loss and would have been disastrous.[46] In theory, the military were expected to contribute most of the resources necessary to transport the *annona* collected in kind or, as was increasingly the case from the early fifth century on, were expected to accept cash payments with which to purchase their own supplies. This practice never completely ended payment in foodstuffs, and historical texts describe Anastasius supplying his field army with *annona militaris* drawn in kind.[47] Irrespective of the nature of the collection, farmers continued to suffer from the army's demands.[48] The degree of this suffering, however, may not be as great as some would propose. A comparison with the burden of the *annona civica* is instructive. Justinianic Egypt was bound to give up 8 million *artabas* of grain, or 8–12% of its total yield, which in cash amounted to about 800,000 *solidi*.[49] Assuming an army presence of 15,000 troops in Egypt, the total army tax burden on the populace would amount to 135,500 *solidi* or, if converted into grain, 1.35 million *artabas*, the equivalent of 2% of all Egyptian production.[50] Despite the obvious shortcomings of such a calculation, the order of magnitude allows scope for comparison. The combined *annonae* burdens do not appear oppressive, as several scholars have noted, and, of these, the military component is relatively light.[51]

The implications for the wider economy, however, remain uncertain. Just how great was the burden of supplying the forces required to protect a vast land territory from invasion? The limited capacity of pre-industrial societies to cope with the maintenance of large standing armies is obvious, and the late Roman Empire was no exception. One recent calculation has estimated that in A.D. 518 the army numbered 301,300 (or 1.6% of the total population of 19.5 million) and cost the fisc 5.558 million *solidi*, or approximately 66% of the State's total budget.[52] In the post-plague world when Justinian was in his final year as emperor, the size of the army has been estimated at 379,300 (2.0% of the total population of 19.5 million), a figure which would have had a total maintenance cost of 7.987 million *solidii*, or 71% of the State's total expenditure.[53] In 518, at the end of Anastasius' relatively stable and prosperous reign, which experienced several reforms, the imperial fisc possessed a massive surplus despite the fact that Anastasius had probably greatly increased the basic military pay. This had resulted in easier recruitment among native imperial populations and quelled unrest in the army, a characteristic feature of the military since the reign of Diocletian. Soldiers were, therefore, less apt to unrest and predation upon local civilians. By the end of

end of the spectrum we find monks of Palestine weaving baskets for their livelihood, and at the other lies the great ecclesiastical centres of the patriarchates, of which there is no better example than that of the Church of Alexandria, especially during the tenure of John the Almsgiver. If his *vita* is to believed, John accumulated gold amounting to 720,000 *solidi* during his patriarchate, or nearly the total value of Egypt's entire annual *annona civica*.[63] Mundell Mango's paper (Chapter 5) illustrates the far-flung trading interests and activities of the clergy at this time, by focusing on the long-distance exchange enterprises that caused products to travel from Egypt to as far as Britain on one hand, and, through the agencies of Nestorian Christians, to China on the other.

As widely travelled as these articles of ecclesiastical trade were the pilgrims who came to visit the Holy Land, who often returned home with physical reminders of the splendid products of the *terra sancta*. Many travellers remained in the Holy Land. Personal piety, no doubt fortified by the turbulent conditions prevailing in the West throughout the fifth century, led those who could afford it to emigrate. The most famous case of such relocation is Melania: after selling her family estate she wondered throughout the western Empire, and finally settled in the Holy City as her grandmother had previously.[64] There she expended large sums on Christian establishments. Although its overall effect is still contested, the notion that Palestine benefitted financially from pilgrimage is beyond dispute.[65] As Kingsley suggests, for example (Chapter 3), such movement of people provided unprecedented positive marketing for Palestine's 'holy' wines. While the impact of the pilgrim trade on the macro-economy of Syria-Palestine is still debated, we can comfortably admit one firm fact: ecclesiastical building was big business. Between the fourth and seventh centuries, houses of worship were erected by the thousand in the Levant. From the provincial churches, like that at Ravenna, which cost 26,000 *solidi*, to Hagia Sophia, which cost Justinian and the Byzantine State approximately 1.73 million *solidi*, labourers from Greece to Egypt benefited by what can only be described as a building boom, in which private acts of piety eclipsed the old euergetism of public building.[66] Theodoret of Cyrrhus describes how such public duties now lay within the bishop's orbit, and provided a list of the structures he built around his town, including bridges, a bathhouse and porticoes.[67]

The economic activities of the new religion were not restricted to the obvious tourism trade and building, but also involved estate ownership and large-scale agricultural production. John of Ephesus described a monastery, located in a village near the Armenian frontier, which planted 20,000 vines a year for three years in the sixth century; after five to six years of diligent cultivation, insufficient jars could be found to contain the wine that the crops yielded.[68] At Samos, excavation has revealed an ecclesiastical establishment producing wine and olive oil on a large scale, and the cargo on the Yassi Ada shipwreck has been linked to production on church estates.[69] Just such a Byzantine period ecclesiastical building has been excavated at Shelomi in N. Israel, and shows that the church's economic interests extended far beyond the monasteries scattered throughout the Judaean Desert.[70] The latter, many equipped with presses and other agricultural installations, served not only the needs of the immediate community, but sold produce as well.[71] Elsewhere in Palestine, wine presses attached to monasteries were built with mass production in mind: the vat at

Caparbaricha in the Jerusalem region, for example, held more than 6,800 litres.[72] The 'army of monks' that guarded the reaches of the central Syrian steppe were not merely wild men and parasites; their building activities and place in the landscape are documented by inscriptions and standing remains, such as those near Hama commemorating the building of the monastic tower.[73] Wherever such houses existed, fields were tilled and desert lands reclaimed on a scale comparable to the great Cistercian efforts in the Medieval West. Under such circumstances, it is hardly surprising to find ecclesiastic establishments entering into relations with the semi-nomadic groups on the imperial fringe, such as those groups which set up long-term encampments around the monastery of Sabas in Palestine. Such contact would not only have been limited to cultural exchange and intellectual awakening, but would have also involved trade, and was perhaps the foundations of the symbiotic relationship between monks and Bedouin seen even today in Sinai. Further to the south, *papyri* offer rare insights into the land-based wealth of Egyptian churches and monasteries, which was based on cultivation, and the leasing of fields and potters' and blacksmiths' workshops.[74]

Among the agents of change were holy men, such as Symeon the Holy Fool of Emesa who lived outside the limits of the 'secular' church. In addition to increasing their influence upon all levels of society throughout Late Antiquity, in life and death these saints founded cult sites and pilgrimage shrines that drew visitors from around the Empire.[75] Most famous of these was the monastery of St. Simeon Stylites in North Syria, the impressive remains of which today testify to the establishment's wealth and influence. Such foundations were sometimes church initiatives, sometimes the initiative of individual monks, and often due to the effort of private individuals. At the other end of the Empire, the Appions of Egypt built a monastery and provided it with a generous annual grain allowance of 1,000 *artabas*; however, Appion clearly did not want all his treasure to be stored in heaven: the family retained control of the monastery, and the monks themselves are found from time to time providing various goods for the estate.[76] What landowner with wasteland on his hands could have resisted the double turn of piety and profit offered by the foundation of religious houses on *agri deserta*, of just the kind we find in the limestone massif or the Syrian steppe, which are studded with monasteries?

The industry of the private individual via the church was also present in the town. The Miracles of St. Artemios depict an urban landscape in Constantinople where private religious foundations are a constant landmark and where they play a significant role in the everyday life of the city, including its economy. Such private intervention in the religious map of Late Antiquity demonstrates the complexity of the period's economy and the entangled relationships between individual and institution that is sometimes difficult to differentiate. In some instances, at least, ecclesiastical activity was an extension of private wealth and an initiative to develop farming and trade.

Commerce, Private Entrepreneurs, and the Open Economy

The extent of social and economic mobility within the world of Late Antiquity is a fascinating intellectual minefield, across which it is wise to tread cautiously. Traditionally, the period has been characterised as one of highly limited socio-economic fluidity for many reasons, not least because society was locked within a rigid caste system. Moreover, taxation is often depicted as higher than during the earlier Roman period, and as a debilitating influence which minimised opportunities for mobility.[77] Although modern archaeological fieldwork has cast serious doubt on the minimalistic theory that high taxation exhausted over-cultivated marginal lands, and that diminished crop yields led to empire-wide rural depopulation in both the West and East,[78] the impression that the farmer's lot in life was so precarious and arduous that economic self-sufficiency prevailed at almost all levels of society is still favoured by many primitivists studying the ancient economy.[79] If we are to accept their battle cry, then shipping was hazardous, overland transport prohibitively expensive, and coins were struck exclusively as a medium to pay military salaries and manage state fiscal affairs during Late Antiquity.[80] The transportation of *annona civica* and *annona militaris*, which demanded regular exchange across different provinces, was politically too sensitive an issue to leave to the 'rough play' of market forces.[81] According to primivitivistic models, the existence of limited commercial trade, such as in Phocaean, Cypriot and African red-slip pottery wares, relied on the pre-existence of established *annona* structures and routes of communication, which were state controlled.[82] No true commercial networks, in which merchants actively stimulated trade, flourished.[83]

Without wishing to reignite the perennial, but unhelpful, debate about the varying quality of data available to historians and archaeologists, it is now broadly accepted that many of the texts used to discuss trade are of limited value, because they selectively refer to 'high-level' tied exchange associated with the State, the Church and wealthy individuals. Even where we do have access to a remarkable set of texts, which supply useful detail about rural production and patronage, and maritime transport, in the form of Libanius' fourth century letters, Liebeschuetz has conceded that "[p]rivate business affairs were not a proper subject for a literary letter. In his correspondence Libanius the business-man is completely eclipsed by Libanius the Sophist".[84] The everyday rhythms of the economy amongst the 'lower class' strata of society are particularly obscure. Even from the 1,784 lines of text preserved in an agricultural account book excavated at Kellis in Egypt, it is difficult to reconstruct the village's economy because written entries are unsystematic and unbalanced.[85]

Although historians' opinions waver, strong grounds do exist to argue that Late Antiquity witnessed substantial horizontal social mobility.[86] Nowhere is the web of contacts between different social and religious groups so evident than within sets of archaeological material culture, the study of which has radically altered the traditional image of late antique exchange. In the place of models arguing that exchange was dominated by the movement of government-subsidised staples and goods of highly specific geographical origin, the belief that large-scale commerce in a very wide range of commodities played an integral role in the complex pattern of the economy is receiving ever-increasing recognition.[87] Without resorting to excavation, for example, Kellis' isolated geographical location in the Daklah Oasis, 300 km away from the Nile (an overland journey of one week), gives the superficial impression that the village must have been entrenched in a self-sufficient economy. The imported African red-slip wares, Nile valley amphorae, and Alexandrine glass recorded on the site present a very different picture.[88]

Agricultural produce and other commodities flowed between different regions for various reasons in Late Antiquity. Although the State imported large quantities of wheat (and probably olive oil, and arguably even wine) to Constantinople as we have seen, the majority of its population would have been obliged to fend for themselves. Even if we accept a low estimate of 300,000 for the capital's population in the fifth century, this means that 73% of its citizens purchased – or perhaps in some cases grew – their own foodstuffs.[89] This reality is reflected in the *Notitia Urbis Constantinopolitanae*, where twenty-one state-owned bakeries are listed in comparison to 113–120 private establishments.[90] In many other major towns population pressure exerted similar inordinate demands on the surrounding countryside; incapable of meeting these, bulk foodstuffs seem to have been shifted both regionally and across longer distances on a regular basis.

In addition to such economic dependence on staple foodstuffs, one gains the distinct impression that the Mediterranean market was also saturated with a broad array of differently spiced and classed oils, wines, sauces and honey, which were sold as semi-luxury produce for their 'exotic' value. The Vandal conquest of N. Africa was accompanied by a significant surge in the volume of imported Eastern foodstuffs reaching Carthage,[91] which cannot be interpreted as tied trade, and Ward-Perkins has emphasised that the continuous flow of Eastern amphorae into the West, following the divide of the Roman Empire, can only logically be explained as the result of commercial transactions.[92] It is extremely improbable that these Eastern amphorae, which reached the West in large quantities during Late Antiquity, were imported to top up daily staple food rations (even following harvest failure), because such long-distance trade must surely have been incredibly inefficient logistically and economically. To these two cases, we may also now add the flow of Eastern imports into Egypt. Much of this trade appears to have been consumer-oriented and developed to meet a market for non-local semi-luxuries.

The freedom and prevalence of the private entrepreneur in satisfying the demand for various commodities has also been identified in the transformation of ship construction in Late Antiquity. The reduction in the number of mortise-and-tenon joints used to build 'shell-first' merchant vessels, a greater reliance on iron nails to secure strakes to frames, the end of investing in lead to sheath and protect hulls (and its replacement with the cheaper medium of pitch),[93] and the overall shift toward frame-first ships, are characteristic features of excavated ships of fourth to mid-seventh century date.[94] These technological changes in ship construction are thought to be related to the status of ship-owners, who were "often independent businessmen with limited assets operating under what amounted to a free enterprise system...These owners needed floating cargo containers that required even less labor and more efficient use of materials than in the past".[95]

Economy, Long-Distance Exchange and the Future

Despite the centrality of the above forms of exchange in moulding the late antique economy, it must be emphasised that our understanding of the macro-economic complexity of the East Mediterranean is at an early stage. The papers presented in this volume should be viewed as an attempt to synthesise some available strands of evidence in order to encourage more detailed and more critical dialogue about various aspects of these exchange systems. Apart from the future discovery of inscriptions, and the much needed sieving of the period's historical documentation, four forms of archaeological evidence stand out as the most promising for improving our knowledge of the subject under discussion. In no particular order these are landscape archaeology, urban archaeology, shipwreck archaeology, and pottery analysis.

Using carefully formulated research strategies, the study of landscapes in different provinces promises to provide a far clearer understanding of the specialised forms and scales of agricultural and industrial activities pursued across the eastern Empire. As long as these include comprehensive pottery recovery and off-site reconnaissance, it ought to be possible to relate rural installations to specific settlement types with greater precision than at present. Analysis of material culture should also clarify the extent to which certain regions were linked to broader exchange systems or confined within a self-sufficient economy. Much of the future success of landscape archaeology will depend on the intensity of the project (preferably including repeat surveys under different visibility conditions) and the incorporation of pottery quantification.[96]

Urban archaeology has a long tradition in the West, which incorporates the analysis of town economies.[97] This area of research is comparatively undeveloped in the East, and although numerous cities have been extensively excavated during the last one hundred years, the urban economy remains virtually a non-subject.[98] Although amphorae assemblages have been quantified in various towns (many of which are discussed in the following papers), enabling issues about regional self-sufficiency and dependence on inter-regional trade to be discussed, few deliberate attempts have been initiated to identify and discuss urban-based specialised industrial production and retail activity. The on-going debate about the economic character of cities in the West has not been reenacted at the other end of the Mediterranean basin. The seventh century shops at Sardis are an outstanding exception (whose importance is clearly enhanced by their excellent level of preservation).[99] However, the extent to which cities were *nuclei* of retail trade and commerce is an extremely rewarding subject. Inscriptions from Korykos in Cilicia,[100] *papyri* from Egypt,[101] and archaeological remains, such as the sixth century dye-works at Jerash,[102] suggest that towns across the Eastern empire witnessed intense commercial activity in both retail and production, the character of which could probably be assessed in useful detail by simply re-analysing many old excavation reports (in the manner adopted by Wilson in this volume; see Chapter 2).

Another area of research, which offers the potential for great scientific strides in the future, is shipwreck archaeology. Despite the exciting data which the study of such 'fine-grained assemblages' promises – including insights into cargo character and volume, amphora content, exchange structures, and merchants' status and origin (identifiable through examining ships' domestic assemblages)[103] – the potential of shipwreck archaeology is far from realised. This is partly because the sub-discipline is site-focused, rather than period specific. Why have no projects attempted to compare the composition of second and third century cargoes with those on fourth century merchant vessels? Why have different sixth century ships not been examined to appraise the impact of the Justinianic plague on long-distance trade? The answer is mainly related to the current tendency for most marine archaeologists to favour data collection over problem-solving, which has meant that analyses of well-preserved sites have taken precedence over the study of wrecks of specific date (irrespective of levels of preservation). More strategic sampling and recording, including survey and limited key-hole excavation, offers the potential for greater progress in the future. For the moment, underwater research in the Sea of Marmara and Israel, in particular, continues to provide access to new data about late antique trade.[104] Serious problems remain, however: available results suggest that almost all excavated and surveyed sites are merchant vessels which were involved in commerce; the absence of luxury cargoes and *annona* ships in the archaeological record in the eastern Mediterranean, not to mention late antique warships, is a sobering indication of the small size, and unrepresentative character, of the available sample.

The final area of research, pottery analysis, is arguably the most influential of all four tools outlined in this paper for examining exchange. Plotting the distribution of specific dated amphorae and fine wares of known provenance on certain types of site continues to clarify trade circulation and penetration, and to reveal aspects of exchange structures. The constant up-dating of such maps leaves little doubt that we are still a long way from obtaining reliable read-outs for the whole empire. This is especially true for inland rural settlements; the recent publication of distribution maps of PRS in Italy (found on both coastal and inland sites) must reflect the wider penetration of other commodities, and we suspect that it is only a matter of time before the question of amphora import into the countryside will demand detailed reconsideration.[105]

The interpretative capability resulting from pottery quantification continues to offer the greatest potential for new results in the field of long-distance exchange. Many sites have now been subjected to this methodology, but the East still continues to lag far behind the West in terms of the variety and number of deposits examined.[106] For example, other than at Caesarea in Israel, no other major urban or rural site has been examined in the East where changes in the relative quantities and types of amphorae and fine wares present over different centuries have been documented. In the case of Caesarea, the deposits which are available for analysis have not been published in as comprehensive a manner as the chronologically diverse data published from Carthage, Benghazi, Rome, Naples, Marseille, and Spain.[107] Thus, although it is currently possible to generalise about levels of local versus imported wares consumed in cities, short-term change is mainly undetectable. Equally evident is that many areas remain very poorly represented, especially Turkey, Cyprus, Syria, and Egypt. Perhaps the greatest development one might hope for in coming decades is the application of quantitative procedures on pottery assemblages from rural sites (villages, farms, estates), which would radically transform our current ignorance about the economic interplay between town and country in the late antique East Mediterranean. To date, Sumaqa in the Carmel of Israel is the only village which has been subjected to this process (as far as we are aware).[108]

In view of the concern that 'cliometrics' (quantitative history derived from the ancient written record) is an unsuitable tool for examining ancient economies, because ancient societies were statistically innocent and data are never presented as part of a systematic series in texts (and, therefore, cannot be easily verified),[109] pottery quantification is even more crucial for discussing orders of magnitude in antiquity. Nevertheless, present analysis is still accompanied by a great deal of subjectivity and variations in standards, which requires detailed consideration: quantification based on estimated vessel-equivalents (eve) seem to be the most accurate technique for obtaining results, but no single procedure will yield equally valid statistics from all types of deposit. Although breakage rates and sherd density amongst fine-wares will generally enable analysis by either eve, sherd count or weight to produce similar results, the quantification of amphora assemblages is more complicated and needs to take composition into greater account:[110] if examined by weight, for example, deposits with a high LR3 presence would cause this thin-walled amphora to be seriously under-represented; analysis by count will also tend to over-represent amphorae of greater volume and hence size. Finally, the question of how many sherds constitute the smallest acceptable sample still requires attention.

Despite the encouraging volume of excavation and survey reports being published, it would be suitable to conclude with a word of caution. As reports appear in ever-greater numbers, from types of site previously poorly known and from regions formerly *terra incognita*, the complexity of the late antique economy becomes increasingly apparent. Given the inevitable limitations of much excavation and interpretation, and the impossibility of obtaining precise statistics about economic activity in Late Antiquity, the impressionistic nature of much of the information available needs to be acknowledged. Only after much future fieldwork, geared toward assessing specific thematic problems, can tentative conclusions be accepted as valid historical patterns. When confronted with the variety of data from various late antique sources in the East Mediterranean, and by the sheer scale of work required to resolve key issues, at present any conclusion must be tempered with Socratic caution: wisdom is the realisation of our current ignorance.

Notes

1	This paper has benefitted significantly from comments offered by Bryan Ward-Perkins, whom we thank profusely. All errors are our own.
2	Storey, 1999: 223–31.
3	Renán, 1864: 96, 251, plate XXXVI; Butler, 1907–1919.
4	Crowfoot and Fitzgerald, 1927: pl. XIV.31 depicts three LR5 and an LR1 amphora with a *dipinto* on the shoulder.
5	Kirwan, 1938: 386.
6	Although numerous surveys of regional landscapes have been conducted in the East, most have been site-focused and have not attempted to relate results to broader Mediterranean-wide economic structures. By contrast, integration is well developed in the West, where a comprehensive body of work has examined the supply of *annona civica* from N. Africa to Rome using historical and archaeological evidence: Tengstrom, 1974; Casson, 1980; Rickman, 1980; Foxhall and Forbes, 1982; Fulford, 1980; 1983; Mattingly, 1988a; 1988b. Sirks' analysis of Roman and late Roman texts (1991a;

199b) offers an excellent foundation for subsequent discussion. In the West, studies of economic self-sufficiency and dependency (based on the quantification of amphora and fine-ware assemblages) have also been developed using fieldwork conducted. For an overview of models on economic self-sufficiency and dependency on imports, see: Fulford, 1987; Tomber, 1993; Reynolds, 1995; for Spain, see Keay, 1984 and Gutiérrez Lloret, 1998. The western urban economy is also a key area of interest: Parkins, 1997; 1998; Whittaker, 1990; 1993.

7   Although soil flotation was conducted by Dauphin (1993: 47) during her excavation of an ecclesiastical farm at Shelomi in north Israel, comparable work is rare in this country. But for elsewhere in Israel, see: Weinstein-Evron and Chaim, 1999 and Lernau, 1999 for palynological analysis and studies of fish bones from the village of Sumaqa in the Carmel; Fradkin, 1997 for fish imports at Sepphoris; Lernau, 1995 for fish remains at the fortress of Upper Zohar in the Negev desert. Gibson's study of landscape archaeology in Israel (1995: 211) concluded that most current survey methods, based on field survey, regional survey and site-catchment analysis, are all fundamentally flawed, because they focus on sites and ignore the relationship between landscape use and associated settlements. More in-depth geomorphological studies have been conducted in southeastern Anatolia: Wilkinson, 1990.

8   Syria: for oil production, see Callot, 1984. Egypt: for wine production, see M. Rodziewicz, 1998a. Recent work in the Wadi Feinan in Jordan has focussed on agriculture and mining activities that include the Roman and Byzantine periods: see Barker, *et al.* 1999. For viticulture around Pella, see Watson, 1996. In Israel, important details about regional economic specialisation can be extracted from the twenty-four surveys published by the Archaeological Survey of Israel. More comprehensive analyses of specific regions are also available – Golan: Urman, 1985, and Ben David, 1998 for olive oil; Samaria: Dar, 1986; Lod: Schwartz, 1991. These studies are largely site-oriented and did not incorporate systematic sherding. Surveys which did examine plough zones and field systems have been conducted at Sataf, in the Golan, and at Dor (Gibson *et al.*, 1991; Dauphin and Gibson, 1992–1993; Gibson *et al.*, 1999). The scant archaeological material available regarding ancient mining activities in the Roman and Byzantine periods is tantalising, as noted in Chrysos, 1993. Mining activity in Byzantium remains an unknown quantity.

9   Recent studies: Banaji, 1992; Kingsley, 1999a; Ward-Perkins, forthcoming. Various articles are also forthcoming in *Late Antiquity and Early Islam. Fifth Workshop. Trade and Exchange in the Late Antique and Early Islamic Near East* (Darwin Press, New Jersey), especially Wickham's paper on 'Trade and Exchange, 550–750: the View from the West'. For Argos, see Abadie-Reynal, 1989; Pella: Watson, 1992; 1995.

10   Abadie-Reynal, 1989: 158–59.

11   The size of the city's population may subsequently have declined by as much as one-half following the Justinianic plague: Mango, 1990: 51.

12   Unlike Rome, the *annona civica* was not specifically a dole for the poor in Constantinople. In addition to the *plebs frumentaria*, imperial officials, the military, and official dignitaries received free distributions. The State also used the lure of hand-outs to encourage settlers to build houses in the capital of the Eastern Empire during its early phase of urban development: Sirks, 1991a: 166, 198, 355. Durliat (1990: 269) has estimated that more than 80,000 of Constantinople's 600,000 population benefited from the *annona civica* in the sixth century.

13   Based on Rickman's suggestion that the wheat *annona* consisted of 5 *modii* of grain in Rome, and assuming that 1 *modius* was the equivalent of 6.5 kg: Rickman, 1980: 261, 263. For the Yassi Ada A dimensions, see Parker, 1992: 454–55.

14   Notably, Keay, 1984: 147 has argued that the State monopolised exchange in imported olive oil in the West: "the presence of African oil amphorae in the *conventus Tarraconensis* represents a successful attempt by the State to profit from its surplus oil, by selling it at a profit at provincial level". Pharr, 1952.

15   Pharr, 1952.

16   *Autobiography*, 279; tr. Norman, 1992: 329.

17   Carignani and Pacetti, 1989: 8, 9, 11. By A.D. 440–480, Eastern amphora occur in equal quantities to N. African containers (each about 30%). This is undoubtedly a reflection of the breakdown in *annona* supplies, which must have occurred following the loss of Africa to the Vandals in 442.

18   Gutiérrez Lloret, 1998: 165.

19   In the well in Rue de la Cathedrale, which probably went out of use in the sixth century, N. African
      wares account for 56% of all amphorae: Moliner and Pournot, 1998: 275, 272. N. African containers
      represented 68% of all amphorae in the well at Cap Titol, which ceased to function sometime
      between the first half of the fifth and the sixth century: Boiron *et al.*, 1998. However, Eastern imports
      are more numerous in many assemblages post-dating the mid-fifth century. Thus, within the well at
      Bon-Jésus in Marseille, abandoned in the second half of the fifth century, Eastern amphorae
      comprised 47% of all amphorae and N. African wares 29.5%: Reynaud *et al.*, 1998. As in Rome, this
      change in consumption patterns is probably related to the loss of the N. African provinces and of
      control over olive oil exports. This created a void, which eastern produce was able to partly exploit.

20   At least in the first three centuries A.D., oil production seems to have been controlled by an urban
      based aristocracy, whose abbreviated names are stamped on batches of Tripolitanian and Tunisian
      amphorae: Mattingly, 1988b: 37, 38, 47.

21   For example, the Dramont E ship wrecked off S. France between A.D. 425 and 455 contained 700–750
      Keay Type 25 and 35 amphorae: Santamaria, 1995: 121, 175, 191. The Isis ship was transporting Keay
      Type 3/5, 25, 31, 35 Tunisian amphorae between Carthage and Italy when she foundered between
      375 and 400 on an offshore shipping lane mid-way between Tunisia and Sicily: Freed, 1994: 22–32;
      McCann, 1994: 51–52.

22   For estate production south of Carthage, Mackensen, 1998. The fifty ARS plates (Hayes forms 50B,
      61B, 64, 65) are the minimum number on the site; it is unknown how many others had already been
      looted: Santamaria, 1995: 79. La Luque B: Liou, 1973.

23   Sirks, 1991a: 166. Sirks argues that after A.D. 534 the eastern capital was also provisioned with N.
      African grain and probably olive oil. Certainly, A.D. 610 Heraclius seized a fleet at Carthage about
      to transport the corn *annona* to Constantinople and used the supplies to support his rebellion against
      Phocas.

24   On gold circulation and taxation in the East Mediterranean, see Banaji, 1996: 41. The population of
      Egypt is discussed in Bagnall and Frier, 1994: 54–56.

25   For summaries of LR7 on all western sites, see Reynolds, 1995: the occasional example is registered
      at sites such as S. Antonino di Petri and Marseille. Saraçhane: Hayes, 1992: 67; the Israeli evidence
      is summarised and discussed in Kingsley, 1999a: 169, tables 14–16.

26   For example, ERS is not registered at Hama in Syria: Lund, 1995; only a handful of Egyptian fine-
      wares were recorded at Saraçhane: Hayes, 1992: 7; three fragments are catalogued at Anemurium:
      Williams, 1989: 27, 57. ERS is known from thirteen sites in Israel, but the highest published quantity
      within a fine-ware assemblage are the four fragments from the Late Byzantine Building at Caesarea:
      Kingsley, 1999a: 17, 169, tables 14–15.

27   ERS bowls seem to be predominant at Tiberias in Palestine during the first half of the eighth century:
      Stacey, 1988–89: 21–22, 26–27. At Ostrakine in Sinai, whereas Cypriot imports accounted for 75% of
      fine-wares during the second half of the sixth or early seventh century, by *c.* 650–685 these had been
      replaced by ERS wares, which represented 82% of all fine-wares: Oked, 1996: 171.

28   The assemblages examined in dumps in Sector 12, Building G at Alexandria are the only quantified
      pottery assemblages so far published from Egypt (Majcherek, 1992: 114–15)). Majcherek has observed
      that Nile valley amphorae comprised only 7–13% of amphora assemblages at this location and that
      the city's great dependence on imports seems to have been to the detriment of Egypt's own
      agricultural hinterland. LR1 reached the Red Sea port of Berenike in the late fourth and fifth centuries:
      Hayes, 1996: 159. Forty-nine LR1 amphorae were excavated at Hermopolis Magna: Bailey, 1998: 122;
      at least another twenty-six were recorded in the southern church at El-Ashmunein, as well as twenty-
      six N. African *spatheia*: Bailey, 1996: 86. LR1 (alongside the Palestinian LR4) was also the most
      common imported amphora registered during rescue excavations in North Sinai: Ballet, 1997: 148.
      The production of LR1 imitations in Nile silt clay, covered with a red slip, at the monastery of St.
      Jeramia at Saqqara post-dates the sixth century and was apparently only used by the local monastic
      community: Ghaly, 1992: p.167–69. Production of LR1 imitation in Mareotis is described by M.
      Rodziewicz, 1998b: 248, fig. 3.1.

29   Empereur and Picon, 1989: 243–44.

30   Cypriot bowls were the most common imported fine-wares in Sinai: Ballet, 1997: 148. Few fine-wares
      were recovered in Building 12 in Alexandria, but Cypriot table-wares were the most common imports

(19 fragments CRS, 3 PRS, 34 ERS): Majcherek, 1992: 87, 91, 92. However, African red-slip vessels were the only imported fine-wares identified in the southern church at El-Ashmunein (187 fragments, compared to 170 examples of ERS): Bailey, 1996: 54, 55, 59.

31   Strabo states that the olive was only cultivated in the Arsinoite nome: 17.I.35; tr, Jones, 1982: 97.

32   Alston, 1998: 183–84 has used data from *papyri*, referring to ninety different types of urban craft, to argue that 28% of the male population of Oxyrhynchus were registered tradesmen. Bagnall, 1993: 86 has used similar sources to estimate that 15–20% of the heads of households were engaged in industrial production in Egypt's late antique cities. Numerous dumps from ivory carving workshops have been recorded across Alexandria. This industry flourished throughout Late Antiquity and certainly into the seventh century. In addition to luxury objects (Cyril, Patriarch of Alexandria, sent an ivory chair to the Patriarch of Constantinople in A.D. 432 or 433), the city's workshops also produced objects used more widely on a daily basis: E. Rodziewicz, 1998: 137, 142.

33   Banaji, 1992: 89, 97 discusses peasants, stone masons and even unskilled workmen in Egypt receiving salaries partly, or even wholly, in gold coin (and the intensification of monetary transactions in the sixth and seventh centuries) and concludes that the "general implication is of a monetary economy that permeated both town and countryside, connecting and unifying them in a lively network of exchanges and making it possible for the State to move progressively to a more thorough going monetisation of the tax system than even Anastasius had wanted or been able to achieve".

34   eg. Angold, 1985: 3.

35   Treadgold, 1995: 195, table 12.

36   Poidebard, 1934; Mouterde and Poidebard, 1945; Parker, 1986; Kennedy and Riley, 1990.

37   Wright, 1968: 70–73.

38   The *annona militaris* continued to be collected and distributed from the fourth-seventh centuries in Egypt, Syria and Mesopotamia, the only regions for which we have evidence: Kaegi, 1985: 592–93.

39   Treadgold, 1995: 149–57, 194–95.

40   *Ibid*: 153.

41   The status of the *limitanei* as front-line soldiers has been questioned. Isaac, 1990: 208–210, and 1998: 125–47, argues convincingly that these troops were army regulars.

42   MacMullen, 1967: 11.

43   Mouterde and Poidebard, 1945: 106–126.

44   Bell, *et. al.*, 1962: 18.

45   Liebeschuetz, 1961: 252.

46   Isaac, 1990: 291–97.

47   Jones, 1964: 460.

48   *Codex Theodosianus* VII.4.30; discussed by Isaac, 1990: 288.

49   Bowman, 1996: 239, Appendix 2 values grain at one-tenth of a *solidus* for the Byzantine period.

50   This calculation, based on Treadgold's pay scale for Justinianic troops is rudimentary (1995: 150), and can only be used for comparative purposes. Numbers of troops stationed in Egypt are unknown and we have used Treadgold's estimate of 176,000 frontier soldiers for the whole of the eastern empire. Assuming these troops were spread evenly over the whole of the thirteen eastern military commands, which of course they were not, one arrives at a total of 13,538, which we have increased to 15,000 for the sake of mathematical convenience; Treadgold, 1995: 60 assumes this includes 5,000 infantry and 10,000 cavalry. For the predominance of cavalry in the Late Roman Empire from the fourth century onwards, see Jones, 1964: 99–100.

51   Bowman 1996: 94; Segrè 1943: 439.

52   Treadgold, 1995: 194, table 12.

53   *Idem.*

54   The plague killed between one-quarter and one-third of the Empire's population: see Allen, 1979: 5–20.

55   Nicasie, 1998: 148 rightly points out that the late Roman army was a mixed blessing for those with whom it came into contact.

56   Segrè, 1943: 410.

57   Dewing, 1960: 283–285; Hendy, 1985: 294–96 and 602–607.

58   Mouterde and Poidebard, 1945: 159–69.

59 MacMullen, 1967: 19–21.
60 Millar, 1998: 119–120; Crone, 1987: 12–51.
61 Jones, 1964: 895.
62 Price, 1991: 20–21.
63 Mango, 1980: 38.
64 Clark, 1984: 38 on Melania's inherited wealth.
65 Hunt, 1982: 137–38.
66 John the Lydian III, 76 (Bandy, 1983) noted that Justinian spent 288,000 *solidi* on the church in only one of the six years its construction took; Treadgold, 1995: 192–93.
67 Schaff and Wace, 1890: 275.
68 Brooks, 1923: 129.
69 Martini and Steckner, 1993: 143–61.
70 Dauphin, 1993.
71 *Spiritual Meadow*: 56; Hirschfeld, 1992: 106–111.
72 Hirschfeld, 1992: 108.
73 Lassus, 1935–36: 28–29.
74 Wipszycka, 1972: 40, 47–49, 52–53.
75 Brown, 1971: 80–101 is still the best introduction to the saint in late antique society; see also Mango, 1980: 105–114.
76 Thomas, 1987: 86–87.
77 Primarily Jones, 1964: 778, 802–823; 1974: 83–87. See Charanis, 1944–45: 39 for an argument that immobility dominated social structures.
78 Traditional studies of the late antique economy ignore the potential for tax demands to actually improve rural prosperity by compelling farmers to cultivate crops more efficiently. The evidence against severe population decline in the East, at least before the Justinianic plague, is now overwhelming. For a detailed critique of the primitivist stance in the West, see Lewit, 1991.
79 Hendy, 1989: 4, 6.
80 On maritime transport conditions, and costs of land transport: Jones, 1964: 312; Garnsey and Saller, 1987: 44. On the monetary economy, see Haldon, 1985: 80–81, and Hendy, 1985: 602; Hendy, 1989: 9.
81 Hopkins, 1983: xxiv.
82 Wickham, 1984: 13; 1998: 284.
83 Durliat, 1998: 115–16.
84 Liebeschuetz, 1972: 83.
85 Bagnall, 1997: 28.
86 MacMullen, 1964. Marcone, 1998: 338, 364, 370 states that inequality was, as ever, the foundation of life in Late Antiquity, and that mobility was a relatively minor phenomenon within a state-coerced environment; however, if vertical mobility was difficult (other than through working in the Church or joining the army), horizontal social fluidity was considerable.
87 Harris, 1993; Paterson, 1998.
88 Bagnall, 1997: 14.
89 Calculated using the figure of 80,000 free distributions in the capital argued by Durliat, 1990: 232 and Sirks, 1991b: 225.
90 Sirks, 1991b: 234.
91 By *c.* A.D. 525–50 East Mediterranean amphora represented 25–30% of assemblages: Fulford, 1983: 9.
92 Ward-Perkins, forthcoming.
93 For an overview of changes in shipbuilding, see Steffy, 1991; Hocker, 1995; Raveh and Kingsley, 1991: 201–203.
94 The earliest ship built frame-first known from the Mediterranean is a fifth or sixth century merchant vessel recently excavated in the harbour of Dor in Israel: Wachsmann and Kahanov, 1997: 4–6. The sixth century seems to have been a transitional period: a ship of the second half of the sixth century from the same site still relied on mortise-and-tenon technology: Kingsley, forthcoming.
95 Steffy, 1994: 85.

96 Barker, 1991: 6–7 and 1995: 2–3 discusses how landscape archaeology can reflect the complex interplay between local, regional and Mediterranean-wide factors, many of which cannot be extrapolated from historical sources.

97 Parkins, 1997; Parkins, 1998; Whittaker, 1990; Whittaker, 1993.

98 For a brief summary of some East Mediterranean sites, see Kingsley, 1999a: 39–43.

99 Stephens Crawford, 1990.

100 Trombley, 1987.

101 Alston, 1998: 183–84.

102 Uscatescu and Martín, 1997: 77 for furnaces from the *tinctoria*.

103 Gibbins, 1990; Parker, 1990.

104 Twenty-two wrecks of late antique date from Israel are discussed in Kingsley, 1999a: 118–137. For wrecks of mid-sixth to mid-seventh century at the entrance to Dor harbour in Israel, see Kingsley and Raveh, 1994; Kingsley and Raveh, 1996; Kingsley, forthcoming; Wachsmann, 1996; Wachsmann and Kahanov, 1997. For the Sea of Marmara, see Kassab Tezgör, 1998.

105 Martin, 1998.

106 For the exemplary material from the West, see Reynolds, 1995, and Kingsley, 1999a: tables 12–13.

107 For an overview of quantified deposits from Caesarea, see Blakely, 1996.

108 Kingsley, 1999b.

109 Whittaker, 1986: 2–3.

110 See Tomber, 1988: 67–69, and Orton and Tyers, 1992.

Bibliography

Abadie-Reynal, C., 1989. 'Céramique et commerce dans le bassin Egéen du IVᵉ au VIIᵉ siècle'. In *Hommes et richesses dans l'empire byzantin. Tome I, IVᵉ-VIIᵉ siècle* (Paris), 143–62.

Allen, P., 1979. 'The Justinianic Plague', *Byzantion* 49, 5–20.

Alston, R., 1998. 'Trade and the City in Roman Egypt'. In H. Parkins and C. Smith (ed.) *Trade, Traders and the Ancient City* (London), 168–202.

Angold, M., 1985. 'The Shaping of the Medieval Byzantine City', *Byz. Forsch.* 10, 1–37.

Bagnall, R.S., 1993. *Egypt in Late Antiquity* (Princeton University Press).

Bagnall, R.S., 1997. *The Kellis Agricultural Account Book (P.Kell IV Gr.96)* (Oxford).

Bagnall, R.S. and Frier, B.W., 1994. *The Demography of Roman Egypt* (Cambridge).

Bailey, D.M., 1996. 'The Pottery from the South Church at El-Ashmunein', *CCE* 4, 47–112.

Bailey, D.M., 1998. *Excavations at El-Ashmunein V. Pottery, Lamps and Glass of the Late Roman and Early Arab Periods* (British Museum, London).

Ballet, P., 1997. 'La céramique romaine. Haut et bas-empire'. In J. Bourriau and D. Valbelle (ed.) *An Introduction to the Pottery of Northern Sinai. Preliminary Results of the Rescue Campaign 1990–1994* (CCE 5, Cairo), 145–49.

Banaji, J., 1992. *Rural Communities in the Late Empire AD 300–700: Monetary and Economic Aspects* (D.Phil Thesis, University of Oxford).

Banaji, J., 1996. 'The Circulation of Gold as an Index of Prosperity in the Central and Eastern Mediterranean in Late Antiquity'. In C.E. King and D.G. Wigg (ed.) *Coin Finds and Coin Use in the Roman World. The 13th Oxford Symposium on Coinage and Monetary History* (Oxford), 41–53.

Barker, G., 1991. 'Approaches to Archaeological Survey'. In G. Barker and J. Lloyd (ed.) *Roman Landscapes. Archaeological Survey in the Mediterranean Region* (Archaeological Monographs of the British School at Rome 2, London), 1–9.

Barker, G., 1995. 'Landscape Archaeology in Italy – Goals for the 1990s'. In N. Christie (ed.) *Settlement and Economy in Italy 1500 BC to AD 1500. Papers of the Fifth Conference of Italian Archaeology* (Oxbow Monographs 41, Oxford), 1–11.

Barker, G. *et al.*, 1999. 'Environment and Land Use in the Wadi Faynan, Southern Jordan: the Third Season of Geoarchaeology and Landscape Archaeology (1998)', *Levant* 31, 255–92.

Bell, H.I. *et al.*, 1962. *The Abinnaeus Archive: Papers of a Roman Officer in the Reign of Constantius II* (London).

Ben David, H., 1998. 'Oil Presses and Oil Production in the Golan in the Mishnaic and Talmudic Periods', *'Atiqot* 34, 1–61. (Hebrew).

Blakely, J.A., 1996. 'Toward the Study of Economics at Caesarea Maritima'. In A. Raban and K. Holum (ed.) *Caesarea Maritima. A Retrospective after Two Millennia* (Leiden), 327–45.

Boiron, R., Chapon, P., Durand, C., Piéri, D., Pournot, J. and Reynaud, P., 1998. 'Le puits du Cap Titol'. In M. Bonifay, M.-B. Carre and Y. Rigoir (ed.) *Fouilles à Marseille. Les mobiliers (Ier-VIIe siècles ap. J.-C.)* (Études Massaliètes, Paris), 252–64.

Bowman, A., 1996. *Egypt After the Pharaohs: 332 BC-AD 642 from Alexander to the Arab Conquest* (London).

Brooks, E.W., (ed. and tr.), 1923. *John of Ephesus. Lives of the Eastern Saints* (Patrologia Orientalis 17, Paris).

Brown, P., 1971. 'The Rise and Function of the Holy Man in Late Antiquity', *JRS* 61, 80–101.

Butler, H.C., 1907–1919. *Syria: Publications of the Princeton University Archaeological Expeditions to Syria in 1904–1905 and 1909. Division II, Sections A and B* (Leiden).

Callot, O., 1984. *Huileries antiques de Syrie du Nord* (Paris).

Carignani, A. and Pacetti, F., 1989. 'Le importazioni di anfore bizantine a Roma fra IV e V secolo: le evidenze di alcuni contesti urbani'. In V. Déroche and J.-M. Spieser (ed.) *Recherches sur la céramique Byzantine* (BCH Suppl. 18, Paris), 5–16.

Casson, L., 1980. 'The Role of the State in Rome's Grain Trade'. In J.H. d'Arms and E.C. Kopff (ed.) *The Seaborne Commerce of Ancient Rome: Studies in Archaeology and History* (Rome), 21–34.

Charanis, P., 1944–1945. 'On the Social Structure of the Later Roman Empire', *Byzantion* 17, 39–57.

Chrysos, E., 1993. 'Cyprus in Early Byzantine Times'. In A.A.M. Bryer and G.S. Georghalides (ed.) *The Sweet Land of Cyprus: Papers Given at the Twenty-Fifth Jubilee Spring Symposium of Byzantine Studies, Birmingham, March 1991* (Nicosia), 3–14.

Clark, E.A. 1984 (tr.). *The Life of Melania the Younger* (New York).

Crone, P., 1987. *Meccan Trade and the Rise of Islam* (Princeton).

Crowfoot, J.W. and Fitzgerald, G.M., 1927. *Excavations in the Tyropoeon Valley, Jerusalem 1927* (Annual of the Palestine Exploration Fund 5, London).

Dar, S., 1986. *Landscape and Pattern. An Archaeological Survey of Samaria 800 BCE-636 CE* (BAR Int. Series 308, Oxford).

Dauphin, C., 1993. 'A Byzantine Ecclesiastical Farm at Shelomi'. In Y. Tsafrir (ed.) *Ancient Churches Revealed* (Jerusalem), 43–48.

Dauphin, C. and Gibson, S., 1992–3. 'Ancient Settlements in their Landscapes: the Results of Ten Years of Survey on the Golan Heights', *BAIAS* 12, 7–31.

Dewing, H.B., 1960 (tr.). *Procopius: Anecdota* (Cambridge, Mass.).

Durliat, J., 1990. *De la ville antique à la ville byzantine. Le problème des subsistances* (École Française de Rome, Rome).

Durliat, J., 1998. 'Les conditions du commerce au VIe siècle'. In R. Hodges and W. Bowden (ed.) *The Sixth Century. Production, Distribution and Demand* (Leiden), 89–117.

Empereur, J.-Y. and Picon, M., 1989. 'Les régions de production d'amphores impériales en Méditerranée orientale'. In *Amphores Romaines et histoire économique: dix ans de recherche* (Ecole Française de Rome, Rome), 223–48.

Foxhall, L. and Forbes, H.A., 1982. '*Sitometreia*: the Role of Grain as a Staple Food in Classical Antiquity', *Chiron* 12, 41–90

Fradkin, A., 1997. 'Long-Distance Trade in the Lower Galilee: New Evidence from Sepphoris'. In D.R. Edwards and C.T. McCollough (ed.) *Archaeology and the Galilee. Texts and Contexts in the Graeco-Roman and Byzantine Periods* (Georgia), 107–116.

Freed, J., 1994. 'The Pottery from the Late-Roman Shipwreck'. In A.M. McCann and J. Freed, *Deep Water Archaeology: a Late-Roman Ship from Carthage and an Ancient Trade Route near Skerki Bank off Northwest Sicily* (JRA Suppl. 13, Michigan), 21–48.

Fulford, M., 1980. 'Carthage: Overseas Trade and the Political Economy, *c.* AD 400–700', *Reading Medieval Studies* 6, 68–80.

Fulford, M., 1983. 'Pottery and the Economy of Carthage and its Hinterland', *Opus* 2, 5–14.

Fulford, M., 1987. 'Economic Interdependence among Urban Communities of the Roman Mediterranean', *World Archaeology* 19, 58–75.

Garnsey, P. and Saller, R., 1987. *The Roman Empire. Economy, Society and Culture* (London).

Ghaly, H., 1992. 'Pottery Workshops of Saint-Jeremia (Saqqara)', *CCE* 3, 161–72.

Gibbins, D., 1990. 'Analytical Approaches in Maritime Archaeology: a Mediterranean Perspective', *Antiquity* 64, 376–89.

Gibson, S., 1995. *Landscape Archaeology and Ancient Agricultural Field Systems in Palestine* (Doctor of Philosophy Thesis, University College, London).

Gibson, S., Ibbs, B. and Kloner, A., 1991. 'The Sataf Project of Landscape Archaeology in the Judaean Hills: a Preliminary Report on Four Seasons of Surveys and Excavation (1987–89)', *Levant* 23, 29–54.

Gibson, S., Kingsley, S. and Clarke, J., 1999. 'Town and Country in the Southern Carmel: Report on the Landscape Archaeology Project at Dor (LAPD)', *Levant* 31, 71–121.

Gutiérrez Lloret, S., 1998. 'Eastern Spain in the Light of Archaeology'. In R. Hodges and W. Bowden (ed.) *The Sixth Century Production. Distribution and Demand* (Leiden), 161–84.

Haldon, J.F., 1985. 'Some Considerations on Byzantine Society and Economy in the Seventh Century', *Byz. Forsch.* 10, 75–112.

Harris, W.V., 1993. 'Between Archaic and Modern: some Current Problems in the History of the Roman Economy'. In W.V. Harris (ed.) *The Inscribed Economy. Production and Distribution in the Roman Empire in the Light of* Instrumentum Domesticum (JRA Suppl. 6, Ann Arbor), 11–30.

Hayes, J.W., 1992. *Excavations at Saraçhane in Istanbul. Vol.2: the Pottery* (Princeton University Press, New Jersey).

Hayes, J.W., 1996. 'The Pottery'. In S. Sidebotham and W. Wendrich (ed.) *Berenike '95. Preliminary Report of the Excavations at Berenike (Egyptian Red Sea Coast) and the Survey of the Eastern Desert* (NWS Publication No. 2, Leiden), 147–78.

Hendy, M.F., 1985. *Studies in the Byzantine Monetary Economy c. 300–1450* (Cambridge).

Hendy, M.F., 1989. *The Economy, Fiscal Administration and Coinage of Byzantium* (Northampton).

Hirschfeld, Y., 1992. *The Judean Desert Monasteries in the Byzantine Period* (New Haven).

Hocker, F., 1995. 'Lead Hull Sheathing in Antiquity'. In H. Tzalas (ed.) *3rd International Symposium on Ship Construction in Antiquity, Tropis III* (Thessaloniki), 197–206.

Hopkins, K., 1965. 'Elite Mobility in the Roman Empire', *Past and Present* 32, 12–26.

Hopkins, K., 1983. 'Introduction'. In P. Garnsey, K. Hopkins and C.R. Whittaker (ed.) *Trade in the Ancient Economy* (London), ix–xxv.

Hunt, E.D., 1982. *Holy Land Pilgrimage in the Later Roman Empire AD 312–460* (Oxford).

Isaac, B., 1988. 'The Meaning of "Limes" and "Limitanei" in Ancient Sources', *JRS* 78, 125–147.

Isaac, B., 1990. *The Limits of Empire. The Roman Army in the East* (Oxford).

Jones, A.H.M., 1964. *The Later Roman Empire 284–602, Vol. II* (Oxford).

Jones, A.H.M., 1974. *The Roman Economy* (Oxford).

Jones, H.L., 1982 (tr.). *The Geography of Strabo* (Harvard University Press).

Kaegi, W.E., 1985. 'The Annona Militaris in the Early Seventh Century', *Byzantina* 13, 589–96.

Kassab Tezgör, D., 1998. 'Prospection sous-marine près de la côte Sinopéene: transport d'amphores depuis l'atelier et navigation en Mer Noire', *Anatolia Antiqua* 6, 443–49.

Keay, S.J., 1984. *Late Roman Amphorae in the Western Mediterranean. A Typology and Economic Study: the Catalan Evidence* (BAR Int. Series 196, Oxford).

Kennedy, D. and Riley, D., 1990. *Rome's Desert Frontier from the Air* (London).

Kingsley, S., 1999a. *Specialized Production and Long-Distance Trade in Byzantine Palestine* (D.Phil Thesis, University of Oxford).

Kingsley, S., 1999b. 'The Sumaqa Pottery Assemblage: Classification and Quantification'. In S. Dar (ed.) *Sumaqa. A Roman and Byzantine Jewish Village on Mount Carmel, Israel* (BAR Int. Series 815, Archaeopress, Oxford), 263–330.

Kingsley, S., forthcoming. *A Sixth Century AD Merchant Vessel in Dor Harbour, Israel (Dor D) – Final Excavation Report* (Oxford).

Kingsley, S. and Raveh, K., 1994. 'Stone Anchors from Byzantine Contexts in Dor Harbour', *IJNA* 23, 1–12.

Kingsley, S. and Raveh, K., 1996. *The Ancient Harbour and Anchorage at Dor, Israel. Results of the Underwater Surveys 1976–1991* (BAR Int. Series 626, Oxford).

Kirwan, L.P., 1938. 'The Pottery'. In W.B. Emery and L.P. Kirwan, *The Royal Tombs of Ballana and Qustul* (Cairo), 386–99.

Lassus, J., 1935–1936. *Inventaire archéologique de la région au nord-est de Hama* (Damascus).

Lernau, G., 1995. 'The Fish Remains of Upper Zohar'. In R.P. Harper (ed.) *Upper Zohar: an Early Byzantine Fort in Palaestina Tertia* (BSAJ, Oxford), 99–105.

Lernau, O., 1999. 'Fish Remains from Horvat Sumaqa'. In S. Dar (ed.) *Sumaqa. A Roman and Byzantine Jewish Village on Mount Carmel, Israel* (BAR Int. Series 815), 379–80.

Lewit, T., 1991. *Agricultural Production in the Roman Economy A.D. 200–400* (BAR Int. Series 568, Oxford).

Liebeschuetz, J.H.W.G., 1961. 'Money Economy and Taxation in Kind in Syria in the Fourth Century A.D.', *Rheinisches Museum für Philogie*, N.F. 104, 242–56.

Liebeschuetz, J.H.W.G., 1972. *Antioch. City and Imperial Administration in the Later Roman Empire* (Oxford).

Liou, B., 1973. 'Direction des recherches archéologiques sous-marines', *Gallia* 31, 571–608.

Lund, J., 1995. 'A Fresh Look at the Roman and Late Roman Fine Wares from the Danish Excavations at Hama, Syria'. In H. Meyza and J. Mlynarczyk (ed.) *Hellenistic and Roman Pottery in the Eastern Mediterranean – Advances in Scientific Studies. Acts of the II Nieborow Pottery Workshop* (Warsaw), 135–61.

Mackensen, M., 1998. 'Centres of African Red Slip Ware Production in Tunisia from the Late 5th to the 7th Centuries'. In L. Saguì (ed.) *Ceramica in Italia: VI-VII secolo. Atti del Convegno in onore di John W. Hayes Roma, 11–13 maggio 1995* (Firenze), 23–39.

MacMullen, R., 1964. 'Social Mobility and the Theodosian Code', *JRS* 54, 49–53.

MacMullen, R., 1967. *Soldier and Civilian in the Later Roman Empire* (Cambridge, Mass.)

Majcherek, G., 1992. 'The Late Roman Ceramics from Sector "G" (Alexandria 1986–1987)', *Études et Travaux* 16, 81–117.

Mango, C., 1980. *Byzantium: the Empire of New Rome* (London).

Mango, C., 1990. *Le Développement urbain de Constantinople (IVᵉ-VIIᵉ siècles)* (Paris).

Marcone, A., 1998. 'Late Roman Social Relations'. In A. Cameron and P. Garnsey (ed.) *The Cambridge Ancient History, Volume XIII. The Late Empire, A.D. 337–425* (Cambridge University Press), 338–70.

Martin, A., 1998. 'La sigillata focese (Phocaean Red-Slip/Late Roman C Ware)'. In L. Saguì (ed.) *Ceramica in Italia: VI-VII secolo. Atti del convegno in onore di John W. Hayes Roma, 11–13 maggio 1995* (Firenze), 109–122.

Martini, W. and Steckner, C. 1993. *Samos 17: das Gymnasium von Samos, das frühbyzantinische Klostergut* (Bonn).

Mattingly, D.J., 1988a. 'The Olive Boom. Oil Surpluses, Wealth and Power in Roman Tripolitania', *Libyan Studies* 19, 21–41.

Mattingly, D.J., 1988b. 'Oil for Export? A Comparison of Libyan, Spanish and Tunisian Olive Oil Production in the Roman Empire', *JRA* 1, 33–56.

McCann, A.M., 1994. 'The Late-Roman Shipwreck: Summary and Conclusions'. In A.M. McCann and J. Freed, *Deep Water Archaeology: a Late-Roman Ship from Carthage and an Ancient Trade Route near Skerki Bank off Northwest Sicily* (JRA Suppl. 13, Michigan), 49–58.

Millar, F., 1998. 'Caravan Cities: the Roman Near East and Long Distance Trade by Land'. In M. Austin, J. Harries and C. Smith (ed.) *Modus Operandi: Essays in Honour of Geoffrey Rickman* (London), 119–38.

Moliner, M. and Pournot, J., 1998. 'Le puits de la Rue de la Cathédrale (îlot 55)'. In M. Bonifay, M.-B. Carre and Y. Rigoir (ed.) *Fouilles à Marseille. Les mobiliers (1er-VIIe siècles ap. J.-C.)* (Études Massaliètes, Paris), 264–75.

Mouterde, R. and Poidebard, A., 1945. *Le limes de Chalcis: organisation de la steppe en Haute Syrie romaine* (Paris).

Nicasie, M.J., 1998. *Twilight of Empire: the Roman Army from the Reign of Diocletian until the Battle of Adrianople* (Amsterdam).

Norman, A.F., 1992. *Libanius. Autobiography and Selected Letters, Volume I* (Harvard University Press).

Oked, S., 1996. 'Patterns of the Transport Amphorae at Ostrakine during the 6th and 7th Centuries', *ARAM* 8, 165–75.

Orton, C.R. and Tyers, P.A., 1992. 'Counting Broken Objects: the Statistics of Ceramic Assemblages'. In A.M. Pollard (ed.) *New Developments in Archaeological Science* (Oxford University Press), 163–86.

Parker, A.J., 1990. 'Classical Antiquity: the Maritime Dimension', *Antiquity* 64, 335–46.

Parker, A.J., 1992. *Ancient Shipwrecks of the Mediterranean and the Roman Provinces* (BAR Int. Series 580, Oxford).

Parker, S.T., 1986. *Romans and Saracens: a History of the Arabian Frontier* (Indiana).

Parkins, H., 1997. 'The 'Consumer City' Domesticated? The Roman City in Élite Economic Strategies'. In H.M. Parkins (ed.) *Roman Urbanism. Beyond the Consumer City* (London), 83–111.

Parkins, H., 1998. 'Time for Change? Shaping the Future of the Ancient Economy'. In H. Parkins and C. Smith (ed.) *Trade, Traders and the Ancient City* (London), 1–15.

Paterson, J., 1998. 'Trade and Traders in the Roman World: Scale, Structure and Organisation'. In H. Parkins and C. Smith (ed.) *Trade, Traders and the Ancient City* (London), 149–67.

Pharr, C., 1952. *The Theodosian Code and Novels and the Simondian Constitutions* (Princeton University Press).

Poidebard, P., 1934. *La trace de Rome dans le désert de Syrie: le limes de Trajan à la conquête arabe: recherches aériennes (1925–1932)* (Paris).

Price, R.M., 1991 (tr.). *Lives of the Monks of Palestine by Cyril of Scythopolis* (Kalamazoo).

Raveh, K. and Kingsley, S., 1991. 'The Status of Dor in Late Antiquity: a Maritime Perspective', *Biblical Archaeologist* 54, 198–207.

Rénan, J. E., 1864. *Mission de Phénicie* (Paris).

Reynaud, P., Bonifay, M., Foy, D., Liou, B., Pelletier, J-P., Piéri, D., Pournot, J. and Rigoir, Y., 1998. 'Le puits de la Rue du Bon-Jésus (îlot 39 N)'. In M. Bonifay, M.-B. Carre and Y. Rigoir (ed.) *Fouilles à Marseille. Les mobiliers (1er-VIIe siècles ap. J.-C.)* (Études Massaliètes, Paris), 197–251.

Reynolds, P., 1995. *Trade in the Western Mediterranean, AD 400–700: the Ceramic Evidence* (BAR Int. Series 604, Oxford).

Rickman, G.E., 1980. 'The Grain Trade under the Roman Empire'. In J.H. d'Arms and E.C. Kopff (ed.), *The Seaborne Commerce of Ancient Rome: Studies in Archaeology and History* (Rome), 261–76.

Rodziewicz, E., 1998. 'Archaeological Evidence of Bone and Ivory Carvings in Alexandria'. In J.-Y. Empereur (ed.) *Commerce et artisanat dans l'Alexandrie héllenistique et romaine* (BCH Suppl. 33, Paris), 136–58.

Rodziewicz, M., 1998a. 'Classification of Wineries from Mareotis'. In J.-Y. Empereur (ed.) *Commerce et artisanat dans l'Alexandrie héllenistique et romaine* (BCH Suppl. 33, Paris), 28–36.

Rodziewicz, M., 1998b. 'Experimental Identification of Local and Imported Pottery in Mareotis'. In J.-Y. Empereur (ed.) *Commerce et artisanat dans l'Alexandrie héllenistique et romaine* (BCH Suppl. 33, Paris), 245–60.

Santamaria, C., 1995. *L'épave Dramont E à Saint-Raphael (Ve siècle ap. J.-C.)* (Archaeonautica 13, Paris).

Schwartz, J.J., 1991. *Lod (Lydda), Israel* (BAR Int. Series 571, Oxford).

Segré, A., 1943. 'Essays on Byzantine Economics, I. The *Annona Civica* and the *Annona Militaris*', *Byzantion* 16, 393–444.

Sirks, B., 1991a. *Food for Rome. The Legal Structure of the Transportation and Processing of Supplies for the Imperial Distributions in Rome and Constantinople* (Amsterdam).

Sirks, A.J.B., 1991b. 'The Size of the Grain Distributions in Imperial Rome and Constantinople', *Athenaeum* 11, 215–37.

Stacey, D., 1988–9. 'Umayyad and Egyptian Red-Slip 'A' Ware from Tiberias', *BAIAS* 8, 21–33.

Steffy, R., 1991. 'The Mediterranean Shell to Skeleton Transition: a Northwest European Parallel?'. In R. Reinders and K. Paul (ed.) *Carvel Construction Technique, Skeleton-first, Shell-first. Fifth International Symposium on Boat and Ship Archaeology, Amsterdam 1988* (Oxbow Monograph 12, Oxford), 1–9.

Steffy, J.R., 1994. *Wooden Ship Building and the Interpretation of Shipwrecks* (Texas A & M University Press).

Stephens Crawford, J., 1990. *The Byzantine Shops at Sardis* (Massachusetts).

Storey, G.R., 1999. 'Archaeology and Roman Society: Integrating Textual and Archaeological Data', *Journal of Archaeological Research* 7, 203–48.

Thomas, J.P., 1987. *Private Religious Foundations in the Byzantine Empire* (Washington).

Tomber, R., 1988. *Pottery in Long-Distance Economic Inference: an Investigation of Methodology with Reference to Roman Carthage* (Doctor of Philosophy Thesis, University of Southampton).

Tomber, R., 1993. 'Quantitative Approaches to the Investigation of Long-Distance Exchange', *JRA* 6, 142–66.

Tengstrom, E., 1974. *Bread for the People. Studies of the Corn-Supply of Rome during the Late Empire* (Lund).

Treadgold, W., 1995. *Byzantium and its Army* (Stanford).

Trombley, F., 1987. 'Korykos in Cilicia Trachis: the Economy of a Small Coastal City in Late Antiquity (*Saec*. V-VI) – a Précis', *The Ancient History Bulletin* 1, 16–23.

Urman, D., 1985. *The Golan. A Profile of a Region during the Roman and Byzantine Periods* (BAR Int. Series 269, Oxford).

Uscatescu, A. and Martín, M., 1997. 'The *Macellum* of Gerasa (Jerash, Jordan): from a Market Place to an Industrial Area', *BASOR* 307, 67–88.

Wace, H. and Schaff, P. (ed.), 1890. A *Select Library of the Nicene and Post-Nicene Fathers of the Christian Church*, (Volume 3, New York) 1–348.

Wachsmann, S., 1996. 'A Cove of Many Shipwrecks: the 1995 INA/CMS Joint Expedition to Tantura Lagoon', *CMS News* 23, 17–21.

Wachsmann, S. and Kahanov, Y., 1997. 'The 1995 INA/CMS Joint Expedition to Tantura Lagoon, Israel', *The INA Quarterly* 24, 3–18.

Ward-Perkins, B., forthcoming. 'Specialised Production and Exchange'. In A. Cameron, B. Ward-Perkins and M. Whitby (ed.) *The Cambridge Ancient History* XIV (*Late Antiquity: Empire and Successors, A.D. 425–600*) (Cambridge).

Watson, P., 1992. 'Change in Foreign and Regional Economic Links with Pella in the Seventh Century AD: the Ceramic Evidence'. In P. Canivet and Rey-Coquais, J.-P. (ed.) *La Syrie de Byzance à 'Islam VII*e*-VIII*e *siècles* (Damascus), 233–48.

Watson, P., 1995. 'Ceramic Evidence for Egyptian Links with Northern Jordan in the 6th-8th Centuries AD'. In S. Bourke and J.-P. Descoeudres (ed.) *Trade, Contact, and the Movement of Peoples in the Eastern Mediterranean* (Mediterranean Archaeology Suppl. 3, Sydney), 303–20.

Watson, P., 1996. 'Pella Hinterland Survey 1994; Preliminary Report', *Levant* 28, 63–76.

Weinstein-Evron, M. and Chaim, S., 1999. 'Palynological Investigations in Sumaqa: 1995–1996'. In S. Dar (ed.) *Sumaqa. A Roman and Byzantine Jewish Village on Mount Carmel, Israel* (BAR Int. Series 815), 365–68.

Whittaker, C.R., 1986. 'Cliometrics and the Historian', *Opus* 5, 1–7.

Whittaker, C.R., 1990. 'The Consumer City Revisited: the *vicus* and the City', *JRA* 3, 110–18.

Whittaker, C.R., 1993. 'Do Theories of the Ancient City Matter?'. In T.J. Cornell and H.K. Lomas (ed.) *Urban Society in Roman Italy* (London), 1–20.

Wickham, C., 1984. 'The Other Transition: from the Ancient World to Feudalism', *Past and Present* 103, 3–36.

Wickham, C., 1998. 'Overview: Production, Distribution and Demand'. In R. Hodges and W. Bowden (ed.) *The Sixth Century. Production, Distribution and Demand* (Leiden), 279–92.

Wilkinson, T.J., 1990. *Town and Country in Southeastern Anatolia* (Chicago).

Williams, C., 1989. *Anemurium: the Roman and Early Byzantine Pottery* (Subsidia Mediaevalia 16, Crescent East).

Wipszycka, E., 1972. *Les resources et les activités économiques des églises en Egypte du IVe au VIIIe siècle* (Brussells).

Wright, W., 1968 (tr.). *The Chronicle of Joshua the Stylite* (Amsterdam).

Chapter 2

Urban Economies of Late Antique Cyrenaica

Andrew Wilson
This paper is dedicated to the memory of John Lloyd

Introduction

Cyrenaica does not figure large in discussions of the ancient economy or trade. In the Greek period Cyrene on occasion relieved famine in Greece with shipments of grain;[1] more generally, literary sources refer to the export of silphium and products derived from it; the scattered references to the other resources of the region (wine, oil, fish, horses, sheep) do not necessarily imply production for export. Archaeologically, the mid-Roman amphorae produced locally at Berenice and Taucheira,[2] and evidently at Ptolemais too,[3] have not been recognised in any quantity outside Cyrenaica. There was, of course, trading contact with the rest of the Empire, but we are looking at a very different picture from the large-scale exports of Africa Proconsularis and Tripolitania. For later antiquity the picture is still less clear. The general view for the third century onwards is of economic decline from which the area was only temporarily rescued by the rebuilding programme of Justinian.[4] Our main literary source, Synesios of Cyrene, bishop of Ptolemais in the early fifth century A.D., offers a view of a province fertile in parts, but increasingly disturbed by nomadic incursions and oppressed by government taxation and mismanagement; and certainly not exporting surplus produce in any quantity. The most detailed modern treatment of late antique Cyrenaica, by Denis Roques, uses Synesios to argue vigorously but unconvincingly that the economy and other aspects of society were flourishing in the late fourth and early fifth centuries;[5] much of his argument reads – to my mind – like an exercise in special pleading. Synesios is not an ideal source for the reconstruction of economic history, and indeed it must be admitted that the relevant literary sources are few; to reconstruct a picture of Cyrenaica in Late Antiquity we are thrown back largely on archaeological data.

Here we are not as well served as we might hope. In common with the rest of North Africa, archaeological investigation in Cyrenaica has concentrated on monumental architecture of the Classical period to the High Empire; late Roman and Byzantine monuments were often regarded as encumbrances to be removed in order to reveal the splendours of the ages before decadence set in. There are honourable exceptions, in the work of Richard Goodchild and particularly the excavations of Berenice (Sidi Khrebish, Benghazi) directed by John Lloyd for the Society for Libyan Studies, and the current Libyan excavations at Tocra by Garyunis University (Benghazi), but for the most part the archaeology of late antique Cyrenaica remains inadequately published and studied.

That is not to say that there is little of it. Most of the visible remains at Taucheira and Apollonia, and to a large extent at Ptolemais as well, belong to the latest periods of those sites. They include a number of structures associated with manufacturing activities that shed some light on economic life in the towns of the Pentapolis in Late Antiquity. It seems worth drawing the data together to see what sort of overall picture they suggest; I should stress, though, that conclusions will be limited and provisional: owing usually to inadequate publication, the chronological evidence for these structures is frequently non-existent or vague in the extreme. I shall examine the cities of the Pentapolis in turn, starting with the two about which we are best informed, Berenice (thanks to the 1970s excavations at Sidi Khrebish), and Taucheira (thanks to the ongoing excavations by Garyunis University). Finally, I shall attempt – tentatively – to deduce a larger context and relate this to wider issues of urban change.

Berenice

Berenice, the westernmost city of the Pentapolis, is the city about whose ordinary urban quarters we are best informed. Excavation in the 1970s revealed an area of prosperous houses of the Hellenistic and Roman periods, that seems to have undergone a radical transformation during the third century A.D.; many houses were abandoned following a possible epidemic in the early third century, and were destroyed around the middle of that century. Subsequently, there was some reoccupation by workshops, on a much reduced scale. The defended circuit of the city was reduced to about a quarter of its former size in the third century, and later rebuilt by Justinian. The aqueduct had been put out of action by the fourth century, or perhaps earlier. The single sizeable late antique building discovered in the 10 ha of excavations is a church, of fortified aspect on the highest point of the site, overlooking the defences, and was built probably in the reign of Anastasius.[6]

The reoccupation during the third century is predominantly of a light industrial character. Kilns, ovens and vats were inserted into buildings, which reused the shells of former houses. Typical of these is the kiln built over the cisterns in the peristyle of Building H following its abandonment and destruction in the early third century. Outside the kiln was a heap of crushed murex shells, and nearby were fragments of unfired pottery. Two other structures, probably ovens, belong to this short-lived occupation phase, which ceased around the middle of the third century.[7]

Building B3, abandoned around the middle of the third century, was also reoccupied by a workshop, making lamps in one or possibly two kilns. Again, this phase was short-lived and does not seem to have lasted much beyond the middle of the third century.[8]

Building P1 was initially a large peristyle house, converted to industrial use in the early third century, before its abandonment in the middle of the third century. This conversion included the insertion into two rooms in the north-west corner of two sets of twelve and six vats, and the building of a kiln and oven for products of uncertain nature in rooms opening onto the peristyle. The vats are each up to 3 m deep and lined with *opus signinum* (Fig. 2.1); evidently they were intended to hold liquids, of which

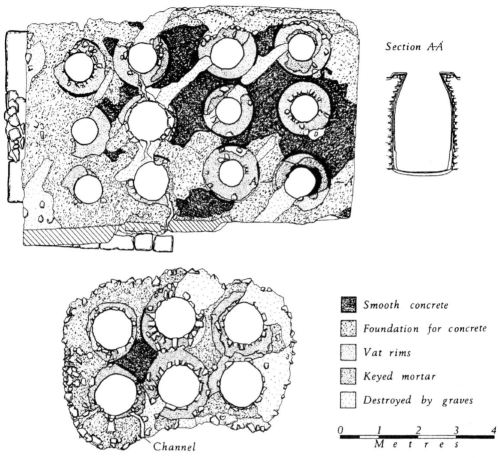

Section A-A'

Smooth concrete

Foundation for concrete

Vat rims

Keyed mortar

Destroyed by graves

0   1   2   3   4
M e t r e s

Channel

Fig. 2.1: Sidi Khrebish (Berenice): plan and section of third-century A.D. vats in Building P1 (from Lloyd 1977, fig. 41; reproduced by kind permission of the Society for Libyan Studies).

olive oil and wine are the two main candidates. I believe wine is the more likely alternative, on the evidence of similar structures from Tocra with seatings for lids (discussed below), suggesting that they are probably fermentation vats.[9]

In the seventh century, a resumption of activity is attested by the reuse of the southern group of vats, and by twenty-seven amphorae from the cistern, which are late variants of Carthage Late Roman Amphora 1, probably reused to transport the liquid produced or stored in the vats. Traces of crude hut walls and another vat to the south-east also date from this late phase.[10]

In a late phase, Building R (also a peristyle house) received a crudely-built circular vat 1.50 m deep, lined with *opus signinum*, which went out of use in the second quarter of the fourth century A.D. An iron crucible was found in room 6.[11] The building was deserted in the fourth century.

Fig. 2.2: Sidi Khrebish (Berenice): early Islamic vats cut through the floor and font of the baptistery of the church. The vat cut through the font (centre) is unfinished, with pick marks visible on the sides. The mouth of the vat to the right has been consolidated with modern cement. (Photo: A. Wilson).

Later still are the two smaller circular vats cut through the baptistery of the late antique church (Fig. 2.2), one of which was 1.20 m deep and lined with *opus signinum*; the other was never completed. A third vat, 2.26 m deep and also lined with *opus signinum*, was sunk through the baptistery floor. This reoccupation of the church, post-dating its deconsecration and partial demolition, can be confidently dated to the early Islamic period.[12] The purpose of these vats is unknown; storage or manufacture of liquids are implied. Oil is perhaps most likely, but even in the early Islamic phase some wine production is not to be entirely excluded (cf. pig bones in early medieval deposits at Germa[13]).

Large dump deposits are today visible by the lighthouse, just inside the third-century wall circuit repaired by Justinian, but have not been excavated. The deposits appear too well sorted to result from secondary redeposition or clearance and probably therefore represent primary dumps; they are likely to be late as they are exposed at the modern ground surface. They include large quantities of deliberately crushed *Murex Trunculus* (much more than is implied by Reese in his discussion of the excavated *Murex* deposits at the site[14]), suggesting that production of purple dye and associated dyeing of wool may have continued into Late Antiquity. Recent fieldwork has established that *Murex* dyeing was an important activity at Berenice's Hellenistic predecessor, Euesperides.[15] Slag derived from metalworking also appears to be present in these late dumps.

Taucheira

We turn now to Taucheira (modern Tocra), the next city to the east of Berenice, to where the provincial headquarters was transferred in the mid-seventh century, prior to the Islamic invasions of 642/5. It was probably chosen as the site of the Byzantine administration's last stand because, alone of the cities of the Cyrenaican coastal plain, it had a water source within its walls.[16]

Recent work by Garyunis University, Benghazi, is helping to develop our understanding of late phases of the site. The excavations have focused on an area close to the centre of the site that seems to have functioned as an industrial zone throughout the city's life, among the earliest recognised features being a Hellenistic kiln.[17] Study of the pottery has still to be completed, and the reports published to date distinguish chiefly between early and late Roman phases, with occupation continuing into the early Islamic period.

The results tell a similar story to that from Berenice. A group of 8 vats, akin to those of Building P at Berenice, went out of use in the mid-third century A.D. These vats are *c.* 3.50 m deep and lined with *opus signinum*, and show seatings for lids allowing them to be sealed (Fig. 2.3).[18] Since no olive pressing structures have been found nearby (such as orthostats, press beds or olive mills), I am inclined to believe that they were more likely to have been used for the fermentation of wine. This suggestion receives some support from the presence a little to the north, though not in strict demonstrable association with the vats, of a feature which I would identify as a wine treading floor – an *opus signinum* floor sloping down to a pair of tanks, with an adjacent cistern mouth (Fig. 2.4). Conceivably,

Fig. 2.3: Tocra: storage vats of the third century A.D. in the industrial quarter excavated by Garyunis University. Note the recessed seating for lids. (Photo: A. Wilson).

Fig. 2.4: Tocra: treading floor (?) lined with opus signinum. *The floor slopes down towards a pair of tanks; to the right is the mouth of a cistern. (Photo: A. Wilson).*

though, a dyeworks could have included such an installation, as suggested for tanks at Carthage where the surrounding floor slopes inward as if to drain spilt dyestuff back into them.[19] The late phases of the building produced much sixth- and seventh-century pottery, and two Islamic coins, one overstruck on a Byzantine coin.

Grain was ground in the vicinity, as evidenced by the finds of a large millstone *c.* 80 cm in diameter, and fragments of other large millstones reused as paving stones in late Roman floors.[20]

Excavations in the 1930s and 1940s, largely unpublished, have brought to light a number of other buildings elsewhere in the city. These include Building 13, to the north of the Byzantine fort, which is sometimes misleadingly referred to as a Roman 'villa'. Remains of a peristyle decorated with Cyrenaican palm leaf capitals are traceable, as well as three vats, a large rectangular tank, and a furnace or kiln in its middle. Chemical analysis of the *opus signinum* from the vats shows similarities with the *opus signinum* of those from the University excavations, and it has therefore been suggested that they are broadly contemporary.[21] While this is possible, I do not think our knowledge of Cyrenaican mortar typologies is sufficiently good to regard this as definite proof of contemporaneity. All that I think can be said at this stage is that from their position within the peristyle the vats and furnace are likely to be secondary additions, and may therefore be late in date (third-century or later?). The kiln or furnace (Fig. 2.5) is a rectangular structure with two compartments; it incorporates tile and *opus signinum*, and shows signs of intense burning. There is no indication as to what was produced within.

Fig. 2.5: Tocra: late kiln or furnace constructed in the peristyle of building 13. The bricks show signs of exposure to extreme heat. Scale: 0.5 m. (Photo: A. Wilson).

Fig. 2.6: Tocra: large olive mill by the wall of a possibly fortified building. Scale: 0.5 m. (Photo: A. Wilson).

Perhaps more securely identifiable as late antique is the large oil mill leaning against what is possibly a fortified building, perhaps a blockhouse of the type found at Ptolemais (Fig. 2.6). Slag and kiln waste nearby attest manufacturing activities in the vicinity.

A little further to the north-east, a building of uncertain function, that may have started life as a set of baths before extensive alterations – including the addition of a possibly Justinianic mosaic floor – contains several tanks or pools lined with *opus signinum*, and fed by channels which are evidently secondary and late. These have been interpreted as pools from a set of baths,[22] although I am unable to think of parallels for the sloping end of one tank, and I wonder whether these too may have served some kind of industrial function.

Ptolemais

The next city to the east is Ptolemais. Originally the port for Barce (El Merj), it grew to surpass Cyrene in importance and became the provincial capital after Diocletian's reforms, from 295/303 to 430/450, when the administration was moved to Apollonia. Excavation has been limited to a number of buildings, but there are tantalising clues as to the city's declining fortunes in Late Antiquity. The aqueduct ceased to function after *c.* A.D. 400, and was repaired by Justinian. At some point, evidently after the period when Synesios wrote, and perhaps after the removal of the capital to Apollonia, the long Hellenistic wall circuit was abandoned for a system of blockhouse defence throughout the rest of the city, where houses were turned into fortified strongholds. Subsequently a reduced circuit was built around the port area, incorporating some of the blockhouse forts.

One of the finest buildings is the so-called Palazzo delle Colonne, a late Hellenistic or Augustan house. It was excavated by the Italians in the first half of this century, but unfortunately the excavations concentrated more on the architecture than on understanding the occupation sequence. Evidently several phases of alterations have confused the picture; a number of *opus signinum* lined vats in the southern part of the villa may not be original (Fig. 2.7), and were in turn clearly sealed by a later flagstone floor. Wells, basins and drainage channels are frequent in this area.[23] There may, therefore, be a broad parallel with Berenice and Taucheira in the introduction of manufacturing/processing activities into what had originally been an elite residence.

The parallels are strengthened by consideration of the building often referred to as Kraeling's 'villa' – an early Roman house where occupation ceased in the mid-third century (coins up to Gordian III). This also contains a group of six circular vats, similar to but shallower than those already discussed (some 1.65 m deep).[24] The date of these vats is not clear, but they seem to pre-date the reoccupation of the villa on a much impoverished scale in Late Antiquity. This Byzantine reoccupation focused on the north end of the complex, while the southern end collapsed, and included the installation of a furnace in what had been a private bath suite. Finds of smithing slag in the vicinity suggested to Kraeling that it was used for melting down metal looted from the abandoned building.[25] Metalworking slag is apparent elsewhere on the site, uncertain. Two further groups of circular vats (numbering four and two), lined with *opus signinum*, with a stone tub nearby, are found a little way to the west of the eastern church.

A building to the west of the Roman Baths was originally published as Byzantine Baths,[29] and contains three *opus signinum*-lined tanks, each overflowing into the next. The interpretation of these as baths has since been rejected (they are clearly unsuitable as pools to sit in),[30] and therefore these tanks also may have had an industrial function, but this again remains unclear. One might think of the sequence of tanks in the fullery of Stephanus at Pompeii as possible parallels.

Cyrene

Cyrene, originally the principal city of the Pentapolis, had lost its pre-eminence by the reign of Diocletian when Ptolemais became the capital. Considerable transformations took place in the third-century, when the agora was invaded by small private dwellings, and it is possibly at this period that the forum (Caesareum) was fortified and turned into barracks.[31] In the fourth century the street along the south side of the Caesareum was blocked by the construction of a lime kiln directly in front of the former public fountain by the south-east corner of the Caesareum.[32]

Industrial structures are suggested by cisterns, vats and ovens in rock-cut chambers overlooking Valley Street; these too may be late, but they are unpublished and it is wholly unclear what they were producing.[33]

Other Sites

Circular vats of the kinds known from Berenice, Taucheira, Ptolemais and Apollonia are also recorded from the fort by the Greek Road near Apollonia, cut into bedrock and apparently lined with *opus signinum*.[34] Again, their date and function are uncertain.

Ceramic Evidence for Imports and Exports

Quantified ceramic assemblages from Cyrenaica are few. The coarse pottery from Berenice indicates occasional contact with Egypt in the fourth and fifth centuries and later (Berenice Late Roman Amphora 6, Coptic fine wares and St. Menas flasks), and sporadic links with the Levant (Palestinian and Gaza amphorae and Late Roman *unguentaria*), but there seems to have been regular commerce with the Aegean. Some 40% of the total coarse pottery (including amphorae) of this period is imported, with Late Roman amphora 1 (from the north-east Mediterranean) accounting for over 13% of the total Late Roman coarse wares, and for 45% of the coarse wares from sixth century levels. Fine pottery imports come mainly from Tunisia and Tripolitania (ARS and TRS), but western coarse wares are scant.[35] Preliminary study of unstratified amphorae from Apollonia suggests a similar pattern of contacts for the sixth- and seventh-centuries;[36] at all sites, recognisably fourth- and fifth-century pottery is relatively sparse. The Tocra material from Boardman's excavations, while a smaller sample, offers a similar picture: the most common amphora is Late Roman 1, with Aegean Late Roman 2 second most common. Fine wares are dominated by African red-slip and Phocaean red-slip (Late Roman C), with some Coptic red-slip, Egyptian A wares, and Cypriot red-slip.[37]

The evidence therefore suggests that Cyrenaica's main commercial links were with the eastern Mediterranean, principally the Aegean, in the sixth- and seventh-centuries, and that it relied heavily on imports. No locally produced amphorae of this period have yet been recognised.

Conclusions

The evidence enumerated can rarely be closely dated, and in some cases can merely be assigned to between the third and seventh centuries A.D.; generic similarities between features, such as the sets of deep vats, may not reflect contemporaneity so much as an enduring regional tradition. Nevertheless, there appear to be certain general trends which can perhaps be linked to a wider picture of urban transformation in Late Antiquity. The preponderance of identifiable production activities from third-century contexts is agricultural – notably the wine (?) vats. Where detailed and extensive excavations have been conducted (Berenice and Taucheira) other activities (murex dyeing and ovens or furnaces for unknown purposes) suggest diversified craft production on a moderate scale in Late Antiquity, probably sufficient for local needs but with little suggestion of significant surplus production for export. However, this picture may be a result of the excavated and published evidence; if future excavations were to reveal more vats and structures associated with artisanal activities, our estimate of their significance might have to be revised upwards accordingly. The larger groups of dated vats, however, seem to be third century; late complexes are smaller. Equally, it is possible that Cyrenaica may have been exporting archaeologically invisible goods (textiles, for example). If it was as one-sidedly reliant on imports as the archaeological picture suggests, and not exporting in return, some of the imports may have arrived as provisions for military garrisons, rather than as market purchases. Agricultural processes continue to operate within towns in the later period, as suggested by the olive mill at Tocra and press elements at Ptolemais.

The partly agricultural nature of urban production highlights a larger feature of urban transformation during the period; a growing convergence of urban and village life. At Cyrene the defended area shrank in Late Antiquity; certain public spaces were separately fortified (the forum/Caesareum). At Ptolemais this process is even more clear; deliberate dismantling, probably in the fifth century, of the Hellenistic wall circuit which had become too long for the available manpower to defend, and its replacement by a number of forts and blockhouses designed to resist nomad raids which, it was accepted, would penetrate the heart of the city.[38]

Urban churches (e.g. Ptolemais) were now fortified in the same manner as those in rural villages (e.g. the pre-Justinianic church at Gasr Libya). The urban blockhouses

Fig. 2.10: Sbeitla (Tunisia): late olive press built across the street. (Photo: A. Wilson).

parallel the rural *gsur*, or fortified farms, of the period.[39] The nature of urban change in Cyrenaica echoes developments further afield in Tripolitania and Africa during the fifth and sixth centuries: a reduction in fortified circuits (Sabratha, Lepcis after the Justinianic fortifications), or a system of blockhouse defence and the conversion of public buildings into forts (Sbeitla, Mactar), and the transformation of other public buildings into installations for processing agricultural produce (Thuburbo Maius, Lepcis).[40] There is a breakdown in civic infrastructure, with aqueducts ceasing to function at Ptolemais and Berenice, and encroachment of private buildings onto public streets (Ptolemais, Mactar, Sbeitla: Fig. 2.10).

These changes occur both in areas subject to Vandal rule (Tunisia) and those outside (Cyrenaica). Broadly speaking, and oversimplifying drastically, I would see this as a response over time to similar factors, both internal and external to late antique society: a decline in the wealth of the curial classes, their increasing unwillingness to shoulder the burdens of municipal office, and their withdrawal to rural estates; the shift of local power from town councils to the church, which had the effect of levelling differences between towns and villages provided that both had bishops; and increased incursions by Berber tribes. In the absence of garrisons to man the wall circuits, blockhouse defence became a more practical option against relatively low-intensity barbarian raids, but in this situation the towns offered little advantage over the villages. We see therefore an increased decentralisation of the population, with the exception of provincial capitals, and a breakdown in the distinction between towns and villages. The conversion of former large residences, such as those at Berenice and Taucheira, and probably Ptolemais as well, into establishments for the processing and storage of agricultural produce – including what at Taucheira has been compared to the fortified farms of the countryside,[41] essentially an urban *gasr* – seems to support this general picture.

But the phenomenon of late antique transformation and its relationship to economic changes in Cyrenaica and elsewhere is still unclear. Much further fieldwork is needed in Cyrenaica both on structures (dating, function, evidence for urban change) and on quantified ceramic assemblages; for the moment, it appears that late antique Cyrenaica was managing to subsist but not exporting in quantity, and was heavily reliant on imports; urban prosperity was drastically reduced from the Roman period, although the centre of gravity may have shifted more in favour of the countryside; but both urban and rural life required an array of fortified structures to counter the threat of raids by the tribes of the interior.

Acknowledgements

I am very grateful to Ahmed Buzaian and Fuaad Bentaher, directors of the Garyunis University excavations at Tocra, for much helpful discussion on site, for showing me round their excavations, and for permission to discuss some of the results here. The views expressed here, and any errors, are mine alone.

Notes

1   *SEG* IX, 2; see Laronde, 1987: 30–33.
2   Riley, 1974: 1976.
3   Personal observation of kiln waste on site.
4   E.g. Reynolds, 1977; Bacchielli, 1981: 183.
5   Roques, 1987.
6   Lloyd, 1977: 31–33.
7   Lloyd, 1977: 99–101, 200–202.
8   Lloyd, 1977: 126–6, 212.
9   Lloyd, 1977: 214.
10   Lloyd, 1977: 143–4, 146–8, 214.
11   Lloyd, 1977: 134.
12   Lloyd, 1977: 189–90.
13   Mattingly *et al.*, 1999: 134.
14   Reese, 1979.
15   Wilson *et al.*, 1999.
16   Jones and Little, 1971: 70–71. See Smith and Crow, 1998 for the Byzantine defences.
17   For preliminary reports see Bentaher, 1994; Buzaian, 2000.
18   Buzaian, 2000: 67–8.
19   Hurst, 1994: 65–6, 83–8.
20   Paving: Buzaian, 2000: 74; large millstone: personal observation.
21   Buzaian, 2000.
22   Bentaher, 1999: 17–28.

23   Personal observation. The vats are mentioned by Pesce, 1950: 64–5 and tav. III, but he gives little further detail.
24   I am not persuaded by Kraeling's interpretation that these "must have served to contain and make immediately accessible water drawn from the [nearby] well" (Kraeling, 1962: 136).
25   Kraeling, 1962: 134, 139.
26   Personal observation. For the reservoir, see Kraeling, 1962: 71.
27   Little, 1979: 41; Ward-Perkins *et al.*, 1986: 147–8, 152.
28   Ward-Perkins *et al.*, 1986: 123–6.
29   Pedley, 1979.
30   Rebuffat *et al.*, 1978: 269, n. 5.
31   Goodchild, 1961; 1971: 74; Bacchielli, 1981: 183–8; Stucchi and Bacchielli, 1983: 111–9.
32   Goodchild, 1971: 75–7.
33   Personal observation. The rock-cut chambers are mentioned by Goodchild (1971: 137; cf. abb. 81) but without further detail.
34   White, 1979: 134, pl. XXIXa.
35   Riley, 1979: 93, 416–8.
36   Riley, 1980.
37   Boardman and Hayes, 1973: 108–118.
38   Kraeling, 1962: 62, 100–7.
39   E.g. Purcaro, 1971.
40   Sbeitla: the forum was fortified, and blockhouses built. Mactar: the South Baths were fortified in the Byzantine period. Thuburbo Maius: olive press in the basement of the capitolium. Lepcis: olive press in the gymnasium adjoining the Hadrianic Baths (personal observation). Cf. Pringle, 1981; Frend, 1985.
41   Smith and Crow, 1998: 37.

Bibliography

Bacchielli, L., 1981. *L'agorà di Cirene, vol. II.1, L'area settentrionale del lato ovest della platea inferiore* (Monografie di archeologia libica 15, Roma).

Bentaher, F., 1994. 'General Account of Recent Discoveries at Tocra', *Libyan Studies* 25, 231–43.

Bentaher, F. and Dobias-Lalou, C., 1999. 'Étude préliminaire d'un bâtiment au sud de l'église orientale à Tocra', *Libyan Studies* 30, 17–28.

Boardman, J. and Hayes, J., 1973. *Excavations at Tocra 1963 – 1965. The Archaic Deposits II and Later Deposits* (Oxford).

Buzaian, A.M., 2000. Excavations at Tocra (1985–1992). *Libyan Studies* 31, 59–102.

Frend, W.H.C., 1985. 'The End of Byzantine North Africa: some Evidence of Transitions'. In *Bulletin archéologique du comité des travaux historiques et scientifiques* n.s. 19 (Histoire et archéologie de l'Afrique du Nord, IIᵉ Colloque International, Grenoble, 5–9 avril 1983), 387–97.

Goodchild, R.G., 1961. 'The Decline of Cyrene and the Rise of Ptolemais: Two New Inscriptions', *Quaderni di archeologia della Libia* 4, 83–95.

Goodchild, R.G., 1971. *Kyrene und Apollonia* (Zürich).

Hurst, H.R., 1994. *Excavations at Carthage. The British Mission, vol. 2.1. The Circular Harbour, North Side: the Site and Finds other than Pottery* (Oxford).

Jones, G.D.B. and Little, J.H., 1971. 'Coastal Settlement in Cyrenaica', *JRS* 61, 64–79.

Kraeling, C.H., 1962. *Ptolemais, City of the Libyan Pentapolis* (The University of Chicago Oriental Institute Publications 90, Chicago).

Laronde, A., 1987. *Cyrène et la Libye hellénistique. "Libykai Historiai": de l'époque républicaine au principat d'Auguste* (Études d'Antiquités africaines, Paris).

Little, J.H., 1979–80. '[Ptolemais]. Excavations in the North-East Quadrant. 1st Interim Report', *Libyan Studies* 11, 37–43.

Lloyd, J.A., (ed.), 1977. *Excavations at Sidi Khrebish, Benghazi (Berenice), Vol. 1, Buildings, Coins, Inscriptions, Architectural Decoration* (Supplements to Libya Antiqua 5, Tripoli).

Mattingly, D.J., al-Mashai, M., Balcombe, P., Drake, N., Knight, S., McLaren, S., Pelling, R., Reynolds, T., Thomas, D., Wilson, A.I. and White, K., 1999. 'The Fezzan Project 1999: Preliminary Report on the Third Season of Work', *Libyan Studies* 30, 129–145.

Pedley, J.G., 1979. 'The Byzantine Baths'. In J.H. Humphrey (ed.) *Apollonia, the Port of Cyrene: Excavations by the University of Michigan 1965–1967* (Supplements to Libya Antiqua 4, Tripoli), 225–43.

Pesce, G., 1950. *Il "Palazzo delle Colonne" in Tolemaide di Cirenaica* (Roma).

Pringle, D., 1981. *The Defence of Byzantine Africa from Justinian to the Arab Conquest*, 2 Vols (BAR International Series 99.1–2, Oxford).

Purcaro, V., 1971. 'Gasr Stillu. Tomba ellenistica e fattoria bizantina nella campagna di Cirene', *Quaderni di archeologia della Libia* 6, 35–41.

Rebuffat, R., Joulia, J.C., Monthel, G. and Lenoir, E., 1978–79 [1987]. 'Note préliminaire sur les grands thermes d'Apollonia', *Libya antiqua* 15–16, 263–77.

Reese, D.S., 1979–1980. 'The Exploitation of Murex Shells: Purple-Dye and Lime Production at Sidi Khrebish, Benghazi (Berenice)', *Libyan Studies* 11, 79–93.

Reynolds, J.M., 1977. 'The Cities of Cyrenaica in Decline'. In P.-M. Duval and E. Frézouls (ed.) *Thèmes de recherches sur les villes antiques d'Occident: Strasbourg, 1er-4 octobre 1971* (Colloques internationaux du Centre national de la recherche scientifique 542, Paris), 53–8.

Riley, J.A., 1974–75. 'Excavations of a Kiln Site at Tocra Libya in August 1974', *Libyan Studies* 6, 25–9.

Riley, J.A., 1976–1977 [1983]. 'Excavation of a Kiln Site at Tocra, Libya in August 1974', *Libya antiqua* 13–14, 235–63.

Riley, J.A., 1979. 'The Coarse Pottery from Berenice'. In J.A. Lloyd (ed.) *Excavations at Sidi Khrebish Benghazi (Berenice) Vol. 2* (Supplements to Libya Antiqua 5, Tripoli), 91–467.

Riley, J.A., 1980–1981. 'Amphoras in the Apollonia Museum Store', *Libyan Studies* 12, 75–8.

Roques, D., 1987. *Synésios de Cyrène et la Cyrénaïque du bas-empire* (Études d'antiquités africaines, Paris).

Smith, D.J. and Crow, J., 1998. 'The Hellenistic and Byzantine Defences of Tocra (Taucheira)', *Libyan Studies* 29, 35–82.

Stucchi, S. and Bacchielli, L., 1983. *L'agorà di Cirene, vol. II.4, Il lato sud della platea inferiore e il lato nord della terrazza superiore* (Monografie di archeologia libica 17, Roma).

Ward-Perkins, J.B., Little, J.H. and Mattingly, D.J., 1986. 'Town Houses at Ptolemais: a Summary Report of Survey and Excavation Work in 1971, 1978–1979', *Libyan Studies* 17, 109–53 (with a contribution by S.C. Gibson).

White, D., 1979. 'The City Defenses of Apollonia'. In J.H. Humphrey (ed.) *Apollonia, the Port of Cyrene: Excavations by the University of Michigan 1965–1967* (Supplements to Libya Antiqua 4, Tripoli), 85–155.

Wilson, A.I., Bennett, P., Buzaian, A.M., Ebbinghaus, S., Hamilton, K., Kattenberg, A. and Zimi, E., 1999. 'Urbanism and Economy at Euesperides (Benghazi): a Preliminary Report on the 1999 Season', *Libyan Studies* 30, 147–168.

Chapter 3

The Economic Impact of the Palestinian Wine Trade in Late Antiquity[1]

Sean A. Kingsley

Introduction

Late Antiquity is perceived widely to be a 'Golden Age' in Palestine's history. Between the fourth and seventh centuries hundreds of new towns and villages were established in response to the pressure exerted by regional population growth. Swamps were drained and replaced by fertile fields, pools of fresh-water dammed, and choice crops cultivated within an extensively terraced landscape.[2] Yet we remain astonishingly ignorant about the stimuli which transformed Palestine from a Roman backwater, whose annual tribute was surpassed within a month by Alexandria (according to Josephus),[3] into an economically vibrant province, and equally ill-informed about the conditions that enabled growth to be sustained. Although polyculture reliant on several commercial crops – most notably grapes, olives, and wheat – has long been acknowledged as a primary source of prosperity, more complex issues concerning the structure of crop production and trade, and how both were affected by wider macro-economic Mediterranean exchange systems, remain unexplained. The study of Palestine's economy, between the date of the foundation of a new Imperial capital at Constantinople in A.D. 330 and the completion of the Arab Conquest in A.D. 641, is remarkably introverted, especially when compared to the healthy debate about long-distance trade generated in the West Mediterranean.[4]

The Byzantine period in Palestine (fourth to mid-seventh centuries A.D.) has interested historians and archaeologists traditionally as a dramatic stage where a struggle for religious supremacy was publicly acted out, as the Jewish heartland became a *terra sancta* for Christians. Consequently, most pre-1980s archaeology concentrated on the material remains of the religious protagonists. The hundreds of churches, chapels, monasteries, hermits' caves, and synagogues identified from historical texts and uncovered during excavations throughout Israel are a legacy to this fascination.[5]

Avi-Yonah's seminal paper on the economy of Byzantine Palestine (published in 1958) typifies how the preoccupation with religious history permeated into other fields of research about the Holy Land. Avi-Yonah regarded the Palestinian economy as an artificial entity sustained by an influx of funds associated with the early Byzantine wave of church construction. Financial capital donated through imperial patronage and by wealthy refugees for the construction of ecclesiastical structures filtered horizontally through the pockets of craftsmen, employed to build churches and monasteries, into various branches of society. In the opinion of Avi-Yonah the East's prosperity was a direct consequence of 'decline' in the West where, with "their jewels handy, the Roman matrons and their husbands could at a moment's notice take ship at Ostia and flee to the East, there to live and build monasteries to their hearts' content". Subsequent prosperity was created by pilgrimage, a form of late antique tourism, and trade in relics.[6] The 'artificial economy' model remains common currency in numerous modern studies,[7] despite the ever increasing realisation that agricultural production is a more appropriate index of the structure of an ancient economy.

Following a phase of intensive excavation conducted in Israel during the last two decades, a wealth of data – unavailable to Avi-Yonah and his contemporaries – enables various branches of Byzantine Palestine's economic portfolio to be appraised more comprehensively. For instance, widespread wheat cultivation encouraged the development of the basalt millstone manufacture industry in the Tiberias region within the Galilee, from where hour-glass shaped products were exported throughout Palestine and even into Cyprus.[8] Olive oil production was equally pivotal to the Palestinian economy. Amongst 365 known Byzantine oil presses, particularly large concentrations existed in central and northern Israel: sixty presses in the Nahariyya zone, 109 installations associated with fifty-eight sites in the western central and lower Golan, fifty-three presses around Netanya, and sixty around Tel Aviv.[9]

Despite primitivistic tendencies to dismiss the role of industry as marginal to the Roman urban economy,[10] the textual and now, increasingly, the archaeological evidence strongly suggests that several such activities deeply affected the prosperity of various strata of society. Palestine was renowned in Late Antiquity for cloth and linen production, tanning and dyeing, and according to the fourth century *Expositio Totius Mundi et Gentium* the cities of Caesarea, Diospolis and Neapolis exported cloth dyed purple.[11] The same source refers to abundant cloth production in Scythopolis, which exported wares throughout the world.[12] This literary evidence is now supported by impressive archaeological remains. A district dated to the second half of the fourth century, and probably associated with dyeing, has been excavated on the threshold of the dismantled triple gateway in the *propylaeum* area of Scythopolis and consists of a complex of heavily plastered brick-built basins inter-connected by ceramic pipes.[13] Coastal cities were particularly advantageously situated to profit from the trade in dyed cloth, and impressive dye-works have been excavated at Dor and Gaza, while an inscription of A.D. 527 from Khirbet Dah-Dah in North Hebron refers to the "shed of Zenonos the tanner from Ascalon", who presumably learnt his trade in the city of his birth.[14]

Glass production was another highly specialised industrial pursuit, and one which reflects the symbiotic economic relationship between town and country. Most documented cases of large-scale glass production are non-urban: a 9 ton glass slab has been excavated in the small town of Beth She'arim in the Galilee,[15] and sixteen single-use kilns of probable seventh century date with twin furnaces at Bet Eli'ezer (located along the coast about 8 km south of Caesarea) could each yield 8–10 tons of glass in a single firing.[16] Production on a smaller scale also occurred in the Jewish village of bemused by the absence of natural conditions suitable for harbour operation in Palestine. The assertion that the shores of Palestine comprised "a stiff, stormy line, down the length of which as there was nothing to tempt men in, so there was nothing to tempt them out", displays a naivety about how ancient mariners successfully adapted to the geomorphology by exploiting minor natural anchorages located behind islets and reefs, or situated north of a protective promontory.[45] Josephus Flavius' infamous statement that Palestine was not a maritime country, and was uninterested in external commerce, was patently untrue even in the Roman period, not to mention Late Antiquity when many Jewish communities were as enticed by the lure of semi-luxury imports as their Christian neighbours (see below).[46] The argument that strict religious observance and geographical factors locked Palestine into an economy oriented around local self-sufficiency is a myth which cannot be sustained by the available evidence for contacts between Palestine and the wider Mediterranean world in either Late Antiquity or any period from the Late Bronze Age onward.[47]

In addition to LR4 and LR5 amphorae depicted onboard ships in a fifth century synagogue mosaic in the House of Kyrios Leontis at Scythopolis, and on a chapel floor dated to the second half of the sixth century at Haditha,[48] both of which are surely based on a realistic awareness of these containers' role in maritime trade, amphorae recovered in harbours and on shipwrecks (Table 3.2) enable some of the sea-lanes

Table 3.2: LR4 and LR5 amphorae recorded in harbours and on shipwrecks in the Mediterranean.

Site	Country	Site Type	Type	Date *	Reference
Cape Andreas	Cyprus	Anchorage	LR5	Byz	McCaslin, 1978: fig. 225-6
Hala Sultan Tekke	Cyprus	Anchorage	LR5	Byz	McCaslin, 1978: fig. 225-6
Keratidhi Bay	Cyprus	Anchorage	LR5	Byz	Morris & Peatfield, 1987: fig. 2, no. 045
Dramont E	France	Wreck	LR4	425-455	Santamaria, 1995: 63, 191
Fos	France	Anchorage	LR5	Byz	Giacobbi-Lequement, 1987: 172
La Palud	France	Wreck	Both	mid/second half 6th	Long & Volpe, 1998: 337-39
Saint Gervais II	France	Wreck	LR5	7th	Jézégou, 1998: 345
Corfu	Greece	Wreck	LR5	4th/5th	pers. comm. D. Kourkoumelis, 1998
Apollonia	Israel	Harbour	Both	5th-7th	Grossmann, 1995: fig. 45.5
Atlit	Israel	Harbour	LR5	Byz	Ronen & Olami, 1978: 36
Caesarea A	Israel	Wreck	LR4	Byz	Raban, 1992: 114
Caesarea B	Israel	Wreck	LR4	Byz	Raban, 1992: 114
Caesarea	Israel	Harbour	LR4	4th-6th	Oleson *et al.*, 1994: figs. 4-5
Dor	Israel	Harbour	Both	6th & 7th	Kingsley & Raveh, 1996: 52-53
Dor A	Israel	Wreck	Both	first half 7th	Kingsley & Raveh, 1996: 63-64
Dor D	Israel	Wreck	Both	second half 6th	Unpublished
Dor E	Israel	Wreck	LR4	6th/7th	Kingsley & Raveh, 1996: 67
Dor F	Israel	Wreck	LR5	first half 7th	Kingsley & Raveh, 1996: 68
Dor G	Israel	Wreck	LR5	first half 7th	Kingsley & Raveh, 1996: 69
Dor J	Israel	Wreck	LR5	6th/7th	Kingsley & Raveh, 1996: 61
Sdot Yam	Israel	Wreck	LR4	Byz	Raban, 1989: 234
Givat Olga	Israel	Wreck	LR4	6th-7th	Edgerton *et al.*, 1980: 13
Iskandil Burnu	Turkey	Wreck	Both	late 6th/7th	Lloyd, 1984: 61
Kekova Oludeniz	Turkey	Wreck	LR5	Byz	Lloyd, 1984: n. 44
Kizilagac Adasi	Turkey	Wreck	LR5	Byz	Lloyd, 1984: n. 44
Serçe Liman	Turkey	Anchorage	LR5	Byz	Lloyd, 1984: n. 44
Yassi Ada A	Turkey	Wreck	LR4	625/6	Bass, 1982: 184, P 73

* Byz = Byzantine

along which Holy Land wines were exported to be traced. Contrary to a view expressed by Zevulun and Olenik that the *"havit*, the typical local storage vessel for wine, was broad-bottomed and therefore ill suited for export of wine by sea",[49] distribution studies prove that overseas exchange unquestionably included the bag-shaped amphora. Late antique wrecks containing cargoes of Palestinian wine amphorae have been surveyed off Israel in anchorages at Dor, Caesarea, and Sdot Yam. A ship recorded at a depth of 40 m off Givat Olga in Israel must have foundered as she tacked out toward an international sea-lane. Wine jars lost during the loading of merchant vessels are also conspicuous in the harbours of Atlit and Apollonia.

The routes used to transport Palestinian wine amphorae West, and the character of the cargoes amongst which it was shipped, cannot be reconstructed at present, particularly in the absence of wrecks containing LR4 and LR5 amphorae recorded between Greece and Sicily. Several primary cargoes of Palestinian wine surveyed off southern Turkey, including a wreck at Iskandil Burnu containing 260 LR5 amphorae and forty-six LR4 examples,[50] demonstrate that large Palestinian consignments arrived in Asia Minor as homogenous cargoes. It may be hypothesised that somewhere in this region, or perhaps even in Greece, amphorae transported as single consignments were broken up, stored in coastal entrepôts, and transported West piecemeal according to vagaries in demand. A complete LR5 amphora found off Corfu marks the position of a late antique sea-lane, along which such wines subsequently travelled.[51] If a wreck dated to between the middle and second half of the sixth century at La Palud off southern France typifies exchange patterns between East and West, then at least some Palestinian wine jars arrived in the West as minor cargo components (in this case apparently via N. Africa): four fragments of LR4 and four LR5 amphorae occur amongst the primary cargo of North African containers (about 90% of all amphorae on the wreck are from the area of modern Tunisia).[52]

After safely reaching port, Palestinian wine was subsequently consumed widely within and beyond the borders of the empire in Late Antiquity, although the picture available is distorted by a preponderance of evidence available for large coastal settlements and comparatively little information published about inland penetration. Most exchange was confined to the Mediterranean basin, where the most substantial deposits have been excavated in major settlements in modern Libya, Egypt, Sinai, Jordan, Cyprus, Turkey, Greece, Italy, France, Sardinia, and Spain (Fig. 3.4). LR4 vessels, however, enjoyed a far wider circulation than LR5. Whereas bag-shaped amphorae have not yet been excavated further west than Lyon in France, LR4 from Gaza and Ashkelon reached Wroxeter in Britain, Augst in Switzerland, and Trier in Germany; huge quantities also passed through Alexandria in Egypt, and some penetrated south to Ballana, and even beyond to Qana in South Arabia.[53]

Forty-six quantified assemblages recorded at twenty-nine sites throughout the Mediterranean basin indicate that the main period of systematic Palestinian wine export began in the late fourth century, followed by an acceleration in the early fifth century.[54] However, the large-scale inter-regional trade in LR4 amphorae clearly preceded the bulk export of LR5. If the quantified amphorae from Beirut typify patterns in other Near Eastern coastal settlements, then a significant quantity of amphorae from the Gaza and Ashkelon region were already being exchanged before the mid-fourth

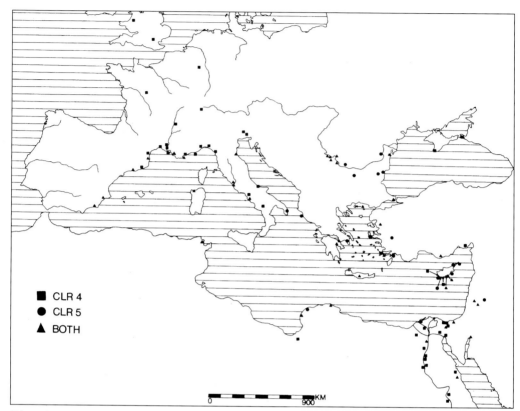

Fig. 3.4: Distribution map of Palestinian wine amphorae in and around the Mediterranean. (Drawing: S. Kingsley).

century: 9.0% of all amphorae at Beirut between A.D. 325–350, which doubled to 18.8% c. A.D. 360–400.[55] Large fifth century deposits excavated at Carthage and Argos (where Palestinian containers account for 45% and 15% of all amphorae respectively), and smaller quantities examined at Capua, El Monastil, Marseille, Naples, Rome and Tarragona (2–9% of all amphorae),[56] convincingly demonstrate that Safrai's argument for fifth century economy decline in Palestine, and a more widespread disruption to trade networks, is incorrect.[57] Rather, the fifth century constituted a pivotal period of economic expansion in the Near East, when new markets developed in response to changing political and cultural demands.

Although our understanding of the chronological and geographical ebb and flow of Palestinian wine export is far from complete at present, consumption remained extensive and continuous in many provinces, even towards the end of Late Antiquity. Palestinian imports accounted for 13% of all amphorae in a deposit dated between 575 and 621 at Calle Solledad in modern Spain, 20% of amphorae of the late sixth century and first half of the seventh century in La Bourse Phase 2B in Marseille, and 16% in late sixth or early seventh century Naples.[58]

Too many variables prevent the cumulative quantity of wine exported from Palestine in any century being realistically estimated, but case studies are helpful in illustrating the scale of much exchange. Relatively large accumulations of Palestinian amphorae have been excavated at Ostrakine in North Sinai (69% of all amphorae), Alexandria (73%, all LR4), Argos (20%), Naples (over 16%), and Rome (11%).[59] What these percentages mean in terms of real volume of consumption is of course not easily determined. Orders of magnitude derived from quantitative studies are notoriously difficult to estimate, let alone substantiate; but they may be postulated hypothetically for certain cities where scholars have been brave enough to speculate about population sizes, and where archaeologists have carefully quantified pottery assemblages. Such models are not presented as fact, of course, but as invitations to an expanded discussion.

A wine consumption model for Carthage, based on Lepelley's suggestion that the population's size stood at about 100,000 people in the fourth century,[60] and Tchernia's estimates for Roman levels of wine consumption, suggest that this city may have demanded about 7.3 million litres of wine annually during Late Antiquity. Using the figure of 10.7%, which Palestinian amphorae represent on average for all quantified amphora deposits dating to Late Antiquity at Carthage, just under 782,000 litres of Palestinian wine may have been consumed annually in this city at certain times during its late antique history. This equates to just under 34,000 full amphorae, or thirty-one annual shipments in a 20 m long merchant vessel capable of transporting 1,100 amphorae, such as the late fourth/early fifth century Yassi Adi B wreck excavated off Turkey.[61]

A similar model for Rome can be formulated using Durliat's estimate that the city's population consisted of 350,000 people in the fifth century and reduced to 60,000 in the sixth century, combined with the figure of 5.9% and 11% for the average Palestinian amphorae quantities recorded respectively in fifth and seventh century deposits. Resultant calculations indicate that Rome may have imported about 1.5 million litres of Palestinian wine annually in the fifth century and just over 480,000 litres in the sixth and early seventh centuries. These estimates convert to about 65,500 fifth century amphorae (or fifty-nine full shiploads annually) and 21,000 amphorae in the later period (nineteen shiploads).[62] In reality, ships' cargoes were almost always composite in character and we ought to at least double the number of merchant vessel crossings accordingly.

Exchange Patterns in Late Antique Palestine

The structures underlying Palestinian wine exports (of which consumption in Carthage and Rome represent only two urban examples) can not be extrapolated easily from the extensive information available. Exactly which strata of society clamoured for these exotic wines is particularly difficult to determine, especially since many important published amphorae accumulations derive from dumps. More revealing contextual data procured from excavations in elite residences, government warehouses, public storerooms, the homes of the city poor, and especially from rural settlements, are rarely available as single sets of information, let alone in combination for intra-settlement comparison.

A prominent trend within current scholarship favours the argument that the late antique economy and long-distance exchange were institutionalised by the State. Thus, the mass export of Tripolitanian oil amphorae to Hispania Tarraconensis before the Vandal period has been interpreted by Keay as a successful state-initiative to profit from surplus taxes not required for distribution as *annona civica*. After its sale in Rome's 2,300 state-owned *mensae oleariae*, oil that originated as tax entered Spain as commercial produce.[63] Wickham has also proposed that commerce was state-dominated and limited in scope: African red slip fine-ware pottery filled opportune spaces amongst fiscal cargoes transporting oil and wheat for the *annona civica* from North Africa to Rome.[64] This model has been adopted to explain the diffusion of Phocaean red-slip fine wares, which may have been shipped from western Turkey to other East Mediterranean provinces on-board empty merchant vessels whose primary service involved transporting wheat required for the *annona civica* from Alexandria to Constantinople.[65] According to these theories limited commerce was thus sustained by pre-existent and well-established state forms of communication.

Durliat is even more dismissive of merchants' ability to actively stimulate trade: apart from state distribution, military supplies, and feeding large cities, only indispensable unavailable commodities such as salt, metals and papyrus travelled over long-distances. Commerce was parasitic on fiscal exchange, itself based primarily on the redistribution of provincial taxes.[66] A slightly more liberal theory associates overseas exchange with urban economic demands. According to theories postulated by Hopkins, and later Reynolds, major cities which had outgrown their hinterlands, or whose lines of supply had been disrupted by local harvest failure, may have been obliged to import large quantities of non-local foodstuffs intermittently or regularly.[67] Just as late antique society is often presented as oppressed within a rigid caste system, so economic immobility is viewed by many historians as a salient characteristic of this period, when the Empire was "a coercive, omnipresent, all-powerful organization that subdued individual interests and levied all resources toward one overarching goal: the survival of the State".[68]

These essentially primitivistic arguments deliberately down-play commerce as a primary force underlying overseas distribution. The obligation to pay regular land taxes in kind to the State within a political economy is admittedly a plausible explanation as the impetus which led to the initial expansion of the Palestinian wine industry. However, as an all-embracing model it does not convince. Even if some wine cargoes were transported to Constantinople on state-commandeered ships for subsidised distribution to sectors of the urban population, following a system initiated in Rome (and perhaps adopted in the East),[69] surely the late antique government would have preferred wine taxes to be commuted swiftly into the preferred medium of gold coin. Rather than inefficiently shoulder the expense of transporting wine to Constantinople, or to state warehouses located along the coast of modern Turkey, the sale in Palestine's ports of surplus wine levies would have served as a more efficient and rational procedure. If this interpretation is correct, private merchants would have entered the exchange chain at an early stage, and most Palestinian wines would have sailed out of the busy Palestinian ports of Gaza, Ashkelon, Caesarea, Apollonia, Dora and Ptolemais as commercial cargoes. The appearance of a steady stream of LR4 amphorae in the second quarter of the fourth century at Beirut, a major port city located along the *annona civica* sea-lane linking Alexandria with Constantinople, may not be a coincidence. Rather, it may reflect the reality of a commercial superstructure overlying the foundation of a state fiscal framework: if, as I suspect is likely, some Palestinian wine was conveyed to Constantinople for purposes of state redistribution, then surplus cargo could have been sold along the way. The merchant vessel carrying the *annona civica* and a commercial cargo is one and the same in this model. Of course, after A.D. 494/5, when tax in kind was commuted to gold coin under Anastasius I,[70] the tax model becomes increasingly difficult to maintain. After this date almost all exports, other than perhaps *annona militaris* rations, can only be interpreted as commercial enterprise.

The extensive consumption of Palestinian wines in the West Mediterranean, following the loss of the Roman dominions to the barbarians and the associated dislocation of state supply lines, can only be explained in terms of the prevalence of commerce. The same is equally true for the escalation in quantities of Near Eastern imports in Vandal North Africa: by the time Belisarius recaptured Carthage in 533, East Mediterranean imports comprised 25–30% of amphorae entering the city.[71] The absence on Palestinian amphorae of *graffiti* or *tituli picti*, sometimes placed on other late antique vessels (such as LR1 and LR2)[72] to verify quality, prevent fraudulent sale, or to denote content and specify the merchant responsible for production or shipping, is another telling set of evidence. This may imply a lack of centralised control over production, and is very different to North African estates, associated with *annona civica* supply, where packaging was stamped. A final indication of the widespread commercial penetration of Palestinian wines is the imitation of LR5 vessels in late antique Egypt.[73] Replication of an amphora type recognisable immediately by shape as a product of the Holy Land, seems to me an indication of market competition (or manipulation) initiated by some Egyptian merchants hoping to profit from the reputation of Palestinian wines. It is difficult to accept that such imitation would have been conceivable in an environment where market forces were restrained, especially since Egypt possessed its own amphora production tradition (LR7 amphorae and Bailey Egyptian Type A).[74]

Even though it would be naive to dispute the likelihood that well-connected urban-based merchants, or commercial agents of the elite, were well-placed to exploit the vulnerability of peasants wishing to dispose of surplus produce – and to profit from the flow of wine between country, town and port – the wine trade seems to have served as a positive economic stimulus amongst many rural communities. Pottery deposits excavated in the Palestinian countryside, where over 80% of society may have lived,[75] have recently revealed two informative socio-economic trends related to the impact of commercial trade. Firstly, small quantities of imported amphorae have been identified consistently in most rural villages. Such consumption patterns typify semi-luxury wine and oil consumption, rather than economic dependence on inter-regional trade to supplement low yields in certain crops. In the Jewish village of Sumaqa in the Carmel mountains, although local Palestinian containers accounted for 92% of the assemblage, an assortment of East Mediterranean wares comprised 8% of amphorae in deposits dated mainly between the mid-fourth and mid-fifth centuries (LR1, LR2, LR3, SUM 1,

Keay Type XXVG, and a Coptic vessel). Small LR3 amphorae proved particularly popular (6.1% of all amphorae).[76] Although amphora assemblages in other villages have been less thoroughly studied, this general trend is supported by evidence from other sites. A Cypriot MR4 amphora has been recorded in the Samaritan village of Antesion, and LR3 vessels are particularly conspicuous at Meiron in the Galilee.[77] LR1 reached a Byzantine farmhouse at Givat Ehud in the Tel Aviv region, and examples were even excavated in a structure interpreted as a tool-shed or watchman's booth at Nahal Beqa' in the Beer Sheva region.[78]

The widespread penetration into rural settlements of non-local fine ware bowls and plates is a second striking trend. Following the cessation of Kfar Hananya ware production in the Galilee during the first half of the fifth century,[79] imports monopolised Palestinian markets. Virtually all bowls and plates used on a daily basis originated in Phocaea in western Turkey and Cyprus, and, to a far lesser extent, Tunisia.[80] These products have been discovered throughout Israel, from the village of Dabiyye in the Golan to Wadi Umm Hashim, deep in the Negev desert.[81] A sample of 568 fine ware fragments excavated in the village of Sumaqa in the Carmel once again provides the clearest evidence available at present about imported volumes: Cypriot red slip bowls accounted for 59% of all fine wares, Phocaean red-slip for 26%, African 6%, and Egyptian less than 0.5%.[82] The deep and extensive commercial penetration into rural Palestine of such semi-luxuries as Mediterranean fine wares almost certainly reflects the import of a wider range of manufactured goods, which are no longer preserved archaeologically (locally unavailable metals, such as iron, copper and bronze, in particular).

Conclusion

The study of the late antique wine trade offers an unusually multifarious insight into the structure of one important branch of Palestine's economic portfolio. Significantly, it advances the debate about the character of the economy beyond the traditional preoccupation within Israeli scholarship with religion as the central cog around which all socio-economic change revolved. In the absence of detailed financial ledgers, systematically maintained accounts, or information about wine prices, our under-standing about the profits derived from exports and the 'wealth' this industry generated, can only be impressionistic. However, several observations about the way the wine trade touched different peoples lives can be proposed.

Not only was late antique Palestine self-sufficient in wine, but many industrial-sized presses mass-produced surpluses. Production was primarily confined to the countryside, and contrary to the often-repeated assertion that overland carriage costs obstructed overland transport, I believe that the roads of Palestine would have been criss-crossed continuously by farmers and merchants travelling between field and market. Many of the distant shores to which their wines travelled, in some instances in impressive quantities, have been mapped. What sectors of society composed the market for such produce is more problematic to fathom. Historical evidence referring to light white Ashkelon wines, prescribed to treat stomach ache, quartan fever, colic, liver disease and eye-infection, clarifies that some produce had a specific, non-recreational function.[83] The quality of other wines may have been more suspect: if vent-holes cut into amphora shoulder's were really designed to reduce carbon dioxide building up, perhaps the grade of the content should be questioned. Could the shipment of immature, fermenting wines point to a pool of somewhat undiscerning customers and to demand outstripping supply? Certainly the attraction of Palestinian wine must have benefited from its association with the land of the Bible, where vineyards spring forth from soils once roamed by the twelve tribes of Israel, and later by Jesus and the Apostles. Local merchants, one suspects, did not have to sweat profusely over marketing strategies. Although the question of consumption requires detailed future study, I would not be surprised if many of the sixty types of wine referred to in the Babylonian Talmud catered intentionally for a diverse hierarchy of tastes and markets.[84]

Perhaps the most surprising result of this study is the pattern of imported wine and oil amphorae, and the abundance of non-local fine wares, in small villages like Sumaqa, which lay at the forefront of the wine trade. The implications of these wares are intriguing. Setting aside the undetermined question of product cost, such conspicuous consumption is clearly not the manifestation of a peasantry scraping a living from limited subsistence farming, from which no surpluses were retained once taxes had been paid. Rather, in addition to the positive impact of the second wave of Romanisation of the Near East associated with the development of Constantinople and its institutions, we may speculate that the well-administered and regulated land tax, a delicate fiscal instrument "which can either stimulate production or kill off the goose that lays the golden egg",[85] was a positive economic catalyst in late antique Palestine. The entire provincial tax burden of late antique Egypt has been estimated at no more than half of the total concentrated surplus agricultural yield.[86] If correct, and if Palestine was a comparable case, numerous village families would have existed well above a basic subsistence threshold. The large deposits of coins found in Palestinian villages also suggest that the rural sector was at least partly monetarised and participated in a wide-ranging market.[87] The imported pottery encountered in the heart of the countryside is a mark of the cultural sophistication achieved by many agricultural communities which, like their urban brethren, chose to identify themselves through a pan-Mediterranean material culture. In this sense, as a commercial crop the humble grape was a potent economic factor in the creation of social fluidity.

Notes

1   This paper is based on research conducted for my doctoral thesis at the University of Oxford (Kingsley, 1999a). I am particularly grateful to my main supervisors, the late John Lloyd and Bryan Ward-Perkins, as well as to Claudine Dauphin – my secular supervisor – for generous advice, support and criticism; the thesis also benefited from additional supervision by Martin Goodman. D. Kourkoumelis kindly provided information about Palestinian amphorae found off Greece, and Shimon Dar permitted me to reproduce Fig. 3.1.

2   For an explanation and detailed description of demographic expansion in Byzantine Palestine, see Dauphin, 1998. Particularly interesting examples of landscape development in late antique Palestine include the draining of swamps at Apollonia (Tsuk and Ayalon, 1995: 140–41) and the construction

of extensive dam systems in the Negev desert, such as along 22 km of the Nahal Hevron (Negev, 1997: 128, 131).

3   *Jewish War* 2.386; tr. St. Thackeray, 1967: 475.

4   Fulford's discussion of long-distance trade between Carthage and Rome (1980; 1987) has been particularly influential on subsequent theory. Both this work, and Keay's analysis of the economy of Spain between the fourth and seventh centuries (1984), rely heavily on pottery studies. Mattingly (1998) has studied large-scale olive oil production in Tripolitania in detail, by quantifying presses and cultivated lands.

5   Summaries of research on synagogues and churches appear in Levine, 1993 and Ovadiah, 1993.

6   Avi-Yonah, 1958: 43.

7   For instance Garnsey, 1998: 158. Shereshevski (1991: 2) simply reiterates the argument when he states that "the Byzantine economy suffered from a basic weakness: investment in non-productive buildings such as churches and monasteries provided seasonal work for a great many laborers, but created a dependency on a steady stream of outside capital. Wealth was concentrated in the hands of the non-productive members of society, especially the priesthood. The pendulum of activity swung from trade and finance to the holy sites, Jerusalem in particular".

8   Williams-Thorpe and Thorpe, 1993: 291–94.

9   Kingsley, 1999a: 82–83, table 3.

10 Jones, 1964: 824–872; 1974: 36–38.

11 *Expositio* XXXI; tr. Rougé, 1966: 165.

12 Supra n.11.

13 Foerster and Tsafrir, 1993: 12.

14 The purple-dye workshop at Dor is discussed by Raban, 1995: 301. Dye pigments excavated in the mid-fifth century workshop at Gaza have been provenanced to the Negev, Sinai, Italy and Greece (Ovadiah, 1969: 196–7). For Khirbet Dah-Dah see Amit, 1991: 162.

15 Brill, 1965.

16 Gorin-Rosen, 1995: 42–43.

17 Sumaqa: Dar, 1999: 44; Sucamina: Hirschfeld, 1998: 20.

18 Scythopolis: Meyers *et al.*, 1995: 70; Jerusalem: Maeir, 1994: 302.

19 Grossmann, 1995: 160.

20 The consumer-city model (Parkins, 1997: 84–87) has not been applied to the Near East, where research into urban economies is remarkably limited.

21 Achziv: Frankel and Getzov, 1997: 65; Tel Tanninim: Stieglitz, 1998: 63; Caesarea: Ayalon, 1979: 179; Kfar Saba: ESI, 1984a; Ashkelon: Israel, 1995a: 104–105; Capernaum: Tzaferis, 1989: 9; Sataf: Gibson *et al.*, 1991: 41, fig. 18.

22 Lernau, 1995: 99.

23 Sepphoris: Fradkin, 1997; Eboda: Tahal, 1995.

24 Broshi, 1986: 46.

25 Tchernia, 1986: 26.

26 Collated in Kingsley (1999a: 88), using Broshi's estimate of Byzantine Palestine's population (1979: 7).

27 Kingsley, 1999a: 89.

28 Kingsley, 1999a: 94.

29 Kingsley, 1999a: 96.

30 Matthews *et al.*, 1990: 21.

31 Fischer, 1985: 196.

32 Dar, 1999: 100–107.

33 Syon, 1998: 7.

34 The Carthage classification system is described in Riley, 1981: 117. Vessel dimensions are taken from Zemer, 1977: 66 and Kingsley, 1999a: appendix 3. LR4 production in Ashkelon is discussed by Israel, 1995b: 106–107.

35 Rabbinical references to the *havith* are touched upon by Vitto, 1987: 48–49. For dimensions, see Zemer, 1977: 69 and Kingsley, 1999a: appendix 3. The Tel Qasile kiln is described briefly by Mazar, 1975; the Horvat 'Uza kilns have been excavated by Ben-Tor, 1966: 2 and more recently by Getzov, 1995: 20.

36   According to Talmudic literature: Vitto, 1987: 48. Nineteen LR5 amphorae containing wheat, Egyptian beans, king walnuts, barley and perhaps olives were excavated in a context of the second half of the fourth century at Meiron in the Galilee: Meyers *et al.*, 1981: 60–72.

37   Adan-Bayewitz, 1986: 92–97.

38   Israel, 1995a: 102.

39   Israel, 1995c: fig. 12.

40   *Natural History* 14.134; tr. Rackham, 1968: 275.

41   Cited in Zevulun and Olenik, 1979: 26.

42   Kingsley and Raveh, 1996: 52.

43   Unpublished data from the 1999 season of the underwater excavations at Dor, directed by S. Kingsley (Somerville College, Oxford), C. Brandon (Nautical Archaeology Society, Portsmouth), Y. Kahanov (The Center for Maritime Studies, University of Haifa), and K. Raveh (Dor Maritime Archaeology Project, Israel).

44   Marseille: Bonifay and Piéri, 1995: 112; Carthage: Opait, 1998: 22.

45   Smith, 1894: 134.

46   *Contra Apion* I.60; tr. St. Thackeray, 1966: 187.

47   The notion that imported foodstuffs and pottery were considered ritually impure by all Jewish communities (Safrai, 1994: 292) is incompatible with the archaeological evidence, which suggests that many late antique settlements in Palestine were occupied by liberal Jews. For complementary historical corroboration of this view, see Neusner, 1994: 42.

48   The upper panel of the floor from Scythopolis depicts two LR5 amphorae on a ship's deck (Zori, 1966: pl.11). Interestingly, one has been represented by red *tesserae*, the other by black cubes; they therefore appear in the two dominant LR5 fabric colours. Furthermore, both containers feature horizontal lines, which faithfully reproduce the ribbing so characteristic of the amphora type. The lower panel of the same mosaic depicts LR4 stowed upside-down on an open deck (Zori, 1966: pl.12). Nine LR4 amphorae appear on a small ship or boat on the Haditha mosaic, located 5 km east of Lod (Avi-Yonah, 1976: pl.6). Both mosaics juxtapose ships and amphorae with Egypt: a Nilometer and inscription mentioning Alexandria occur on the former example, and a walled city alongside a Greek inscription referring to Egypt appears on the Haditha floor. Although both are part of broader Nilotic imagery, I suspect that the structural inclusion of maritime motifs reflects an understanding of the importance of Palestinian trade with Egypt through Alexandria.

49   Zevluin and Olenik, 1979: 28.

50   Lloyd, 1984: 61.

51   Pers. comm. D. Kourmoumelis, 1998.

52   Long and Volpe, 1998: 317, 336–39. The sample of transport amphorae recovered includes 180 substantial fragments of North African Keay Type LV and LXII vessels, as well as two LR1 and three LR2 fragments. The secondary Near Eastern consignment, including the Palestinian amphorae, thus represents 7% of the total cargo. It is not impossible that these containers were galley stores owned by a Near Eastern merchant responsible for the crossing.

53   LR5 – Lyon: Bonifay and Villedieu, 1989: 18, 20–21. LR4 – Wroxeter: Riley, 1979: 221; Augst: Martin-Kilcher, 1994: 439; Trier: Riley, 1979: 221; Alexandria: Majcherek, 1992: 106; Ballana: Kirwin, 1938: pl. 111, no.10; Qana: Sedov, 1992: fig. 2, nos. 1 & 5.

54   Figures compiled in Kingsley, 1999a: tables 12–13.

55   Based on the Aub-Leverhulme excavations, Reynolds, 1997–1998: 54.

56   Carthage: both mid-fifth century, in the Canadian excavations (Hayes, 1980b: 205) and Cistern D27 (Riley, 1981: 90); Argos (Abadie, 1989: 54); Capua, late fifth century (Reynolds, 1995: 340); El Monastil, *c.* 400–475 (Reynolds, 1995: 181); Marseille, *c.* 400–450 (Bonifay, 1986: 302–303); Naples, Vico Carminiello ai Mannesi *c.* 440 (Arthur, 1985: 250); Rome, Schola Praeconum 430–440 (Whitehouse *et al.*, 1982: 60); Tarragona, Vila-Roma 450/475 (Reynolds, 1995: 180, 282–3).

57   Safrai, 1998.

58   Calle Soledad: Reynolds, 1995: 182, 264–5; Marseille: Bonifay, 1986: 303–304; Naples: Arthur, 1985: 255.

59   Ostrakine, *c.* 550 to early seventh century: Oked, 1996: 168–9; Alexandria Sector G, sixth-to-seventh centuries: Majcherek, 1992: 106, 116–7; Argos, sixth century: Abadie, 1989: 54; Naples, late sixth/

early seventh century: Arthur, 1985: 255; Rome, Schola Praeconum *c.* 600–650: Whitehouse *et al.*, 1985: 186.

60   Lepelley, 1981: 48.

61   The figure of 10.7% for Carthage is based on thirteen deposits excavated along the Theodosian Wall (Neuru, 1980), in the cisterns (Riley, 1981), at Salammbo (Peacock, 1984: table 1), in the Circus (Tomber, 1988), and at Bir el Knissia (Freed, 1993a: 85; 1993b: 112; Kalinowski, 1993: 159, 162, 165, 167). These are tabulated in Kingsley, 1999a: table 12. The calculation uses Tchernia's estimate that men consumed a minimum of 146 lt of wine annually, and women half that quantity (1986: 26). For the sake of convenience the figure assumes an equal male, female and child population size of 33,333 each. Amphora numbers are estimated using an average LR4 and LR5 volume capacity of 23 lt. Yassi Ada B wreck amphora capacities are based on Parker, 1992: 455.

62   Durliat, 1990: 112, 117. The quantified deposits in Rome derive from the Schola Praeconum excavations (Whitehouse *et al.*, 1982: 60; 1985: 186), the Crypta Balbi, Porticus Liviae, and Temple of Magna Mater (Carignani *et al.*, 1986: 38; Carignani and Pacetti, 1989: 8–9, 11). See note 61 for the general background of this calculation.

63   Keay, 1984: 414, 424.

64   Wickham, 1984: 13; 1998: 284.

65   Ward-Perkins, forthcoming.

66   Durliat, 1998: 115–7.

67   Hopkins, 1983: 90, 92; Reynolds, 1995: 123.

68   Tainter, 1988: 141.

69   Edict 11.2.2 in the Theodosian Code issued in A.D. 364, and repeated in 365 and 377 (Pharr, 1952: 296), states that wine levied locally through tax was sold to specific sectors of society in Rome at one fourth of the market price. There is no evidence that Constantine's distribution of wine, meat and garments, alongside loaves of bread at Constantinople in A.D. 330 (*Malalas* 13.322–323; Jeffreys *et al.*, 1986: 175), was a long-term strategy maintained in the eastern capital as an integral part of the *annona civica*.

70   *Malalas* 16.394; tr. Jeffreys *et al.*, 1986: 221.

71   Fulford, 1980: 71.

72   Derda, 1992.

73   Imitation LR5 amphorae were produced both in the Abu Mena region (Empereur and Picon, 1992: 50) and along the Nile (Bailey, 1998: 137). Five workshops manufacturing imitation LR5 amphorae have been identified along Lake Mareotis (Empereur and Picon, 1998: 85,-88). One of these is located in the geographical sphere of a village and wine press; amphorae found in close proximity to the port of Marea, and along the eastern mole, suggest that such imitations (and their produce) were traded intra-regionally.

74   Bailey, 1998: 125–129.

75   Hirschfeld, 1997: 37.

76   Kingsley, 1999b: 270–273, table 1b.

77   Antesion: Fowler, 1990: 37, no.3; Meiron: Meyers *et al.*, 1981: pl. 6.4 – no.4, pl. 8.13 – nos.2, 4.

78   Givat Ehud: Hizmi, 1992: 293, fig. 4; Nahal Beqa': Katz, 1994: fig. 113, no.5.

79   Adan-Bayewitz, 1993: 239.

80   Hayes, 1972; 1980a; for Tunisian ARS see also Mackensen, 1998.

81   Dabiyye: Killebrew, 1991: fig. 2; Wadi Umm Hashim: Haiman, 1986: 203, no.4.

82   Kingsley, 1999b: 274–80, table 11.

83   Mayerson, 1993: 173.

84   Wine varieties are mentioned by Broshi, 1984: 26–27.

85   Whittaker and Garnsey, 1998: 277.

86   Bagnall, 1993: 172.

87   About 1,000 late sixth and early seventh century coins were recovered from a deposit located just outside the synagogue in the village of Korazin (ESI, 1984b: 67). Some 458 coins were excavated from residential units and the synagogue in the village at Sumaqa in the Carmel. Mints represented within the corpus include Aquileia, Thessalonica, Nicomedia, Cyzicos, Heraclea, Constantinople, Antioch, Alexandria and Carthage (Kindler, 1999: 347–361).

Bibliography

Abadie, C., 1989. 'Les amphores protobyzantines d'Argos (IVᵉ-VIᵉ siècles)'. In V. Déroche and J.-M. Spieser (ed.) *Recherches sur la céramique byzantine* (BCH Suppl. 18, Paris), 47–56.

Adan-Bayewitz, D., 1986. 'The Pottery from the Late Byzantine Building and its Implications (Stratum 4)'. In L.I. Levine and E. Netzer (ed.) *Excavations at Caesarea Maritima 1975, 1976, 1979 – Final Report* (Qedem 21, Jerusalem), 90–129.

Adan-Bayewitz, D., 1993. *Common Pottery in Roman Galilee. A Study of Local Trade* (Ramat-Gan).

Ahlström, G.W., 1978. 'Wine Presses and Cup-Marks of the Jenin-Megiddo Survey', *BASOR* 231, 19–49.

Amit, D., 1991. 'Khirbet Dah-Dah', *ESI* 9, 162–163.

Amit, D., 1992. 'Khirbet Hilal', *ESI* 10, 150–151.

Arthur, P., 1985. 'Naples: Notes on the Economy of a Dark Age City'. In C. Malone and S. Stoddart (ed.) *Papers in Italian Archaeology IV. Part IV. Classical and Medieval Archaeology* (BAR Int. Series 246), 247–260.

Avi-Yonah, M., 1958. 'The Economics of Byzantine Palestine', *IEJ* 8, 39–51.

Avi-Yonah, M., 1976. 'The Haditha Mosaic Pavement', *Sefunim* 5, 61–66.

Ayalon, E., 1979. 'The Jar Installation at Khirbet Sabiya', *IEJ* 29, 175–181.

Bagnall, R.S., 1993. *Egypt in Late Antiquity* (Princeton University Press).

Bailey, D.M., 1998. *Excavations at El-Ashmunein V. Pottery, Lamps and Glass of the Late Roman and Early Arab Periods* (London).

Bass, G.F., 1982. 'The Pottery'. In G.F. Bass and F.H. van Doorninck (ed.) *Yassi Ada I. A Seventh Century Byzantine Shipwreck* (Texas A & M University Press), 155–188.

Ben-Tor, A., 1966. 'Excavations at Horvat 'Usa', *'Atiqot* 3, 1–3.

Bonifay, M., 1986. 'Observations sur les amphores tardives à Marseille d'après les fouilles de la Bourse (1980–1984)', *RAN* 19, 269–305.

Bonifay, M. and Piéri, D., 1995. 'Amphores du Ve au VIIe s. à Marseille: nouvelles données sur la typologie et le contenu', *JRA* 8, 94–120.

Bonifay, M. and Villedieu, F., 1989. 'Importations d'amphores orientales en Gaule (Vᵉ-VIIᵉ siècle)'. In V. Déroche and J.-M. Spieser (ed.) *Recherches sur la céramique byzantine* (BCH Suppl. 18, Paris), 17–46.

Brill, R.H., 1965. 'Beth She'arim', *IEJ* 15, 261–262.

Broshi, M., 1979. 'The Population of Western Palestine in the Roman-Byzantine Period', *BASOR* 236, 1–10.

Broshi, M., 1984. 'Wine in Ancient Palestine – Introductory Notes', *Israel Museum Journal* 3, 21–40.

Broshi, M., 1986. 'The Diet of Palestine in the Roman Period – Introductory Notes', *Israel Museum Journal* 5, 41–56.

Carignani, A., Ciotola, A., Pacetti, F. and Panella, C., 1986. 'Roma. Il contesta del tempio della Magna Mater sur Palatino'. In A. Giardina (ed.) *Societa romana e impero tardoantico. Le merci gli insediamenti* (Rome), 27–43.

Carignani, A. and Pacetti, F., 1989. 'Le importazioni di anfore Bizantine a Roma fra IV e V secolo: le evidenze di alcuni contesti ribani'. In V. Déroche and J.-M. Spieser (ed.) *Recherches sur la céramique Byzantine* (BCH Suppl. 18, Paris), 6–10.

Dagan, Y., 1998. 'Khirbet el-'Alya (B)', *ESI* 17, 94–100.

Dagan, Y. and Avganim, A., 1998. 'Nahal Zanoah (Site 04/12)', *ESI* 17, 127–129.

Dar, S., 1999. *Sumaqa. A Roman and Byzantine Jewish Village on Mount Carmel, Israel* (BAR Int. Series 815, Oxford).

Dauphin, C., 1998. *La Palestine byzantine. Peuplement et populations, Vols I-III* (BAR Int. Series 726, Oxford).

Derda, T., 1992. 'Inscriptions with the Formula "God's Grace [is] a Gain" on Late Roman Amphorae', *ZPE* 94, 135–152.

Dothan, M. and Freedman, D.N., 1967. *Ashdod I. The First Season of Excavations 1962* ('Atiqot, Jerusalem).

Durliat, J., 1990. *De la ville antique à la ville byzantine. Le problème des subsistances* (École Française de Rome, Rome).

Durliat, J., 1998. 'Les conditions du commerce au VIe siècle'. In R. Hodges and W. Bowden (ed.) *The Sixth Century. Production, Distribution and Demand* (Leiden), 89–117.

Edgerton, H.E., Linder, E. and Tur-Caspa, Y., 1980. *Side Scan Sonar Survey for Ancient Wrecks along the Israeli Mediterranean Coast – November 1978* (Research Report No.1, Haifa).

Empereur, J-Y. and Picon, M., 1992. 'La reconnaissance des productions des ateliers céramiques: l'exemple de la Maréotide', *CCE* 3, 3–92.

Emperur, J.-Y. and Picon, M., 1998. 'Les ateliers d'amphores du Lac Mariout'. In J.-Y. Empereur (ed.) *Commerce et artisanat dans l'Alexandrie héllenistique et romaine* (BCH suppl. 33, Paris), 75–91.

[ESI], 1984a. 'Kfar Sava', *ESI* 2, 60–61.

[ESI], 1984b. 'Korazin', *ESI* 1, 64–67.

Fischer, M., 1985. 'Kh. Zikrin, 1982–1984', *IEJ* 35, 194–98.

Foerster, G. and Tsafrir, Y., 1993. 'The Bet She'an Excavation Project (1989–1991). City Center (North)', *ESI* 11, 3–12.

Fowler, A., 1990. 'The Pottery of Zur Natan'. In *Publication of the Texas Foundation for Archaeological and Historical Research* (Houston), 34–51.

Fradkin, A., 1997. 'Long-Distance Trade in the Lower Galilee: New Evidence from Sepphoris'. In D.R. Edwards and C.T. McCollough (ed.) *Archaeology and the Galilee. Texts and Contexts in the Graeco-Roman and Byzantine Periods* (Georgia), 107–116.

Frankel, R., 1999. *Wine and Oil Production in Antiquity in Israel and other Mediterranean Countries* (Sheffield Academic Press).

Frankel, R. and Getzov, N., 1997. *Map of Akhziv (1), Map of Hanita (2)* (Jerusalem).

Freed, J., 1993a. 'Pottery from *Sondage* 1'. In S.T. Stevens (ed.) *Bir el Knissia at Carthage: a Rediscovered Cemetery Church. Report No.1* (JRA Suppl. 7, Michigan), 73–90.

Freed, J., 1993b. 'Pottery from below the Tangent Circle Mosaic'. In S.T. Stevens (ed.) *Bir el Knissia at Carthage: a Rediscovered Cemetery Church. Report No.1* (JRA Suppl. 7, Michigan), 111–117.

Fulford, M., 1980. 'Carthage: Overseas Trade and the Political Economy, *c.* AD 400–700', *Reading Medieval Studies* 6, 68–80.

Fulford, M., 1987. 'Economic Interdependence among Urban Communities of the Roman Mediterranean', *World Archaeology* 19, 58–75.

Garnsey, P., 1998. *Cities, Peasants and Food in Classical Antiquity. Essays in Classical Antiquity* (Cambridge University Press).

Getzov, N., 1995. 'Horvat 'Uza', *ESI* 13, 19–21.

Giacobbi-Lequement, M-F., 1987. 'La céramique de l'épave Fos 1', *Archaeonautica* 7, 169–191.

Gibson, S., Ibbs, B. and Kloner, A., 1991. 'The Sataf Project of Landscape Archaeology in the Judaean Hills: a Preliminary Report on Four Seasons of Surveys and Excavation (1987–89)', *Levant* 23, 29–54.

Gichon, M., 1993. *En Boqeq. Ausgrabungen in Einer Oase am Toten Meer, Band 1* (Mainz am Rhein).

Gorin-Rosen, Y., 1995. 'Hadera, Bet Eli'ezer', *ESI* 13, 42–43.

Grossmann, E., 1995. *Maritime Investigation of Tel-Michal and Apollonia Sites* (Doctor of Philosophy Thesis, Macquarie University).

Haiman, M., 1986. *Map of Har Hamran – Southwest (198) 10–00* (Jerusalem).

Hayes, J.W., 1972. *Late Roman Pottery* (British School at Rome, London).

Hayes, J.W., 1980a. *A Supplement to Late Roman Pottery* (British School at Rome, London).

Hayes, J., 1980b. 'Late Roman Pottery: a Fifth Century Deposit from Carthage. Summary of Amphorae Types: 1M7', *Antiquités Africaines* 16, 205.

Hirschfeld, Y., 1997. 'Farms and Villages in Byzantine Palestine', *DOP* 51, 33–71.

Hirschfeld, Y., 1998. 'Tel Shiqmona – 1994', *ESI* 18, 19–20.

Hizmi, H., 1992. 'A Byzantine Farmhouse at Givat Ehud, near Modi'in', *Liber Annuus* 42, 289–96.

Hopkins, K., 1983. 'Models, Ships and Staples'. In P. Garnsey and C.R. Whittaker (ed.) *Trade and Famine in Classical Antiquity* (Cambridge), 84–109.

Israel, Y., 1995a. 'Ashqelon', *ESI* 13, 100–105.

Israel, Y., 1995b. 'Survey of Pottery Workshops, Nahal Lakhish-Nahal Besor', *ESI* 13, 106–107.

Israel, Y., 1995c.'The Economy of the Gaza-Ashkelon Region in the Byzantine Period in the Light of the 3rd Mile Estate', *Michmanim* 8, 119–132. (Hebrew).

Jeffreys, E., Jeffreys, M. and Scott, R., 1986. *The Chronicle of John Malalas* (Melbourne).

Jézégou, M.-P., 1998. 'Le mobilier de l'épave Saint-Gervais 2 (VIIᵉ s.) à Fos-sur-Mer (B.-du-Rh)'. In M. Bonifay, M.-B. Carre and Y. Rigoir (ed.) *Fouilles à Marseille. Les mobiliers (Iᵉʳ-VIIᵉ siècles ap. J.-C.)* (Études Massaliètes, Paris), 343–352.

Johnson, B.L., 1988. 'The Pottery'. In G.D. Weinberg (ed.) *Excavations at Jalame* (Columbia), 137–226.

Jones, A.H.M., 1964. *The Later Roman Empire 284–602, Vol. II* (Oxford).

Jones, A.H.M., 1974. *The Roman Economy* (Oxford).

Kalinowski, A., 1993. 'Pottery from Unit 4000'. In S.T. Stevens (ed.) *Bir el Knissia at Carthage: a Rediscovered Cemetery and Church. Report No.1* (JRA Suppl. 7, Michigan), 155–177.

Katz, O., 1994. 'Be'er Sheva, Nahal Beqa' 1', *ESI* 12, 96–97.

Keay, S.J., 1984. *Late Roman Amphorae in the Western Mediterranean. A Typology and Economic Study: the Catalan Evidence* (BAR Int. Series 196, Oxford).

Killebrew, A., 1991. 'Pottery from Dabiye', *'Atiqot* 20, 66–73.

Kindler, A., 1999. 'Summary of Twelve Years of Numismatic Finds in the Excavations of Sumaqa (1983–1995)'. In S. Dar, *Sumaqa. A Roman and Byzantine Jewish Village on Mount Carmel, Israel* (BAR Int. Series 815, Oxford), 347–361.

Kingsley, S.A., 1999a. *Specialized Production and Long Distance Trade in Byzantine Palestine* (D.Phil Thesis, University of Oxford).

Kingsley, S., 1999b. 'The Sumaqa Pottery Assemblage: Classification and Quantification'. In S. Dar (ed.) *Sumaqa. A Roman and Byzantine Jewish Village on Mount Carmel, Israel* (BAR Int. Series 815, Archaeopress, Oxford), 263–330.

Kingsley, S. and Raveh, K., 1996. *The Ancient Harbour and Anchorage at Dor, Israel. Results of the Underwater Surveys, 1976–1991* (BAR Int. Series 626, Oxford).

Kirwin, L.P., 1938. 'The Pottery'. In. W.B. Emery, *The Royal Tombs of Ballana and Qustul* (Cairo), 386–399.

Lepelley, C., 1981. *Les cités de l'Afrique romaine au bas-empire, tome II* (Paris).

Lernau, G., 1995. 'The Fish Remains of Upper Zohar'. In R.P. Harper (ed) *Upper Zohar: an Early Byzantine Fort in Palaestina Tertia* (BSAJ, Oxford), 99–105.

Levine, L.I., 1993. 'Synagogues'. In E. Stern (ed.) *The New Encyclopedia of Archaeological Excavations in the Holy Land, Vol. 4* (Jerusalem), 1421–1424.

Lloyd, M., 1984. *A Byzantine Shipwreck at Iskandil Burnu, Turkey: Preliminary Report* (MA Thesis, Texas A and M University).

Long, L. and Volpe, G., 1998. 'Le chargement de l'épave 1 de la Palud (VIᵉ s.) à Port-Cros (Var). Note préliminaire'. In M. Bonifay, M.-B. Carre and Y. Rigoir (ed.) *Fouilles à Marseille. Les mobiliers (Iᵉʳ-VIIᵉ siècles ap. J.-C.)* (Études Massaliètes, Paris), 317–342.

Mackensen, M., 1998. 'New Evidence for Central Tunisian Red Slip Ware with Stamped Decoration', *JRA* 11, 355–370.

Maeir, A.M., 1994. 'The Excavations at Mamilla, Jerusalem, Phase I (1989)'. In H. Geva (ed.) *Ancient Jerusalem Revealed* (Jerusalem), 299–305.

Majcherek, G., 1992. 'The Late Roman Ceramics from Sector "G" (Alexandria 1986–1987)', *Études et Travaux* 16, 81–117.

Martin-Kilcher, S., 1994. *Die Romischen Amphoren aus Augst und Kaiseraugst. 2: Die Amphoren fur Wein, Fischsauce, Sudfruchte (Gruppen 2–24) und Gesamtauswertung* (Augst).

Matthews, E., Neidinger, W. and Ayalon, E., 1990. 'Preliminary Report on the 1989 and 1990 Excavation Seasons at Zur Natan'. In *Publication of the Texas Foundation for Archaeological and Historical Research* (Houston), 4–28

Mattingly, D.J., 1988. 'The Olive Boom. Oil Surpluses, Wealth and Power in Roman Tripolitania', *Libyan Studies* 19, 21–41.

Mayerson, P., 1993. 'The Use of Ascalon Wine in the Medieval Writers of the Fourth to the Seventh Centuries', *IEJ* 43, 169–73.

Mazar, A., 1975. 'Excavations at Tell Qasile, 1973–1974', *IEJ* 25, 77–88.

McCaslin, D., 1978. *Hala Sultan Tekke 4. The 1977 Underwater Report* (Studies in Mediterranean Archaeology XLV.4, Goteborg).

Meyers, E.M., Meyers, C.L. and Hoglund, G., 1995. 'Sepphoris (Sippori), 1994', *IEJ* 45, 68–71.

Meyers, E.M., Strange, J.F. and Meyers, C.L., 1981. *Excavations at Ancient Meiron, Upper Galilee, Israel 1971–72, 1974–75, 1977* (Cambridge).

Morris, C.E. and Peatfield, A.D., 1987. 'Pottery from the Cyprus Underwater Survey, 1983', *RDAC*, 199–212.

Ne'eman, Y., 1990. *Map of Ma'amit (54) 15–20* (Jerusalem).

Negev, N., 1997. 'Nahal Hevron – Dams', *ESI* 16, 128–131.

Neuru, L., 1980. 'Late Roman Pottery: a Fifth Century Deposit from Carthage', *Antiquités Africaines* 16, 195–213.

Neusner, J., 1994. *Purity in Rabbinic Judaism. A Systematic Account* (Atlanta).

Oked, S., 1996. 'Patterns of the Transport Amphorae at Ostrakine during the 6th and 7th Centuries', *ARAM* 8, 165–175.

Oleson, J.P., Fitzgerald, M.A., Sherwood, A.N. and Sidebotham, S.E., 1994. *The Harbours of Caesarea Maritima. Results of the Caesarea Ancient Harbour Excavation Project 1980–85. Volume II: the Find and the Ship* (BAR Int. Series 594, Oxford).

Opait, A., 1998. 'New Pottery from the Circular Harbour of Carthage', *CEDAC* 18, 21–35.

Ovadiah, A., 1969. 'Excavations in the Area of the Ancient Synagogue at Gaza (Preliminary Report)', *IEJ* 19, 193–198.

Ovadiah, A., 1993. 'Early Churches'. In E. Stern (ed.) *The New Encyclopedia of Archaeological Excavations in the Holy Land, Vol. 1* (Jerusalem), 305–309.

Parker, A.J., 1992. *Ancient Shipwrecks of the Mediterranean and the Roman Provinces* (BAR Int. Series 580, Oxford).

Parkins, H., 1997. 'The 'Consumer City' Domesticated? The Roman City in Élite Economic Strategies'. In H.M. Parkins (ed.) *Roman Urbanism. Beyond the Consumer City* (London), 83–111.

Patrich, J. and Zafrir, Y., 1986. 'Horvat Bet Loya', *ESI* 4, 11–14.

Peacock, D.P.S., 1984. 'The Amphorae: Typology and Chronology'. In M.G. Fulford and D.P.S. Peacock (ed.) *The Avenue de President Habib Bourguiba, Salammbo: the Pottery and other Ceramic Objects from the Site. Vol. 1.2* (Sheffield), 116–140.

Pharr, C., 1952. *The Theodosian Code and Novels and the Simondian Constitutions* (Princeton University Press).

Raban, A., 1989. *The Harbors of Caesarea Maritima. Results of the Caesarea Ancient Harbor Excavation Project, 1980–1985. Volume I: the Site and the Excavations* (BAR Int. Series 491, Oxford).

Raban, A., 1992. 'Sebastos: the Royal Harbour at Caesarea Maritima – a short-lived Giant', *IJNA* 21, 111–124.

Raban, A., 1995. 'Dor-Yam: Maritime and Coastal Installations at Dor in their Geomorphological and Stratigraphic Context'. In E. Stern, *Excavations at Dor, Final Report, Volume IA. Areas A and C: Introduction and Stratigraphy* (QEDEM 1, Jerusalem), 285–354.

Rackham, H., 1968. *Pliny. Natural History* (Harvard University Press).

Reynolds, P., 1995. *Trade in the Western Mediterranean, AD 400–700: the Ceramic Evidence* (BAR Int. Series 604, Oxford).

Reynolds, P., 1997–1998. 'Pottery Production and Economic Exchange in Second Century Berytus: some Preliminary Observations of Ceramic Trends from Quantified Ceramic Deposits from the Aub-Leverhulme Excavations in Beirut', *Berytus* 43, 35–110.

Riley, J., 1979. 'The Coarse Pottery from Benghazi'. In J.A. Lloyd (ed.) *Sidi Khrebish Excavations. Benghazi (Berenice) Vol. II* (Tripoli), 91–449.

Riley, J.A., 1981. 'The Pottery from the Cisterns 1977.1, 1977.2, 1977.3'. In J.H. Humphrey (ed.) *Excavations at Carthage 1977, Conducted by the University of Michigan. Volume VI* (Ann Arbor), 85–124.

Ronen, A. and Olami, Y., 1978. *'Atlit Map* (Jerusalem).

Rougé, J., 1966. *Expositio Totius Mundi et Gentium* (Paris).

Safrai, Z., 1994. *The Economy of Roman Palestine* (London).

Safrai, Z., 1998. *The Missing Century. Palestine in the Fifth Century: Growth and Decline* (Leuven).

Santamaria, C., 1995. *L'épave Dramont E à Saint-Raphael (Vᵉ siècle ap. J.-C.)* (Archaeonautica 13, Paris).

Sedov, A.V., 1992. 'New Archaeological and Epigraphical Material from Qana (South Arabia)', *Arabian Archaeology and Epigraphy* 3, 110–135.

Seligman, J., 1994. 'Jerusalem, Pisgat Ze'ev (East A)', *ESI* 12, 52–54.

Shereshevski, J., 1991. *Byzantine Urban Settlements in the Negev Desert* (Beer-Sheva V, Ben-Gurion).

Shourkin, O., 1997. 'Jerusalem, Pisgat Ze'ev E', *ESI* 16, 99.

Smith., G.A., 1894. *The Historical Geography of the Holy Land* (London).

St. Thackeray, H., 1966. *Josephus I. The Life. Against Apion* (Harvard University Press, 4th ed.).

St. Thackeray, H., 1967. *Josephus II. The Jewish War, Books I-III* (Harvard University Press, 4th ed.).

Stieglitz, R.R., 1998. 'A Late Byzantine Reservoir and *Piscina* at Tel Tanninim', *IEJ* 48, 54–65.

Syon, D., 1998. 'A Wine Press at Akhziv', *'Atiqot* 34, 85–99. (Hebrew).

Tahal, G., 1995. 'Avedat', *ESI* 14, 130–133.

Tainter, J.A., 1988. *The Collapse of Complex Societies* (Cambridge University Press).

Tchernia, A., 1986. *Le vin de l'Italie romaine. Essai d'histoire economique d'après les amphores* (Rome).

Tomber, R.S., 1988. 'Pottery from the 1982–83 Excavations'. In J.H. Humphrey (ed.) *The Circus and a Byzantine Cemetery at Carthage, Volume I* (Michigan), 437–538.

Tsuk, T. and Ayalon, E., 1995. 'Herziliya Tunnel', *ESI* 14, 140–141.

Tubb, J.N., 1986. 'The Pottery from a Byzantine Well near Tell Fara', *PEQ*, 51–65.

Tripolitanian types appear in contexts throughout the Mediterranean and form part of the large oil vessel dump at Monte Testaccio, where a major deposit dating from the Severan period represents *annona* shipments of African oil.[3]

While these western examples have generated considerable scholarly interest, the eastern Mediterranean production of olive oil largely remains a mystery. Heichelheim argued that the oil of Syria and Palestine was of no great reputation in antiquity as far as the written sources are concerned.[4] However, with Constantine's foundation of a grand, new capital on the Bosphorus, a steady food supply was required and olive oil formed a staple element of this requirement. Since Africa did not bear the burden of supplying grain for both the eastern and western capitals, it seems unlikely that the African and Spanish provinces were expected – or even able – to meet the yearly demands of the new city. Certainly after the Vandal conquest of Africa, there could be no state-organised shipments of oil from the African provinces. If the capital depended on Egyptian grain and the high quality wine of Palestine, from where did Constantinople receive its olive oil?

One suggestion concerning the regional supply of a significant volume of olive oil within the eastern Mediterranean in Late Antiquity was posited by Georges Tchalenko, whose monumental study (*Villages Antique de la Syrie du Nord*) served as a catalyst for scholarship of North Syria. During his years of work amongst the so called 'Dead Cities' of the limestone hills between Antioch (Antakya) and Beroia (Aleppo), Tchalenko studied the remains of more than 450 Roman and Byzantine villages. In his opinion the architecturally elaborate remains constructed of large ashlars and the temples and numerous churches presented a picture of general prosperity in Late Antiquity. Based primarily on dated inscriptions, Tchalenko believed occupation extended from the second through to the seventh centuries A.D. (ending at the time of the Arab conquest), but boomed in the fifth and sixth centuries, a time traditionally viewed as one of decline. He argued that the villages' prosperity should be attributed to their exploitation of an olive monoculture; in this view Tchalenko may have been strongly influenced by the North African material cited above, of which he was certainly aware. This thesis has been challenged in some details in the past two decades.[5] Excavations in the limestone massif at the village of Dehes proved that occupation did not cease with the Arab conquest, but continued into the ninth century. Through his work at this site and elsewhere in the limestone massif, Tate has also demonstrated that a monoculture did not exist. The numerous livestock troughs in houses throughout the region and finds of remains of domestic animals in excavations have shown that the villagers followed a common Mediterranean mixed agricultural regime in antiquity. Various crops were cultivated in combination with stock raising. Importantly, however, although Tate argues his case for mixed farming, he does not deny that the olive held an important place in the village economy. Nevertheless, he does not believe that the produce of the region was exported for overseas consumption. The prosperity of the region, according to Tate, is to be viewed primarily as a result of local demographic growth.[6] The State played a role in this development but only at a local level; the zone located to the east of the limestone massif saw increasing militarisation during Late Antiquity, and Antioch to the west held a strategically vital place in the supply and maintenance of eastern armies. In response to the factors of town growth, regional security, or the input of resources into the frontier region from Diocletian onwards, landowners invested their own wealth to develop sedentary agriculture.[7]

As we have seen, the pendulum has swung considerably away from Tchalenko's olive monoculture produced for export overseas to Tate's polyculture based on local and regional demand. The issue requires more detailed investigation.

The Basis of Syria's Late Antique Rural Wealth

The period of the fourth-fifth centuries A.D. does appear to have been a period of generalised prosperity following the disruptions of the third century A.D. when Roman Syria suffered Persian devastation and the eruption of Zenobia's revolt. Syrian cities and towns grew during the years of relative peace between A.D. 300 and 500: Antioch had covered an area of 90 hectares within its walls during its Hellenistic heyday, while late Roman Antioch covered 600 hectares. Apamea (Afamia), to the immediate south of the jebels was, like Antioch, already a thriving city in the Hellenistic period. However, Justinian refortified the city with a circuit enclosing a 3 km^2 area. Unsurprisingly, the two-century period from A.D. 300–500 also corresponds with the peak period of building and occupation in the limestone massif.[8]

The area of North Syria investigated in this study is dominated by a broken chain of hills running from the region of Cyrrhus (Nabi Uri) in the north to Apamea in the south, Antioch in the west to Beroia in the east (Fig. 4.1). Five major jebels are located in this region: Siman, Bariša, Il A'la, Wastani, and Zawiye. These hills rise to a maximum elevation of 600–800 m. There are no perennial streams or bodies of surface water amongst the jebels, and rainfall, while plenteous in comparison with the eastern steppe they border, is limited to between 400 and 600 mm per year. With the notable exception of the plain of Dana between the Jebels Wastani and Zawiye, few areas of open land suitable for the cultivation of cereals exist in the region. The broken nature of the terrain caused villages to be connected to one another by tracks, rather than roads. The difficult terrain further complicated communications with the cities that ringed the escarpment.

At first glance these limestone uplands, largely denuded of soil and containing only small areas of arable land, seem ill-suited to supply food for an empire. However, closer examination and comparison with cultivation patterns in other regions, in particular the North African jebels, shows it is precisely this landscape on which we should focus. As survey work around Lepcis Magna in Tripolitania has demonstrated, the hill country behind that coast was increasingly developed for oleiculture during the Imperial period, probably due to the fact that the region can support this type of exploitation, although marginal areas (under 150 mm of annual rainfall) necessitate intensive water management. The olive possesses some drought tolerance and an ability to grow in a range of soils and is thus an ideal crop for such conditions. Consigned to marginal lands with a relatively low rainfall, the olive can not only exist but thrive.

Within the limits of the 400–600 mm rainfall zone of the Syrian jebels (which is much greater generally than that received by any region of Tripolitania), mature trees would

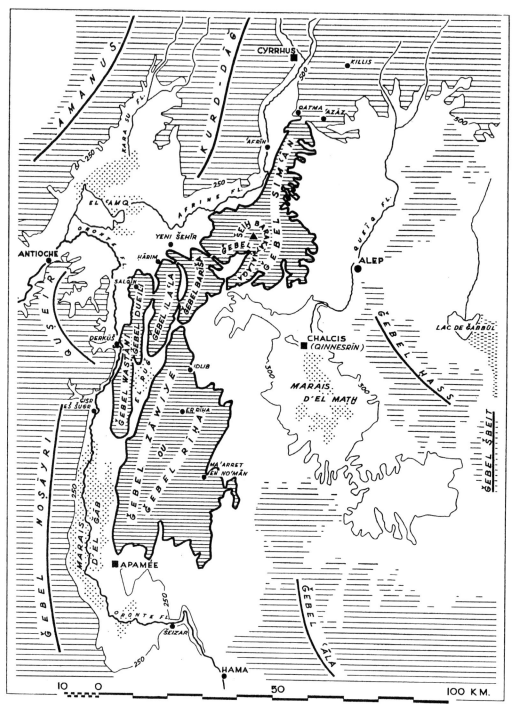

Fig. 4.1: North Syrian Cities (from Tchalenko, 1953: pl. XXXIX).

generally require no irrigation. Rainwater was collected and stored in cisterns which are common features among the region's village remains and were used (as they are today) for domestic consumption or for limited agricultural activities. The *terra rossa* soil of the region, while mostly restricted to pockets contained within decaying formations of limestone, is fertile. Groves of olives also allow other crops to be grown beneath or between trees, or for animals to be grazed among them. Although the hills are a barrier to traffic, cities surround this upland area, and it is easy to see how villages in the jebels would be in a position to market goods both among the villages and to the surrounding urban areas. Rarely do more than a few kilometres separate one village from another, which made travel among them less difficult than the terrain initially suggests. A major Roman road running from the coast via Antioch to Chalcis (Qinnasrin), a city and important military post on the eastern steppe, linked the villages to the rest of northern Syria (Fig. 4.1). Roads linked the region with Cyrrhus in the north and Apamea to the south.[9] The presence of these arteries meant that the villages were not entirely isolated, but had access to the larger market towns of Seleucia-Pieria and Antioch in the west, Beroia and Chalcis to the east. From Antioch to Beroia (across the width of the entire limestone massif region) is approximately 90 km, which is 3–5 days travel by road in antiquity, depending on the mode of transport used.[10]

Evidence for olive production abounds in this region. Tchalenko, declining to estimate, simply stated that the presses in the area are 'innumerable'.[11] Tate's survey of forty-five villages in the Jebels Siman, Halaqa, Bariša and il A'la yielded 245 presses.[12] He surmised that many more presses are buried, while others have gone unnoticed in the tumble of the less well-preserved houses. Most villages contain one or more processing installation. Many villages contain a large number of installations for their relatively small size, a pattern typified by Behyo where Tchalenko counted thirty-seven presses.[13] At nearby Qabloze, famous for its great early Christian basilica, Tchalenko recorded only five or six farms, but twenty presses in the immediate vicinity. The village of Qirqbize, located on a spur on Jebel il A'la (Fig. 4.1), covers an area of approximately 100 x 200 m and consists of twenty-two houses. Here Tchalenko noted eight press installations, including the large lever and screw press studied in detail by Callot (Fig. 4.3).[14] Although these presses are not as large-scale as those of the African provinces, they are nevertheless indicative of surplus production. One does not require an expensive press installation to process olive oil for subsistence purposes. Based on a comparison with larger North African presses, this Syrian example could process perhaps between 2,500 and 5,000 litres of olive oil during the annual pressing season.[15] If one accepts that twenty litres of olive oil per year is a reasonable figure for consumption, then this press alone could have supplied the needs of between 125 and 250 people.[16] The village itself is small, containing twenty-two houses and a total of fifty-one rooms. Even if we assume that four people cohabited per room, the population of the whole village would only amount to only 204 people. Thus, one press alone potentially sufficed to supply the needs of the entire settlement for a year. While the other presses in Qirqbize are smaller in scale, their mere existence is a clear indication of surplus production.

How may one link such evidence for surplus production to the wider issue of East Mediterranean trade? In the cases of Spain and Africa, the thread that has connected

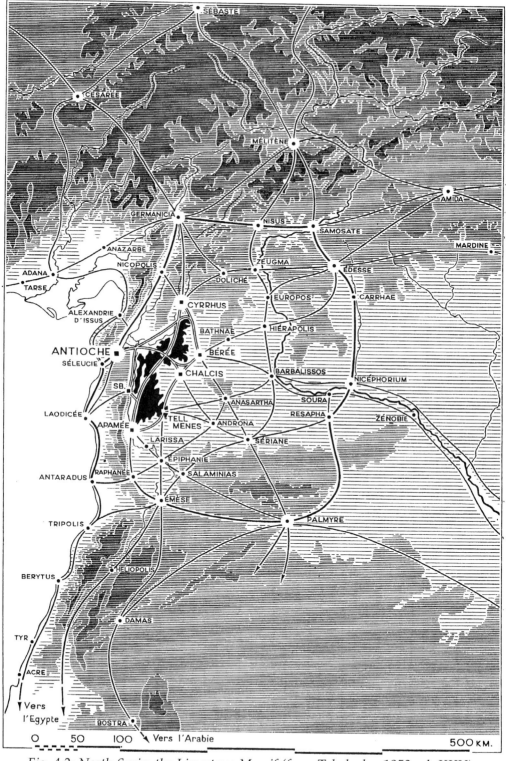

Fig. 4.2: North Syria: the Limestone Massif (from Tchalenko, 1953: pl. XXV).

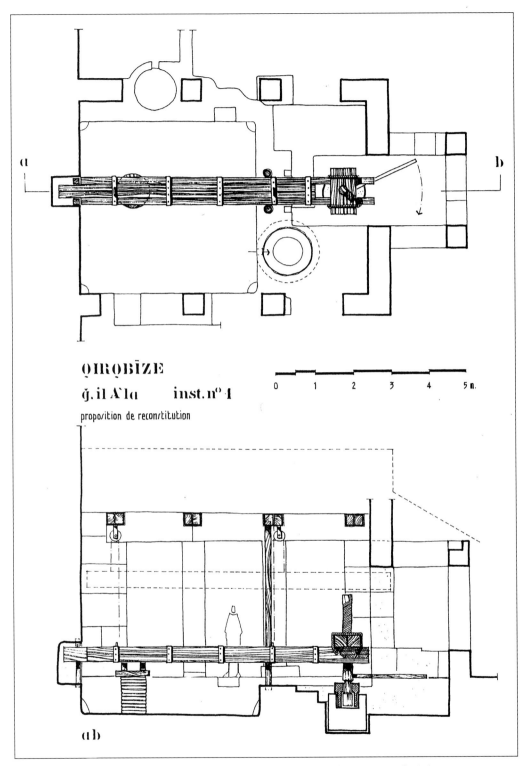

QIRQBĪZE

ǧ. il A'la　　inst. nº 1

proposition de reconstitution

Fig. 4.3: Lever and screw press (from Callot, 1984: pl. 61).

Fig. 4.5: Mosaic depicting a boat carrying amphorae (Apamea Archaeological Museum, Syria).

Oil and Wine?

The relationship between LR1 and North Syria has traditionally been viewed with an eye towards the exploitation of the olive. This study has developed this correlation by discussing parallels between this region and others noted for oil production across the Mediterranean. Support for oil as a content of many LR1 jars emerges from inscriptions on vessels. *Graffiti* on a jar from the Yassi Ada wreck has been interpreted as signifying olive oil.[35] At Qustul in Egypt, an inscription on another jar was read as *elaiou*.[36] This jar type has not been subjected to scientific content analysis, and so any evidence regarding content must remain speculative on the basis of the jars themselves. However, there are reasons to consider wine as also playing a role not only in the regional economy, but also in wider Mediterranean exchange. While Palestine was the noted eastern wine producer in Late Antiquity (see Kingsley, this volume), there is evidence to suggest that Syria also participated in the long-distance trade of wine. The export of wine from North Syria by Late Antiquity had a long history stretching at least as far back as the Hellenistic period and in the early Imperial period Laodicea (immediately to the south of Antioch) was a producer of wine sought after as far afield as East Africa and Arabia.[37] Laodicea's famed vineyards, that clung to the hills behind the town, continued to

Fig. 4.6: Roller crusher installation (from De Vogüé, 1865–77: pl. 113).

produce wine, some of which was exported, throughout Late Antiquity. Alexander Tralles in the seventh century recommended Laodicean wine for kidney ailments.[38] The export of Apamean wine was known in the Roman period and finds of presses in its *territorium* (see below) indicate that production continued without interruption between the fourth and sixth centuries. Antioch also produced wine of repute.[39] There may have been little or no distinction in the produce of the two cities, in the same way that wine referred to as 'Gazan' in historical texts actually included produce grown and packaged outside the city's *territorium*.[40] Probably much of the better wine processed in North Syria was traded as 'Laodicean'.

While numerous presses in the limestone massif are certainly oil presses (based on their physical characteristics of raised, circular press bed, square or rectangular collecting vats and associated rotary mills of *trapetum* or *mola olearia* type), a recent study has challenged the identification of certain installations from North Syria traditionally identified as oil presses. The types in question are those that use stone rollers in processing (Fig. 4.6). Callot publishes such installations from North Syria as oil mills, and pre-industrial evidence from Greece supports the hypothesis that olive oil could be processed using rollers.[41] However, evidence from Israel suggests that such roller crushers were used in wine production. The flat surfaces within the roller presses as well as their circular collecting vats are more typical of wineries than oil installations.[42] In light of the presence of other mill types, the *trapetum* and *mola olearia*, where a few examples are representative of many more now lost, it is unnecessary to identify the roller crushers as oil installations to demonstrate extensive olive processing.[43] Tate argued convincingly for a mixed agricultural economy of stocking, as well as grain, oil and wine production; while the evidence for olive cultivation is widespread and well known, little attention has been paid to the possibility of extensive viticulture, despite the favourable climate (vines flourish on the Jebel Zawiye today) and the textual evidence described above. While oil presses are abundant, wine presses are rarely discussed in the North Syrian context; the lone example given attention is the large, industrial scale press at El Bara in the territory of Apamea, probably of fourth century date.[44] Beyond this press, archaeological evidence for wine production has been left largely unexplored in North Syria. Re-identification of the numerous roller installations as wineries accords with the model of a mixed agricultural economy argued by Tate and creates a strong case for the possibility of surplus wine production to accompany oil.[45]

The critical problem of press function remains a challenging one, especially since presses could serve multiple uses. In some cases installations could be used for both wine and oil, although in an environment of specialised production for the market this is unlikely. Without further excavation of presses where botanical remains may provide clues to press function and more extensive survey within the limestone massif to determine relationships among installation types, this question will remain un-answered.

There would seem little reason to attempt such a revision of the prevailing interpretation were it not for the increasing evidence that the LR1 jar carried wine as one of its principal contents. Amphorae finds from the inner harbour of Carthage included pitch lined LR1 amphora sherds, which must have carried wine and not oil, since pitch was used to waterproof wine jars and to flavour the wine, but not for oil.[46] The fact that LR1 jars carried wine, at least part of the time, also may explain why such vessels appear in oil producing regions such as North Africa. Pitched LR1 vessels were also found in excavations at Ballana.[47] In the seventh century Yassi Ada wreck, examples of LR1 were similarly pitched.[48] While the LR1 jar has been associated with oil due to the hypothesis of a surplus production of this commodity in North Syria, there are grounds to modify this theory. In my opinion, this amphora type carried a wide variety of agricultural products from the North Syria region (including Cilicia, Cyprus and the Cyclades). Its main contents, however, were oil and wine.

The Potential for Surplus

An attempt to quantify the output of the hill villages is difficult, not only owing to the incomplete nature of the archaeological record, but also due to the uncertain identification of known press examples. The amphora evidence supports reinterpreting many presses as wine installations, but a further division of presses has crucial implications for the region's economic character. If a significant portion of the North Syrian presses were indeed used for wine production, then we must consider the output of olive oil to be lower than once thought and that of wine higher. Since at present it is impossible to know what proportion of presses in the limestone massif should be re-identified, one could argue that in attempting to calculate possible surpluses we have reached an impasse. Identification of wine presses at the expense of oil installations reduces the overall potential for a surplus of olive oil, and vice versa.

Based on the scant evidence available, we can however propose tentative estimates of production capability. Using the 245 presses identified in forty-five villages we can begin to attempt quantification based on overall press types, by establishing that on average 5.4 presses are associated with each village. The area surveyed was a good cross section of the Jebels Siman, Halaqa, Bariša, il Al'a, and Zawiye; only Jebel Wastani does not figure in the calculations. Furthermore, due to the rapid chronological development of the massif villages, which occurred over a relatively short span of time, we can be confident that most presses were in use contemporaneously during the peak period of settlement between the fourth and sixth centuries. There are 700 villages in the region and an estimate based on 5.4 presses per village yields a total 3,780 for all the villages. Even if one rounds down press numbers to an average of five per village (a reduction of nearly 10% from Tate's findings), the region would contain 3,500 presses. If this calculation is erroneous, it is more likely to be conservative than liberal, because many presses are buried or destroyed, especially in the valleys where there has been greater settlement continuity.

The calculated number of presses, nearly 3,800, is vastly greater than that estimated for the city of Lepcis Magna in North Africa (1,500), which specialized in the production and export of oil. The density of presses is vastly higher in Syria, with 1.5 presses per square km, three times that around Lepcis Magna-Oea, where the density is 0.5 presses per square km.[49] While the presses of the two regions differ from one another in terms of size, the smaller Syrian examples are considerably more numerous. Surplus production may be argued for on the basis of two points. We have noted above the presence of LR1 amphorae kiln sites along the Syro-Cilician coast. Another crucial factor is that whereas the whole of the territory of Lepcis Magna is represented by the estimate of 1,500 presses, Antioch-Apamea (whose territory included the southern portion of the Jebel Zawiye) greatly exceeds this figure even though it is based on data obtained from only a portion of the two cities' *territoria*.

Roman Syria was known for its vast city territories.[50] While it is true that the limestone massif is an important and territorially significant component of the Antiochene hinterland (and to a lesser degree, Apamean), the hill country under investigation does not comprise a majority of either city's rural area. In the case of Antioch, the total territory belonging to the city comprised about 4,000 km². Within this area was the rich valley of the Orontes, the fertile coastal plain towards Seleucia and Daphne, the productive valley of the Afrin River as far as the territory of Cyrrhus, and the southern extent of the Amanus range. The Jebels Siman, il A'la, Bariša, Wastani and northern Zawiye belonged to Antioch; the combined area of these jebels is roughly 2,500 km², or approximately only 60% of the total (exluding the southern portion of Zawiye, which belonged to Apamea). Thus, the total number of presses in the whole Antiochene territory could potentially increase to 6,000.

Apamea's territory was equally vast: perhaps 4,000 km² of lands including the villages of southern Jebel Zawiye and the vast sweep of Orontes river valley and plains opening to the Syrian steppe. The Apamean hinterland encompassed the southern Jebel Zawiye and the Jebel Nosayri, another group of hills comparable in character to the limestone massif and thus a possible centre of oil and wine production. The city territory also contains a significant area of plains and Orontes river bottom lands.

Strabo (16.2.10) noted that the city supplied the Seleucid cavalry and its lands were probably utilised in antiqiuty more for livestock rearing and cereal culture than viticulture and oil. In view of this evidence, one may estimate a press density around Apamea lower than the 1.5 per km^2 of Antiochene territory, but comparable to that of Lepcis Magna-Oea (0.5 per km^2), a total of 2,000 presses. Thus the two hinterlands of Antioch and Apamea could yield a combined 8,000 presses.

Conclusions

The above analysis sheds light on the background underlying Syria's role in provisioning urban centres throughout the late antique Mediterranean. In the eastern provinces, prosperity based on exploitation of the land owed much to the ability to move a limited range of agricultural products in universal demand over long distances: namely wine and oil. We possess tangible evidence about production in the *territoria* of two of the greatest cities of Late Antiquity, Antioch and Apamea. The large number of press remains indicate that a significant surplus of wine and oil was produced in the city hinterlands. While much of this produce was consumed within the region, a sizeable quantity was shipped to destinations throughout the Mediterranean. The coastal zones nearby provided the link between producer and consumer: kilns manufacturing LR1 amphorae. Finds of this type of container overseas are an index of the importance of the export trade in agricultural commodities within and indeed beyond the Mediterranean basin. Syria, then, takes its place as an economic focal point for the late Roman and early Byzantine period, "a land overflowing with grain, wine and oil".[51]

Many questions remain. We do not fully know what social factors were at work in the limestone massif, and possess little information about the agents responsible for carrying out the export trade. The abundance of small presses in modest-sized villages stands in contrast to the massive African presses and oil factories.[52] The North Syrian villages may represent the small late Roman farmer operating outside the estate, producing for the market. Regarding the merchants who trafficked in oil, we have virtually no evidence. Both questions are likely to remain elusive even in the light of new archaeological evidence. At present, we also cannot be certain how deeply integrated into a wider economy the Syrian cities were and we cannot fully appreciate the scale of the trade, nor its overall range. Until additional archaeological evidence is unearthed and quantified, such issues will remain obscure. An obvious starting point is a thorough examination of the limestone massif presses. Excavation of LR1 kiln sites and further quantification of LR1 sherds recorded outside the production area will shed additional light on the nature of this exchange. Nevertheless, a mosaic is slowly being revealed piece by piece.

Placed at the centre of imperial policy from the fourth century on, with a population that expanded into the sixth century, and constituting a major centre of government and military supply and organisation, Antioch and its surroundings boomed in Late Antiquity. The two-way relationship between urban and rural economic growth is best represented in North Syria by the hundreds of village communities, which shared in the fortunes of the urban centres dependent upon them. Yet this web of exchange is only a microcosm of the greater imperial network, which demanded the movement of foodstuffs to the imperial vortex at Constantinople and to the farthest reaches of military involvement, such as the Danube river zone, a scenario that is reminiscent of the early Empire when Spanish oil nourished legions on the Rhine and joined African oil on the tables of Rome.

With the gradual decline of Rome in the West and the shift of the locus of power to the city of Constantinople, much nearer at hand to Antioch, the New Rome proved to have as voracious an appetite as old Rome: immense quantities of grain, wine and oil were demanded for the populace. The grain and oil dole was maintained in Late Antiquity in the new capital, creating demand which local sources could not meet. Vandal control of North Africa necessitated the replacement of African oil by the produce of Greater Syria (including Cyprus and Cilicia). This situation was naturally exploited throughout the East, but especially in Oriens, where the urban elite figured prominently in imperial circles from the fourth to seventh centuries and where the well developed urban character of the land, especially the coast, facilitated efficient communications and exchange. The ubiquitous Syrian merchant no doubt also played an important role.[53] While the shipments of LR1 to the Danubian provinces may be explained as part of state supply, that in the West, in Britain, Spain and southern Gaul must have been purely commercial. The vast number of presses, which at the moment we cannot estimate with certainty, must nevertheless have numbered upwards of 8,000 in the combined hinterlands of Antioch and Apamea. This number represents an extraordinary level of activity on the land in late antique Syria which must be equally valid for other North Syrian centres such as Cyrrhus, Laodicea and Beroia. As the Syrian cities developed and expanded during the relative peace and stability of the late Roman/early Byzantine period, they enjoyed communications and integration with the wider Mediterranean. Demographic growth in the urban environment demanded expansion of the rural zone, intensification and exploitation of more marginal areas. Wine must be added to the already established olive oil as a product exported from North Syria in Late Antiquity, as it had been throughout earlier periods (especially that from Laodicea). The strong probability that a significant portion of the press remains from the limestone massif are in fact wine installations fits well with both the ceramic evidence and the written sources.

The emerging mosaic, however, is like a few *tesserae* in the corner of a wider carpet. In the middle of the composition, still hidden, lie mechanisms and merchants, scope and scale. In one corner, the presses, vessels, villages and peasants of a Syrian landscape unfold. In another corner, distant cities like Carthage and Constantinople receive the fruits of Syria's labour. Whatever the final picture may be, the quest promises to yield a fruitful harvest for the study of the late antique economy.

Notes

1   Remesal Rodríguez, 1999: 27.
2   For the fine on Lepcis see Mattingly, 1985: 27; Mattingly, 1988: 37 on the figures from Lepcis.
3   Mattingly, 1995: 153–155.

4   Heichelheim, 1938: 132.
5   Callot, 1984 and Tate, 1992.
6   Tate, 1993: 332.
7   Tate, 1992: 220.
8   Will, 1997:108; Foss, 1997: 189–269.
9   Tchalenko, 1953: 104–105.
10   Casson, 1974: 191 discusses travellers on horseback moving 16–26 miles (25.6–41.6 km) per day. Peasants travelling on foot obviously would be significantly slower.
11   Tchalenko, 1953: 40.
12   Tate, 1992: 243.
13   Tchalenko, 1953: 360; Callot, 1984: 120 states that only ten of these installations are presses, the others are roller crushers.
14   Tchalenko, 1953: 320; Callot, 1984: pl. 61.
15   Mattingly, 1993: 491.
16   Foss, 1997: 201 accepts Tate's figures, 1992: 183.
17   Described in Riley, 1981a: 117.
18   Egloff, 1977: 110, 112.
19   Finds of LR1: Anderin, Dr. Nigel Pollard, 2000: personal communication; Dehes: Orssaud, 1980: 240 Type 1. Ashdod: Dothan and Freedman, 1967: 34–35, fig. 14.2; Caesarea: Riley, 1975: 33; Jerusalem: Crowfoot and Fitzgerald, 1929: 81 and pl. XIV.29.
20   Egypt: Kellia, Egloff, 1977: 110, 112; Meröe (Soba): Welsby, 1998: 92; Axum: De Contenson, 1963: 8, 11 and pl. XIII, b–c.
21   Anemurium: Williams, 1989: 95; Istanbul: Hayes, 1992: 64; Athens: Robinson, 1959: 82 and 84, 115 [M 333] and pls. 32, 58; Rome: Pensabene, 1985: 190–200; Benghazi: Riley, 1979: 212–216; Apollonia: Riley, 1981b: 75; Italy: Riley, 1979: 214; Carthage: Riley, 1982: 116; southern France (Marseille and Arles): Bonifay, 1989: 660–662; Spain: Keay, 1984: 654, Type LIII.
22   Britain: Peacock and Williams, 1986: 186; Danube: Pacetti, 1995: 278–279. See also Karagiorgou this volume.
23   Bonifay, 1989: 660–663.
24   Reynolds, 1995: 390–391.
25   Tocra: Reynolds, 1995: 389; Berenike: Reynolds, 1995: 384; Carthage: Reynolds, 1995: 371; Marseille, Bonifay, Congès and Leguilloux, 1998: 663.
26   Adams, 1962: 251.
27   Empereur and Picon, 1989: 236–243.
28   Tchalenko, 1953: 21, 28-30, pl.CXXXIV 23,24,25).
29   Callot, 1984: 105–114.
30   Gatier, 1995: 36. For a caravan of mule drivers on what seems to be a regular route, see Sarason, R., 1993. *The Talmud of the Land of Israel: Demai* (New York), 49.
31   Such as at Nessana, *P. Ness.* 89, Kraemer, (1958).
32   Mosaic of a camel carrying an amphora was found at Kissufim in Palestine: Cohen, 1977: 234–235.
33   Dr. M. Mango, 2000 personal communication. The mosaic is displayed in the Museum at Apamea.
34   Strabo XVI, 2.7, ed. H.L. Jones (London, 1917–1932); Rougé, 1986: 40.
35   Van Alfen, 1997:202.
36   Emery and Kirwan, 1938: 401–405, pl. 117.
37   Strabo comments on the vines of Laodicea (XVI, 2.9). Exports to East Africa (Adulis): *Periplus Maris Erythraei* 6; Arabia: *Periplus* 49.
38   Alexander Tralles, *Oeuvres Médicales* IV (tr. F. Brunet, 1937: 177).
39   Liebeschuetz, 1972: 45.
40   Mayerson, 1994: 250–255.
41   Callot, 1984: 21–23, pl. 24; for Greek roller evidence, see note 40 in Frankel, 1999: 88–89.
42   Frankel, 1999: 87–88.
43   Mattingly and Hitchener, 1993: 443.
44   Lutz, 1922: 23, provides the Latin inscription: Nectaros succos, Baccheia munera, cernis/Quae bitis genuit sup aprico sole refecta.

45   Wine presses are known at Deir Dehes; their form is remarkably similar to roller installations.
46   *Geoponica* (VI.4), edited Beckh 1895.
47   Emery and Kirwan, 1938: 389.
48   Bass, 1982: 181.
49   Mattingly, 1988: 35.
50   Bowersock, 1989: 66.
51   *Expositio Totius Mundi et Gentium* 31 (tr. West, 1924:161).
52   Mattingly, 1995: 142.
53   West, 1924: 183–187.

Bibliography

Adams, W.Y., 1962. 'An Introductory Classification of Christian Nubian Pottery,' *Kush* 10, 245–288.

Bass, G. F., *et al.*, 1982. *Yassi Ada: a Seventh-Century Byzantine Shipwreck* (College Station).

Bonifay, M., Congès, G. and Leguilloux, M., 1989. *Amphores romaines et histoire économique: dix ans de recherche: actes du colloque* (Collection de l'École française de Rome 114), 660–663.

Bowersock, G., 1989. 'Social and Economic History of Syria under the Roman Empire'. In J.-M. Dentzer and W. Orthman (ed.) *Archéologie et histoire de la Syrie. 2: la Syrie de l'époque achéménide à l'avènement de l'Islam* (Paris), 63–80.

Callot, O., 1984. *Huileries antique de Syrie du Nord* (Paris).

Casson, L., 1974. *Travel in the Ancient World* (London).

Cohen, R., 1977. 'Kissufim', *IEJ* 29, 254–256.

Crowfoot, J.W. and Fitzgerald, G.M., 1929. 'Excavations at the Tyropoeon Valley, Jerusalem', *Palestine Exploration Fund Report for 1927*.

De Contenson, H., 1963. 'Les fouilles à Axoum en 1958. Rapport préliminaire', *Annales d'Ethiopie* 5, 1–16.

Dothan, M. and Freedman, D.N., 1967. *Ashdod I, the First Season of Excavation 1962* ('Atiqot 7, Jerusalem).

Egloff, M., 1977. *Kellia: la poterie copte. Quatre siècles d'artisanat et d'échanges en Basse-Égypte* (Genève).

Emery, W.B. and Kirwan, L.P., 1938. *The Royal Tombs of Ballana and Qustul* (Cairo).

Empereur, J-Y. and Picon, M., 'Les regions de productions d'amphores imperials en Mediterranée orientale'. In *Amphores romaines et histoire économique: dix ans de recherche. Actes du colloque* (Collection de l'École française de Rome 114), 236–243.

Foss, C., 1997. 'Syria in Transition: A.D. 550–750: an Archaeological Approach', *DOP* 51, 189–270.

Frankel, R., 1999. *Wine and Oil Production in Antiquity in Israel and other Mediterranean Countries* (Sheffield).

Gatier, P.-L., 1992. 'Villages du Proche-Orient protobyzantin (4me-7 ème s.). Étude régionale.' In King, G.R.D. and Cameron, A., *The Byzantine and Early Islamic Near East, II: Land Use and Settlement Patterns* (New Jersey), 17–48.

Hayes, J., 1992. *Excavations at Saraçhane in Istanbul*, Volume II (Princeton).

Heichelheim, M., 1938. 'Roman Syria'. In T. Frank (ed.) *Economic Survey of Ancient Rome IV*, 123–257.

Keay, S., 1984. *Late Roman Amphorae in the Western Mediterranean: a Typology and Economic Study: the Catalan Evidence* (BAR Int. Series, Oxford).

Kraemer, C.J., 1958. *Excavations at Nessana 3: Non-literary Papyri* (Princeton).

Liebeschuetz, J.H.W.G., 1972. *Antioch: City and Imperial Administration in Later Empire* (Oxford).

Lutz, H.F., 1922. *Viticulture and Brewing in the Ancient Orient* (Leipzig).

Mattingly, D.J., 1985. 'Olive Oil production in Roman Tripolitania'. In D.J. Buck and D.J. Mattingly, *Town and Country in Roman Tripolitania* (Oxford), 27–46.

Mattingly, D.J., 1988. 'Oil for Export?', *JRS* 2, 33–56.

Mattingly, D.J. and Hitchener, B., 1993. 'Technical Specifications for some North African Olive Presses'. In M.-C. Amouretti and J.P. Brun, *La production du vin et de l'huile en Meditérranée* (Bulletin de Correspondance Hellénique Suppl. 26, Paris), 439–462.

Mattingly, D.J., 1995. *Tripolitania* (London).

Mayerson, P., 1994. *Monks, Martyrs, Soldiers and Saracens: Papers on the Near East in Late Antiquity* (Jerusalem).

Oikonomou, A., 1996. 'Proviomichanikes techniks paragogis elaioladou stin periochi tis Petrinas Lakonias'. In *Proceedings of a Conference on 'Elia kai Ladi'* (Kalamata, 7–9 May 1993, Athens), 362–371.

Orssaud, D., 1980. 'Déhès (Syrie du nord) campagnes I-III (1976–1978): recherches sur l'habitat rural. La ceramique', *Syrie* LVII, 234–266.

Pacetti, F., 1995. 'Appunti su alcuni tipi di anfore orientale della prima età bizantina centri di produzione, contentuti, cronologia e distribuzione,' *Atlante Tematico di Topographia Antica* Suppl. I, 273–294.

Peacock, D.P.S. and Williams, D.F., 1991. *Amphorae and the Roman Economy: an Introductory Guide* (London).

Pensabene, P., 1985. 'The Schola Praeconum II. Appendice I. Le anfore con iscrizioni cristiane', *PBSR* 53, 163–210.

Remesal-Rodriguez, J., 1998. 'Baetican Olive Oil and the Roman Economy'. In S. Keay, *The Archaeology of Early Roman Baetica* (JRA Suppl. 29, Ann Arbor), 183–200.

Reynolds, P., 1995. *Trade in the Western Mediterranean, AD 400–700* (BAR Int. Series, Oxford).

Riley, J.A., 1975. 'The Pottery from the First Session of Excavation in the Caesarea Hippodrome', *BASOR* 218, 25–63.

Riley, J.A., 1979. 'The Coarse Pottery from Berenice'. In J. Lloyd (ed.) *Excavations at Sidi Khrebish, Benghazi (Berenice) II* (Supplement to Libya Antiqua V), 91–465.

Riley, J.A., 1981a. 'The Pottery from Cisterns 1977.1, 1977.2, 1977.3'. In J. Humphrey (ed.) *Excavations at Carthage VI, 1977, Conducted by the University of Michigan* (Ann Arbor), 85–124.

Riley, J.A., 1981b. 'Amphoras in the Apollonia Museum Store,' *The Society for Libyan Studies 12th Annual Report*, 75–78.

Riley, J.A., 1982. 'New Light on Relations between the Eastern Mediterranean and Carthage in the Vandal and Byzantine Periods: the Evidence from the University of Michigan Excavations'. In *Actes. Colloque sur la céramique antique, Carthage, 23–24 juin 1980* (Paris), 111–124.

Robinson, H.S., 1959. *The Athenian Agora V, Pottery of the Roman Period.* (Princeton).

Rougé, J., 1986. 'La navigation intérieure dans le Proche Orient antique'. In P. Louis (ed.) *L'homme et L'eau en Méditerranée et au Proche Orient* (Lyon), 39–49.

Tate, G., 1992. *Les campagnes de la Syrie du nord du IIe au VIIe siècle* (Paris).

Tchalenko, G., 1953–1958. *Villages antique de la Syrie du nord I-III* (Paris).

Van Alfen, P., 1996. 'New Light on the 7th-c. Yassi Ada Shipwreck: Capacities and Standard Sizes of LRA1 Amphoras' *JRA* 9, 189–213.

Welsby, D., 1998. *Soba II: Renewed Excavations within the Metropolis of the Kingdom of Alwa in Central Sudan* (London).

West, L.C., 1924. 'Commercial Syria under the Roman Empire,' *TAPA* 55, 159–189.

Will, E., 1997. 'Antioche, un metropole d'Asie', *Syrie* lxxiv, 99–113.

Williams, C., 1989. *Anemurium: the Roman and Early Byzantine Pottery* (Toronto).

Chapter 5

Beyond the Amphora: Non-Ceramic Evidence for Late Antique Industry and Trade

Marlia Mundell Mango

In a recent article I attempted to show that there exists diverse evidence for early Byzantine trade extending from Ireland in the West to Manchuria in the East (Fig. 5.1).[1] The main subject of that article was Byzantine maritime trade with the East, which interlocked with Byzantine exchanges with the West. I described this 'Byzantine trade' as the movement of Byzantine goods eastward from the Empire, and of oriental goods westward into the Empire, irrespective of the identities of their carriers or middlemen – Axumites, Himyarites, Persians: many being Nestorian Christians. I also argued that the Sasanian takeover of Himyar and Axum in 570 and 599, respectively, from where Red Sea trade was controlled, resulted in more expensive trade rather than no trade. The evidence for this far-flung trade, of which Alexandria remained the hub as in earlier Roman times, is both textual and archaeological. In the sixth century Cosmas Indocopleustes described trading mechanisms and goods exchanged. Those brought from the East included aromatics and spices, silk, ivory, precious stones and shells. Available to be sent to the East were Tyrian purple, linen, papyrus, tin, copper, silver, glass and wine – all favoured exports in the Roman past.

Archaeological evidence of this activity includes the staples of trade discussion, namely amphorae and coins. Byzantine amphorae have been found in Britain, Nubia, Axum, Himyar and, most recently, in the port of Zanzibar. As yet unclassified Mediterranean amphorae have been found at about twenty sites in India. In India and Sri Lanka gold and copper coin evidence of Byzantine trade, from 450–640 (300–640 in Sri Lanka), occurs particularly in the south, where international trade was concentrated.[2] Furthermore, limited but significant finds of Byzantine gold coins dating into the seventh century have been made in China.[3] The relevant archaeological evidence both inside and outside the Empire for this extensive trade (Fig. 5.1) goes beyond pots and coins, and includes, for example, the trade-linked Byzantine and related artefacts (weights, scales, possibly stamps) excavated in Nubia and Axum.[4]

In the following paper I shall consider some of the Byzantine products of this international trade which, given the distances involved, can only be described as luxury trade. In so doing, I should like to go beyond the amphora, so often taken by scholars as the sole indicator of late antique circulation and exchange,[5] to examine the evidence offered by other materials which represent a higher level of financial investment in both inter-regional and international trade. Of the Byzantine products available for

Fig. 5.2: Byzantine copper-alloy lamp excavated at Matara in Axum (from F. Anfray, 1967. 'Matara', Annales d'Ethiopie *7, fig. 10).*

Fig. 5.3: Copper-alloy amphora from household hoard found in Syria (?). (Photograph: M. Mango).

basins, ewers, and other domestic utensils, have been excavated in burials (Fig. 5.5). Often deposited with the cast copper-alloy objects were amethysts, cowrie shells and elephant ivory rings – all transported from India or Africa, undoubtedly via Byzantium and possibly up the Rhine (Fig. 5.1).[17]

The Nubian/Axum and European finds are somewhat similar in type and appearance (Figs. 5.4–5). The former may well have originated in Egypt and, in fact, the European finds have for long been called 'Coptic',[18] due to a perceived resemblance with objects in the Cairo Museum published by Strzygowski in 1909.[19] The dating of the Nubian finds has been controversial, mostly because it is generally thought that the deposition of grave goods points to the period before the Byzantine-sponsored Christian conversion of the X-culture people in the mid-sixth century.[20] However, grave goods are not unknown in Christian burials inside the Empire[21] and typologically the metalware in question could well date to the sixth century or later. Besides, many of the objects are decorated with crosses.

The manufacture and circulation of the said objects in Europe were originally attributed on the basis of related coin finds to the period *c.* 500–560.[22] Yet the Italian finds are said to be in Lombard graves and therefore post-date 568; one basin occurs in the Sutton Hoo royal burial of the 620s;[23] and finds in Tarragonna are associated with

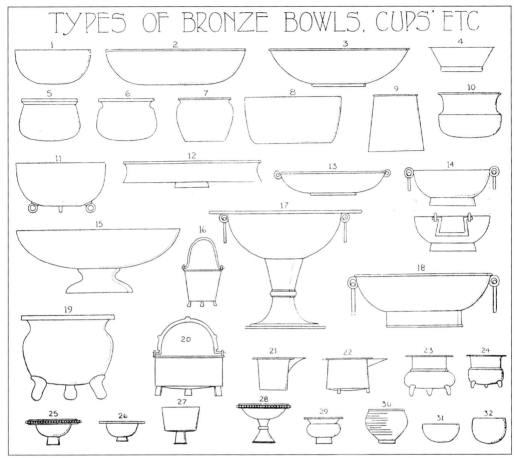

Fig. 5.4: Byzantine (?) copper-alloy vessels excavated at Ballana and Qustul in Nubia (from Emery and Kirwan, 1938: fig. 100).

a coin hoard of *c.* 650. It is now generally acknowledged that the European finds context is late sixth and seventh century.[24] Mention may also be made of a related small series of hammered and decorated brass buckets, many with Greek inscriptions, which have been found in Britain (Sutton Hoo, Winchester, Isle of Wight) and Spain, as well as in late Roman Palestine and Mesopotamia.[25]

Finds of copper-metal vessels within the Empire complement the 300-odd exports enumerated above. Two groups of finds are informative. On the one hand, there are the 100-odd vessels excavated in mostly seventh century contexts at Sardis.[26] These include cauldrons, flasks and jugs (Figs. 5.6–7), lighting devices and censers. On the other hand, there is an exceptional cache of related items, all probably from a single household (reportedly in Syria) and now dispersed in many directions,[27] which was said to have originally contained 250 pieces (Fig. 5.3). There are stylistic and other indications that these objects probably date to the sixth century; one with a Greek

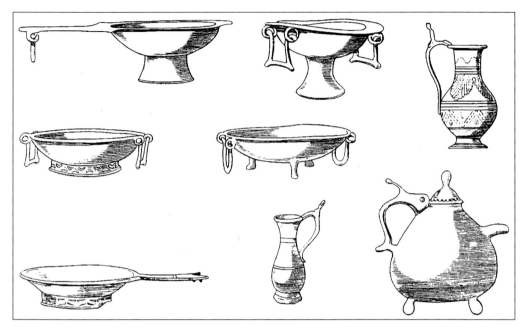

Fig. 5.5: Byzantine copper-alloy vessels exported to Europe where they have been excavated in tombs (from Bruce Mitford, 1983: fig. 531).

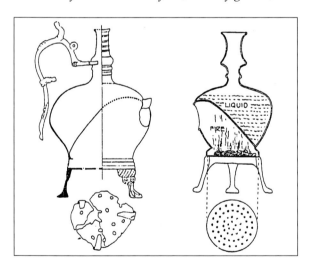

Fig. 5.6: Byzantine copper-alloy samovars excavated at: Sardis (left) and Nubia (right) (fromWaldbaum, 1983: pl. 34 no. 522, and Emery and Kirwan, 1938: pl. 93 D, fig. 114).

inscription (preceded by a cross) was said to have held a coin of Justinian.[28] In some cases these objects (lampstands, tripods, amphorae, etc.) differ from the exports in type and decoration. In sum, between the exports and the local finds, the variety and volume of Byzantine copper metalworking in the fifth-seventh centuries is noteworthy, although comprehensive study remains to be done. Where were these objects produced?

Centres of Metalware Production

The copper-alloy exports to Europe have common typological and decorative features; as noted above, some have Greek inscriptions suggesting an eastern manufacture.[29] All the metalware in question may be divided into two main groups, according to manufacturing techniques – casting and hammering. The exports and the lighting devices found locally, in the Empire, are mostly cast copper-alloys.[30] Items of hammered sheet metal (such as flasks and cauldrons) are often of unalloyed copper.[31]

Two features characterise the early Byzantine copper-metal work overall. Taking both the broad view within Late Antiquity and the long view into the eleventh century, for example, one is struck by uniformity and continuity. Types found in early seventh century Sardis (Fig. 5.7A-B, D-E)[32] reappear between the ninth and eleventh centuries at Corinth[33] and at Constantinople, where a copper flask (Fig. 5.7G), similar to one from a seventh century shipwreck at Dor (Fig. 5.7F), was found containing a hoard of eleventh century coins.[34] Of course, uniformity of types for hammered vessels such as cauldrons and flasks (Figs. 5.7) cannot be explained in terms of travelling and durable moulds. During Late Antiquity, a new design in hammered sheet-metal samovars (having a tall, narrow neck with convex moulding) is found at two distant sites (Fig. 5.6), at Sardis[35] and in Nubia.[36] During the same general period, the technical innovation of the crenellated seam appears apparently out of nowhere, probably as early as the third century in hammered vessels, contemporaneously in West and East and is widespread, particularly in the East by the sixth and seventh (Figs. 5.7b, e-f, 11). Eventually it is taken to Scandinavia by the eighth century and, at some unknown time, to India where it is still used today as it is also in the Middle East.[37] One final element in the manufacturing equation to consider with regard to uniformity is the state weapons factories, such as that at Sardis (see below). Army supplies may have included some domestic items and regional factories could explain conformity to standard vessel types.[38] Thus, uniformity or repetition of types could be explained by state influence/control and/or circulation by trade.

Leaving aside the question of the sources of copper (i.e. mines, etc.[39]), we shall consider places of manufacture. The locations of state factories of arms, armour and parade armour, working in several types of metal, are given in the *Notitia Dignitatum* for the Western and Eastern Empires. Private workshops are harder to locate. For example, discounting the earlier description of the copper-metal exports discussed above (Figs. 5.2, 4–5, 6b) as 'Coptic', therefore Egyptian, it is impossible to identify a particular city or cities as their manufacturing centre, despite the fact that Alexandria is here called the hub of East-West trade.[40] We can, however, consider the *type* of place where they may have been made. Unlike silversmiths, who were apparently exclusively urban, goldsmiths (making jewellery) and coppersmiths operated in both city and village, the latter undoubtedly for local consumption.[41] Regarding the distribution of industries within the city, the law book of Julian of Ascalon lists the spaces required between various types of workshops and other buildings, particularly dwellings. Emission of smoke, steam and odours, as well as the threat of fire, were taken into consideration. For example, limekilns had to be up to 47 m apart and potters up to 14 m. Glass makers were to be placed outside the city or built-up areas within.[42] While glass vessels and window panes were sold in shops E 12–13 on the central *decumanus*

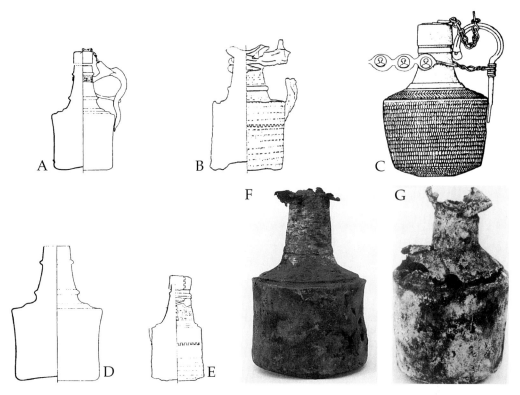

Fig. 5.7: Copper jugs and flasks excavated at Sardis (A-B, D-E), Alassa, Cyprus (C), Dor shipwreck (F); Istanbul, containing hoard of eleventh century coins (G). B, E-F with crenellated seam. (A-B, D-E: from Waldbaum, 1983: pl. 35, nos. 526, 528–530; C: from Flourentzos, 1996: pl. XLII; F: photograph S. Kingsley; G: Asgari, 1985: fig. 15).

maximus at Sardis,[43] they were made elsewhere (although probably locally in or around the city).[44] Scythopolis may offer a model: one of the shops in the porticoed *exedra* (the *Sigma*), which was newly built in 507 in the stylish central section of the city, sold glass lamps,[45] while the recently discovered glass factory was situated outside the centre, by the north-east wall of the city.[46] This segregation of heavy industry from light industry/ retail conformed to a Roman model;[47] it was the Umayyads who broke this system by installing their factories on prime property in the city centre. Again, Scythopolis provides examples, such as the pottery factory built on the Byzantine agora.[48]

A similar segregation of heavy industry from light industry/retail may have existed for Byzantine metalworkers. Many copper-metal objects (see above) were excavated in the Byzantine shops of Sardis, also situated on the *decumanus maximus*.[49] Shops E 9–11 are considered to have comprised a single metalwork business, suggested by the series of 127 locks found in one unit (Fig. 5.8). Overall, finds indicate that locks were repaired, but not made in the shops;[50] the location of this and other metalworking within the city is a subject of speculation. The imperial arms factory at Sardis may have been situated on the north-east edge of the city by the circuit wall, where a survey in 1979 revealed an area with concentrations of slag;[51] an inscribed copper-alloy dagger sheath discovered in the city in a seventh century context may have been made in this factory.[52] Contemporary with the dagger sheath found at Sardis are arms (six iron swords, two spearheads, five shield bosses) uncovered in a Byzantine shop (or possibly a workshop) with some unspecified industrial installations outside the west wall of Jerusalem.[53] In his Oration on Antioch, Libanius refers to numerous workshops in the quarters outside the city gates.[54] Elsewhere, at Justiniana Prima, metalworking-retail shops – of two iron smiths (with agricultural tools and forging hearths) and a jeweller (with moulds, punches, anvil, scales) – were found on the main streets,[55] but the production of the iron metal probably took place elsewhere.[56] In Constantinople, the copper workers were from an early period situated opposite St. Sophia in the centre of the city, an area where the church of St. Mary Chalkoprateia was built in the fifth century.[57] Whether all stages of copper production took place on these centrally located premises is unclear. Forging and other shaping and repair operations may (as at Sardis and Justiniana Prima) have been based in the city centre, together with retailing. Julian of Ascalon stipulates only 1.56 m distance for forging workshops; in the seventh century a forger operated on the *cardo maximus* (the portico of Domninos) of Constantinople.[58] But the heavier smelting, alloying and casting of the metal may well have taken place further away.

Circulation of Metalware

A. Maritime Trade Known from Written Evidence
Having considered where the copper-alloy metalware was produced in an urban context,

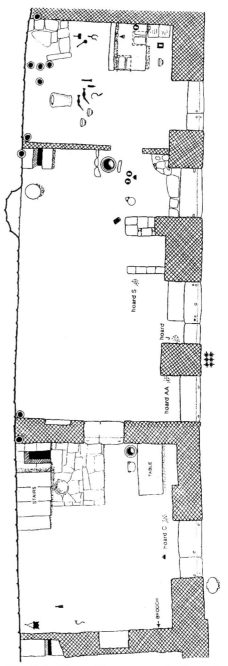

Fig. 5.8: Plan of ironmonger's shops E 9–11 at Sardis, where locks (found in E 11) were repaired (from Stephens Crawford, 1990: figs. 329, 344).

if not geographically, we shall turn now to the question of its trading context in the sixth/seventh century, when much of the material considered above was made and/or traded. We look first to Constantinople on the basis of the Miracles of St. Artemius, composed probably between 656 and 668.[59] Several Miracles concern people involved in trade and foreign travel. The author states at the outset that many who sought the care of Artemius (who specialised in male disorders) "came from Alexandria, Africa and Rhodes for help".[60] All arrived there by ship. One was in Constantinople on business from Chios; his ship was to sail from Hebdomon (a suburb). Another two, George and Theodore, were from Rhodes where both either lived or had property. Theodore owned his own ship, which sailed to Constantinople at least four times during two years. Menas, who was there in the reign of Maurice (582–602), was a stevedore from Alexandria who injured himself loading full wine amphorae (*magarika*) onto a ship docked at Argyropolis (Tophane) just beyond Galata. Two other Alexandrians are mentioned, one of whom was the guardian of what was now the main granary of Constantinople. Another man came from Africa on behalf of his sick son, who remained at home. The last, Theoteknos, was a fifty year old shipbuilder (*naupegos*) who stayed some time at Constantinople awaiting a miraculous cure and finally sailed off to Gaul in his own ship accompanied by the saint himself, according to the Miracles.[61] So, in the mid-seventh century when the Miracles were compiled, Constantinople is portrayed as a city still visited by people from afar (Fig. 5.9), some of them engaged in commerce (such as trade in wine).

We turn now to our second commercial centre, Alexandria, as portrayed in the *Life of John the Almsgiver*, patriarch from 610–620.[62] Various stories revolve around ships and merchants; one of the latter is a *gallodromos*, specialising in trade with Gaul (chapter 36); several ships sink or cargoes are lost (chapters 8, 25, 26, 28), but that is doubtless stage-setting for acts of charity and miracles. The *Life* (chapter 28) states that the patriarchal church owned a fleet of over thirteen ships, each with a capacity of 10,000 *modii*.[63] The church also owned ships twice that size: during a famine at Alexandria, two 'gazelles' (*dorkones*) which could carry 20,000 *modii*[64] were sent to Sicily (Fig. 5.9) to procure grain (chapter 11). Two stories illustrate the different levels of commerce represented by these two types of ships.

The first story (chapter 8) concerns one 'gazelle' which sailed from Alexandria with 20,000 *modii* of grain to Britain (Fig. 5.9), where there was a famine. Upon arrival the captain agreed to a payment of 1 *solidus* per *modius* for half the cargo, while the rest of the payment was made in an unspecified number of tin ingots. On his return to Alexandria, the captain stopped in Cyrenaica and removed 50 lbs. of the tin to sell to an associate there (Fig. 5.9); the punch-line was that the tin had miraculously changed to pure silver. It should be noted that among thousands of pottery sherds excavated at Tintagel in Cornwall (Fig. 5.1) are many from eastern Mediterranean amphorae and African red-slip and Phocaean red-slip fine wares, which, it is plausibly suggested, derived from trade in Cornish tin for Mediterranean oil and/or wine via the Atlantic.[65] The story recounted here introduces the additional possibility of trade in grain. The vastly inflated price of the grain in this case was presumably occasioned by famine; elsewhere grain sold at 30 *modii* per *solidus*.[66] The entire cargo of 20,000 *modii*, with a normal value of 667 *solidi*, was sold at 20,000 *solidi*, half of which was paid in cash and

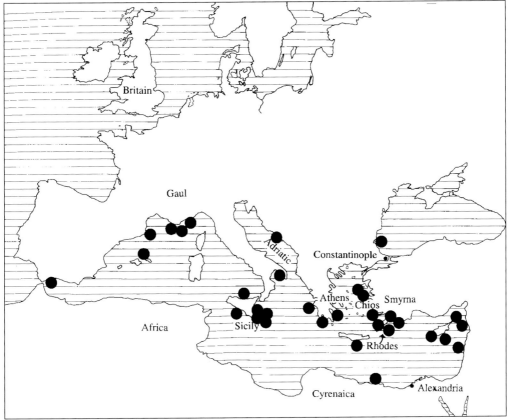

Fig. 5.9: Map showing fifth-seventh century shipwrecks and sites, and areas mentioned in the Miracles of St. Artemius, *the* Life of John the Almsgiver *and two fifth century horoscopes. (The solid dots denote the position of shipwrecks). (Drawing A.A. Wilkins).*

the other half in tin ingots which weighed in excess of 50 lbs. The entire amount of tin may have been considerably higher. In the case of the more valuable silver, 2,500 lbs was equivalent to 10,000 *solidi*. A supply of *solidi* available in Britain could be explained by continuous Mediterranean-British trade:[67] the same fifth-to-seventh century pottery types seen at Tintagel have been found at thirty sites altogether in south-west Britain and Ireland (Fig. 5.1).[68] If, in normal circumstances, the Mediterranean grain, wine and other imports were cheaper than the British tin (see below), payment in gold *solidi* may have been needed to make up the difference.

The second story (chapter 28) relates to high-value mixed cargoes directly relevant to the present subject. This story took place during a storm, when the entire fleet of over thirteen ships of 10,000 *modii* capacity were forced to dump their cargoes in the Adriatic (Fig. 5.9). They carried dried goods (*xerophorta*), clothing (*himatia*), silver (*argyros*; probably silver plate) and "other objects of high value" (*pragmata anagkaia*).

The total value lost was said to have been thirty-four *kentenaria*, the equivalent of 3,400 lbs of gold, a subject to which we shall return. Two other written accounts of similar mixed cargoes, which may be described as genuine, support the veracity of the fictional account given in the Life, with which they share many striking similarities in detail. They are contained in horoscopes dated to 475 and 479, respectively.[69] Both concern shipments of goods from Alexandria, the earlier one to Athens, the later to Smyrna (Fig. 5.9). The horoscopes were drawn up to reassure anxious Alexandrian (?) merchants based abroad awaiting the delayed shipments. The first voyage originated, apparently, in Cyrenaica where a merchant vessel took on board a shipment of camels, before stopping at Alexandria for high-grade textiles (*kortinas phrontalia kai akoubetalia*) and items of silver (*argyra basternia*: silver litters). The ship sailed to Athens via Rhodes, but was forced to jettison heavy cargo (the camels?) when it encountered a storm. The second ship left Alexandria with a cargo made up of little birds (*pterota tina, strouthia*), books or leaves of papyrus (*biblia tina e chartas, charten liton*), objects of bronze and kitchen utensils (*skeue chalka, skeue mageirika*) and a chest full of medicines (*iatrika skeue, pharmakotheken pepleromenen*). This ship too was caught in a storm and broke up so that the cargo was transferred to another ship. The "medicines" of the horoscope correspond in general to the "dried goods" of the patriarchal ships (perhaps pepper and other exotic items imported from the East via Alexandria); the silver and/or copper wares and textiles are included in both the Life and horoscopes. All, together with the papyrus books, may be seen as high-value cargoes, possibly typical of Alexandrian exports.

The exact value of these shipments cannot be determined, but a rough estimation may be made on the basis of the figure given for the lost cargoes of the patriarchal ships (Table 5.1). The total value lost was said to have been 34 *kentenaria*, the equivalent of 3,400 lbs of gold. If the fleet had consisted of fifteen ships (a maximum estimate), each would have been worth 227 lbs. that is 16,344 *solidi* per ship, a very high amount. Some calculations concerning the value of the cargo may be made. Another story in the *Life of John the Almsgiver* (chapter 27) relates that a bishop set aside 30 lbs. of gold (2,160 *solidi*) to buy a silver service at Alexandria. At the approximate current bullion value of silver, four *solidi* per pound, this service would have weighed a maximum of 540 lbs, nearly the exact weight of inventoried domestic silver donated to churches at Auxerre in 603–621/3.[70] If the silver on the ships in the Adriatic took the form of four sets of silver plate on each ship, it would account for over half the value: 8,640 *solidi* out of 16,344 *solidi*, or 120 lbs. out of a total of 227 lbs. per ship. Equally, the "clothing" in the cargo may have been as expensive as the luxurious bed covering (*gonachion/pallion*) that John was given by a well-wisher, which cost 36 *solidi* or half a pound of gold, as against the cheaper cover called a *syridion* (made in Syria) which cost only 1/4 *solidus* (chapter 19). Silk garments owned in the mid-sixth century by the widow of a *cubicularius* at Constantinople were worth twice as much, namely one pound of gold (72 *solidi*) each;[71] 100 such garments would have been worth 100 lbs. of gold. If, therefore, the silver and the garments on each ship were worth 220 lbs., at least part of the other 50 lbs. could be explained by the third item listed. As mentioned above, the dry goods (*xerophorta*) may have been spices and aromatics imported from the East via Alexandria.[72] That everything carried by the ships was valuable may be implied by the phrase "other objects (also) of high value". If so, this story may be a plausible account of the highest end of the shipping market in this period. The loss was a tragedy for the church of Alexandria and its programme of charitable works. The cargoes of the horoscope ships sailing from Alexandria to Athens and Smyrna would have been of comparable value.

As mentioned above, stories in the *Life of John the Almsgiver* illustrate different levels of commerce represented firstly by two types of ships (the 'gazelle' with a 20,000 *modii* capacity and the smaller ship with a 10,000 *modii* capacity) and, secondly, two types of cargo (agricultural commodities and high-value goods). Thanks to a local famine, the grain transported to Britain in the 'gazelle' enjoyed the inflated value of 20,000 *solidi* (half paid in cash, half in tin ingots). Normally this cargo would have been worth 667 *solidi*; grain carried on a 10,000 *modii* ship would, therefore, have been worth 334 *solidi*. The wrecked ship found at S. Gervais carrying 6,000–8,000 *modii* of grain (see below) measured 20 m in length. This, in turn, is similar in size to the contemporary ship wrecked at Yassi Ada off the southwest coast of Asia Minor with a cargo of about 900 amphorae (with a maximum capacity of 1,200) which, had they all contained wine, would have had an aggregate value of 70 *solidi* according to G. Bass, less than a pound of gold.[73] The relatively low figures of 334 and 70 *solidi* for grain and wine transported on 10,000 *modii* ships, respectively, are in sharp contrast to those relating to the patriarchal ships bearing mixed cargoes to the Adriatic (Table 5.1). Each of these had goods valued at 16,344 *solidi*, despite being of the same size as the amphora-carrying ships. Other tales in the *Life of John the Almsgiver* (chapters 8, 20) relate stories of merchants who each bought an (unspecified) cargo or a business for 10 lbs. (720 *solidi*).

B. Maritime Trade Known from Archaeological Evidence: Shipwrecks

Bearing these various stories in mind, we shall now look at contemporary late antique shipwrecks (Fig. 5.9). In Parker's publication there are thirty-seven from this general period (fifth-seventh century) spread across several regions, in descending order of frequency: Sicily (8), Cyprus (6), France (5), Turkey (4), with seven spread across various Greek islands. Other countries include Spain, Libya, Syria, Israel, Italy, Croatia, and Bulgaria.[74] Places mentioned in the *Miracles of St. Artemius* and the *Life of John the Almsgiver* – Chios, Rhodes, Gaul, the Adriatic – are all represented, except for Constantinople and Alexandria (Fig. 5.9). Almost all reported cargoes are of amphorae, with a few interesting exceptions. The 15–18 m ship found at S. Gervais (Site B) off France carried 6,000–8,000 *modii* of grain (*Triticum sp.* mixed with *Agrostemma sithago*) stowed loosely when it went down around A.D. 600–625; it also carried amphorae containing local pitch.[75] It may have been transporting grain from Italy, Africa or Spain to Arles which had no grain; the pitch may have been collected in south-west Gaul. The ship was similar in construction to the eastern vessel at Yassi Ada (of *c.* 626) and slightly smaller than the ships in the patriarchal fleet at Alexandria which held 10,000 *modii* (as against the 'gazelle', which carried 20,000, and the earlier Roman capacity of 10,000–50,000). The wreck at Marzamemi, Sicily carrying marble (Proconnesian and Thessalian) from two different quarries, and having therefore a mixed cargo, is well-known;[76] a Byzantine wreck at Taranto (A) in South Italy carried millstones.[77]

Three other wrecks had cargoes directly relevant to the present subject of metalware and recall the *"ergomoukia argyra"* and *"skeue chalka"* of the horoscopes and the *"argyros"*

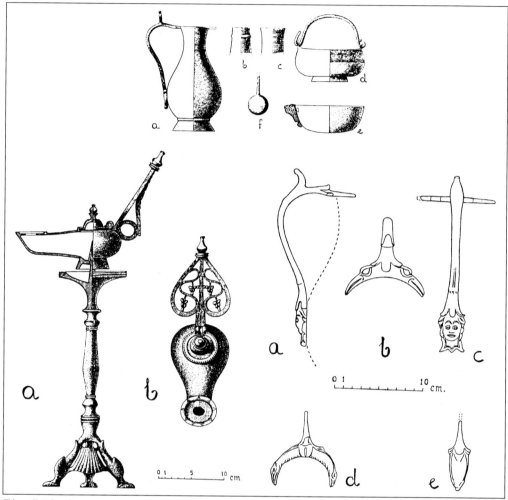

*Fig. 5.10: Copper-alloy objects from the Plemmyrion shipwreck near Syracuse, Sicily
(from Kapitän and Fallico, 1967: figs. 7, 9–10).*

of the patriarchal fleet, all involved in storms which threatened shipwreck. These
include cast bronze lamps, a lampstand, censers, pitchers (Fig. 5.10), recovered from
the ship sunk at Plemmyrion opposite Syracuse in Sicily.[78] Although it has been
suggested that these objects may have been for the use of the ship's crew, the level of
craftsmanship and decoration is superior to that of the hammered copper cauldrons
and flasks found on other shipwrecks at Yassi Ada, Dor (Fig. 5.7F) and near Ravenna.[79]
The bronze items at Plemmyrion may well have been cargo. Another wreck at Favaritx
off Spain, carried, as its excavators suggested, Byzantine bronzes and pottery belonging
to a metalworker from Egypt or Syria who was en route to the Balearic Islands; much
of the metalware found has since been stolen.[80] The third ship, at Grazel (Site B;

Fig. 5.11: Copper-metal objects and fragments (basin, bowls) from the Grazel shipwreck off S. France (from Solier, 1981: figs. 9–11).

Gruissan) in France carried metal objects (Fig. 5.11), many now gone, and 101 Byzantine coins dating up to A.D. 631.[81] The cargo of this last ship may, therefore, represent the type of international trade operating during the period when Byzantine bronze objects were being exported to Europe.

In sum, various types of evidence relating to late antique glass and copper-metalware deserve further study concerning their production and circulation both locally and as exports. Neither glass nor copper-metalware is per se a luxury material, except when specially prepared (for example, by 'bleaching' or by inlay) or when used in special circumstances (for example, when considered luxuries by foreign elites) as revealed in burials outside the empire, in Europe, Nubia and China. Although

Table 5.1: List of comparative values for different cargoes, 5th–7th centuries A.D.

Cargo	Ship Capacity	Ship Length	Value in *solidi*	Origin	Destination	Findspot	Source
Wine	822 amphorae	20 m	70	Black Sea	Syria?	Yassi Ada	---
Grain	6–8,000 *modii*	20 m	200–267	Italy/Africa/Spain?	Arles?	S. Gervais	---
Grain	10,000 *modii*	---	333?	Mediterranean	Mediterranean	---	Jones, 1964: 446
Grain (famine)	20,000 *modii*	---	10,000 + tin	Alexandria	Britain	---	John the Almsgiver
Tin (50 lbs.)	---	---	?	Britain	Cyrenaica	---	John the Almsgiver
Silver, clothing, dried goods	10,000 *modii*	---	16,344	Alexandria	Adriatic	---	John the Almsgiver
Camels, textiles, silver	---	---	---	Alexandria	Smyrna	---	Horoscope A.D. 475
Birds, books (papyrus, bronzes, medicine	---	---	---	Alexandria	Smyrna	---	Horoscope A.D. 479

metalware cargoes feature in only three out of thirty-seven recorded shipwrecks of the fifth-seventh centuries (Fig. 5.9), most of which held amphorae, they were much more valuable than wine, oil or other agricultural commodities carried by the amphorae. This conclusion is based on evidence from three similarly-sized ships (Table 5.1). If the *Life of John the Almsgiver* is to be believed, one luxury cargo (of silver plate, dried goods and clothing) was valued at over 16,000 *solidi*. By contrast, a shipment of grain was worth 334 *solidi* and another of wine, only 70 *solidi* (exemplified by the Yassi Ada A ship). Only some of the high-value cargoes were durable enough to survive in the archaeological record. But the written sources cited above show that although shipping high-value cargoes could be a very risky enterprise, the rewards were, in turn, far greater than those obtained from the more common commodities. For a more balanced view of late antique economy and exchange, both types of enterprise should be viewed together.

Notes

1   Mundell Mango, 1996.
2   Sewell, 1904: 591–631; Carson, 1980: 20–23; Gupta, 1984: 37–43; Berghaus, 1991: 108–121; Walburg, 1991: 164–167; Berghaus, 1993: 548–549; Morrisson, 1995: 83.
3   Thierry and Morrisson, 1994.
4   Mundell Mango, 1996: 153–155.
5   E.g. Peacock and Williams, 1986.
6   Thierry and Morrisson, 1994: 132–135.

7   Where the glass (Marshak and Anazawa, 1989: fig. p. 53 lower right) may be compared with Byzantine examples preserved in Venice: Philippe, 1970: fig. 74.

8   Thierry and Morrisson, 1994: 132, 140; for late antique purple glass see, e.g. Buckton, 1984: no. 1.

9   Biek and Bayley, 1979: 6–16.

10   Thierry and Morrisson, 1994: 132–135.

11   Vickers, 1996; Stern, 1997.

12   Rodziewicz, 1984: 249–251.

13   Mundell Mango, 1994, 1996, 1998.

14   Mundell Mango, 1996: 153–154.

15   The term copper-metal (which I owe to Anna Bennett) is used here to cover both alloyed (bronze, brass, etc.) and unalloyed copper.

16   Emery and Kirwan, 1938; Mundell Mango, 1998: 216–217.

17   One related find is in the Ukraine: Richards, 1980.

18   E.g. Werner, 1938.

19   E.g. nos. 9040–9042.

20   Kirwan, 1982.

21   Mundell Mango, 1998: 210, 216.

22   Werner, 1938.

23   Bruce Mitford, 1983: 732–752.

24   *Ibid;* Périn, 1992: 43

25   Mundell Mango *et al.,* 1989.

26   Walbaum, 1983: nos. 490–618, *passim.*

27   See Mundell Mango, forthcoming 1.

28   Personal examination of a half dozen objects from the hoard, including the inscribed ewer and two amphorae, including the one illustrated here in Fig. 3.

29   Mundell Mango *et al.,* 1989: 298–305.

30   Bruce Mitford, 1983: 732–752; Waldbaum, 1983: nos. 577–618.

31   Waldbaum, 1983: nos. 490–552 *passim.*

32   Waldbaum, 1983: nos. 515–517, 523–526, 528–530. A related jug was found at Alassa, Cyprus; Flourentzos, 1996: pl. XLII. I should like to thank Tassos Papacostas for drawing this object to my attention.

33   Davidson, 1952: 72–74, nos. 548, 552–559. For the dating see also Mundell Mango, 1994.

34   For the Dor flask see Kingsley and Raveh, 1996: 6., pl. 6. CU. The Istanbul flask is too fragile to have been much older than the coins; Asgari, 1984: 79–80, figs. 15–19.

35   Waldbaum, 1983: no. 522.

36   Emery and Kirwan: 1938: no. 790, pl. 93 D, fig. 114.

37   Mundell Mango, forthcoming 1.

38   Mundell Mango *et al.,* 1989: 305.

39   On which see recently, Yener, 1993.

40   It has been suggested that the brass buckets may have been made at Antioch: Mundell Mango, 1995.

41   Mundell Mango, 1984: 128–130.

42   Saliou, 1996: 32–42.

43   Crawford, 1991: 78–86.

44   Van Saldern, 1980: 36–37.

45   Bar-Nathan and Mazor, 1992: 42–44.

46   Mazor and Bar-Nathan, 1998: 26–29.

47   Waldbaum, 1983: 9.

48   Mazor and Bar-Nathan, 1998: 17–21.

49   Waldbaum, 1983; Crawford, 1990.

50   Crawford, 1990: 71–78.

51   Waldbaum, 1983: 9.

52   Waldbaum 1983: no. 8.

53   Maeir, 1993: 62.

54   Festugière, 1959: 30, Libanios Oration XI. The Antiochikos: see Festugiere, 1959: 33– 35, 56–58.

55   Popovic, 1990: 295–296.
56   Manning, 1976: 143.
57   Mundell Mango, forthcoming 2.
58   Crisafulli and Nesbitt, 1997: 147–149.
59   Crisafulli and Nesbitt, 1997: 7. For the importance of this source for seventh century Constantinople, see C. Mango, forthcoming 1.
60   Crisafulli and Nesbitt, 1997: 221.
61   Crisafulli and Nesbitt, 1997: *Miracles* 4–5, 9, 27, 32, 35, 60.
62   Festugière, 1974.
63   Festugière, 1974, 594: XXVIII.11.
64   Festugière, 1974, 550: VIII.32.
65   Thomas, 1993: 93–96.
66   Guillou, 1977: 382; Jones, 1986: 446.
67   Tin was charged at a higher rate than lead in the Anazarbus tariff list; Dagron and Feissell, 1987: 180–81, no. 109, lines 14–15. On Roman and Byzantine currency in use in Sri Lanka, see Mundell Mango, 1996: 156–157.
68   Thomas, 1981.
69   Dagron and Rougé, 1982. No cargo is mentioned on a third ship sailing to Constantinople.
70   Mundell Mango and Bennett, 1994: 54.
71   Mundell Mango, 1984, 109.
72   Mundell Mango, 1996: 148.
73   Bass and van Doorninck, 1982: 315 and note 25.
74   Parker, 1992: (Sicily) nos. 245, 401, 671, 787, 833, 1092; (Cyprus) nos. 203–204, 212, 1145; (France) nos. 268, 483, 782, 1001; (Turkey) nos. 111, 351, 518, 1239; (Greek islands) nos. 71, 215, 795, 884, 889, 900, 1244; (Spain) nos. 397, 446; (Libya) no. 660; (Syria) no. 59; (Israel), no. 367; (Italy) no. 1131; (Croatia) no. 902; (Bulgaria) no. 738.
75   Parker, 1992: no. 1001.
76   Parker, 1992: no. 671.
77   Parker, 1992: no. 1131.
78   Parker, 1992: no. 833; Kapitan and Fallico, 1967: 91–97.
79   Bass and van Doorninck, 1982: 269–73; Kingsley and Raveh, 1996: 62–63, 68, 72, fig. 47, pls. 59.CU1, 60.CU2, 61.CU3, 70.CU3, 71.CU5; Maioli, 1986.
80   Parker, 1992: no. 397.
81   Parker, 1992: no. 483; Solier, 1981: 27–31.

Bibliography

Asgari, N., 1985. 'Istanbul temel kazilarindan haberler – 1984', *Aristirma Sonuclar Toplantisi* III (Ankara).

Bar-Nathan, R. and Mazor, G., 1992. 'The Bet She'an Excavation Project (1989–1991). City Centre (South) and Tel Iztabba Area', *ESI*, 11, 33–51.

Bass, G. and van Doorninck, F.H., 1982. *Yassi Ada I, a Seventh-Century Byzantine Shipwreck* (College Station).

Berghaus, P., 1991. 'Roman Coins from India and their Imitation'. In A.K. Dja (ed.) *Third International Colloquium. Coinage, Trade and Economy* (Indian Institute of Research in Numismatic Studies, Anjaneri), 108–121.

Berghaus, P., 1993. 'Etudes et travaux', *Bulletin de la Société Française de Numismatique* 48, 548–549.

Biek, L. and Bayley, J., 1979. 'Glass and other Vitreous Materials', *World Archaeology*, 11, 1–25.

Bruce Mitford, R.L.S., 1983. *The Sutton Hoo Ship-Burial* (London).

Buckton, D., (ed.), 1984. *The Treasury of San Marco, Venice* (Milan).

Carson, R.A.G., 1980. 'Late Roman and Early Byzantine Solidi from India', *Numismatic Digest* 4, 20–23.

Crawford, J.S., 1990. *The Byzantine Shops at Sardis* (Cambridge, MA).

Crisafulli, V.S. and Nesbitt, J.W., 1997. *The Miracles of St. Artemios. A Collection of Miracle Stories by an Anonymous Author of Seventh-Century Byzantium* (Leiden).

Dagron, G. and Feissel, D., 1987. *Inscriptions de Cilicie* (Paris).

Dagron, G. and Rouge, J., 1982. 'Trois horoscopes de voyages en mer (5e siecle après J.-C.)', *Revue des Etudes Byzantines*, 40, 117–133.

Davidson, G.R., 1952. *Corinth XII. The Minor Objects* (Princeton).

Emery, W.B. and Kirwan, L.P., 1938. *The Royal Tombs at Ballana and Qustul* (London).

Festugière, A.J., 1959. *Antioche paienne et chretienne. Libanius, Chrysostome et les moines de Syrie* (Paris).

Festugière, A.J., 1974. *Léontios de Néapolis, Vie de Syméon le Fou et Vie de Jean de Chypre* (Paris).

Flourentzos, P., 1996. *Excavations in the Kouris Valley. II. The Basilica of Alassa* (Nicosia).

Guillou, A., (ed.), 1977. *La cosidetta cronaca siriaca di Giosue la Stilita in Civilta bizantina dal IV al IX secolo* (Bari).

Gupta, P.L., 1984. 'Early Byzantine Solidi from Karnataka', *Numismatic Digest* 8.1, 37–43.

Jones, A.H.M., 1986. *The Later Roman Empire, 284–602. A Social, Economic and Administrative Survey* (Baltimore).

Kapitän, G. and Fallico, A.M., 1967. 'Bronzi tardoantichi dal Plemmyrion presso Siracusa', *Bottetino d'Arte* 52, 90–97.

Kingsley, S. and Raveh, K., 1996. *The Ancient Harbour and Anchorage at Dor, Israel. Results of the Underwater Surveys, 1976–1991* (BAR Int. S626, Oxford).

Kirwan, L.P., 1982. 'The X-Group Enigma', *Meroitica* 6, 191–204.

Maeir, A., 1993. 'Jerusalem, Mamilla (2)', *ESI* 12.

Maoili, M.G., 1986. 'Cervia (Ravenna). Relitto bizantino o altomedievale', *Bolletino d'Arte*, 37–38, 14–16.

Mango, C., forthcoming. *Constantinople: Urban Development*.

Manning, W.H., 1976. 'Blacksmithing'. In D. Strong and D. Brown (ed.) *Roman Crafts* (London), 143–153.

Mazor, G. and Bar-Nathan, R., 1998. 'The Bet She'an Excavation Project – 1992–1994. Antiquities Authority Expedition', *ESI* 17, 7–36.

Marshak, B. and Anazawa, W., 1989. 'Some Notes on the Tomb of Li-Xian and his Wife under the Northern Zhou Dynasty at Guyuan, Ningxia and its Gold-Gilt Ewer with Greek Mythological Scenes Unearthed there', *Cultura Antiqua* 41, 49–58.

Morrisson, C., 1995. 'La diffusion de la monnaie de Constantinople: routes commerciales ou routes politiques?'. In C. Mango and G. Dagron (ed.) *Constantinople and its Hinterland* (Aldershot), 77–89.

Mundell Mango, M., 1984. *Artistic Patronage in the Roman Diocese of Oriens, 313–641 A.D.* (DPhil Thesis, Oxford University).

Mundell Mango, M., 1994. 'The Significance of Byzantine Tinned Copper Objects'. In *Thymiama sti mneme tis Laskarinas Mpoura* (Athens), 221–228

Mundell Mango, M., 1995. 'Artemis at Daphne'. In S. Efthymiades, C. Rapp and D. Tsougarakis (ed.) *Bosphorus. Essays in Honour of Cyril Mango* (Byzantinische Forschunger XXI), 263–282.

Mundell Mango, M., 1996. 'Byzantine Maritime Trade with the East (4th-7th Centuries)', *ARAM* 8, 139–163.

Mundell Mango, M., 1998. 'The Archaeological Context of Finds of Silver in and beyond the Eastern Empire'. In N. Cambi and E. Marin (ed.) *Acta XIII Congressus Internationalis Archaeologiae Christianae*. II (Vatican City and Split), 207–252.

Mundell Mango, M., forthcoming 1. *The Sevso Treasure. Part Two.* (Ann Arbor)

Mundell Mango, M., forthcoming 2. 'The Commerical Map of Constantinople', *Dumbarton Oaks Papers.*

Mundell Mango, M., Mango, C., Evans, A.C. and Hughes, M., 1989. 'A 6th-Century Mediterranean Bucket from Bromeswell Parish, Suffolk', *Antiquity* 63, 295–311.

Mundell Mango, M. and Bennett, A., 1994. *The Sevso Treasure. Part One* (Ann Arbor).

Parker, A.J., 1992. *Ancient Shipwrecks of the Mediterranean and the Roman Provinces* (Bar Int. S580, Oxford).

Peacock, D.P.S. and Williams, D., 1986. *Amphorae and the Roman Economy* (London)

Périn, P., 1992. 'A propos des vases de bronze "coptes" du VIIe siècle en Europe de l'Ouest: le pichet de Bardouville (Seine-Maritime)', *Cahiers Archéologiques* 40, 35–50.

Philippe, J., 1970. *Le monde byzantin dans l'histoire de la verrerie (Ve-XVIe siècle)* (Bologna).

Popovic, I., 1990. 'Les activités professionnelles à Caricin Grad vers la fin du Vie et le début du VIIe siècle d'après les outils de fer'. In B. Bavant, V. Kondic and J.-M. Spieser, *Caricin Grad. II* (Belgrade and Rome), 269–306.

Richards, P., 1980. *Byzantine Bronze Vessels in England and Europe: the Origins of Anglo-Saxon Trade* (Ph.D. Thesis, Cambridge University Library).

Rodziewicz, M., 1984. *Les habitations: romaines tardives d'Alexandrie à la lumière des fouilles polonaises à Kom el-Dikka.* Alexandrie III. (Warsaw).

Saliou, C., 1996. *Le traité d'urbanisme de Julien d'Ascalon (VIe siècle)* (Paris).

Sewell, R., 1904. 'Roman Coins found in India', *Journal of Royal Asiatic Society*, 591–631.

Solier, Y., 1981. *Les Epaves de Gruissan* (Archaeonautica 3, Paris).

Stephens Crawford, J., 1990. *The Byzantine Shops at Sardis* (Archaeological Exploration of Sardis Monograph 9, Cambridge, MA).

Stern, M., 1997. 'Glass and Rock crystal: a Multifaceted Relationship', *JRA*, 10, 192–206.

Strzygowski, J., 1909. *Koptische Kunst* (Cairo).

Thierry, F. and Morrisson, C., 1994. 'Sur les monnaies byzantines trouvées en Chine', *Revue Numismatique*, 6e ser. 36, 109–145.

Thomas, C., 1981. *A Provisional List of Imported Pottery in Post-Roman Western Britain and Ireland* (Redruth)

Thomas, C., 1993. *Tintagel, Arthus and Archaeology* (London).

Van Saldern, A., 1980. *Ancient and Byzantine Glass from Sardis* (Cambridge, MA).

Vickers, M., 1996. 'Rock Crystal: the Key to Cut Glass and Diatreta in Persia and Rome', *JRA* 9, 48–65.

Walburg, R., 1991. 'Late Roman Copper Coins from India'. In A.K. Dja (ed.) *Third International Colloquium. Coinage, Trade and Economy* (Indian Institute of Research in Numismatic Studies, Anjaneri), 164–167.

Waldbaum, J.C., 1983. *Metalwork from Sardis: the Finds through 1974* (Cambridge, MA).

Werner, J., 1938. 'Italisches und koptisches Bronzegeschirr des 6. und 7. Jahrhunderts nordwarts der Alpen'. In Crome, J.F. *et al.* (ed.) *Mnemosynon Theodor Wiegand* (Munich), 74–86.

Yener, K.A., 1993. 'Byzantine Silver Mines: an Archaeometallurgy Project in Turkey (with a contribution on the pottery finds by A. Toydemir)'. In S.A. Boyd and M. Mundell Mango (ed.) *Ecclesiastical Silver Plate in Sixth-Century Byzantium* (Washington, D.C.), 155–168.

Chapter 6

The Economy of Late Antique Cyprus

Tassos Papacostas

Introduction

> "...and her inhabitants, toiling their land and trading with foreign nations, were growing in both prosperity and wealth...they were founding temples and churches, building magnificent dwellings, surrounding their cities with walls and renovating fortifications".

This is more or less all that Archimandrite Kyprianos has to say about non-ecclesiastical matters in late antique Cyprus in his *Chronological History*, published in Venice in 1788.[1] Although surprisingly succinct as a comment on a relatively long period that stretches from the reign of Constantine (324–37) to the Arab raids of the mid-seventh century, the archimandrite's statement encapsulates the essence of late antique Cyprus as this is revealed by archaeology. The rest of the eighteenth century historian's account of this period is focused on two events which concern the island's ecclesiastical history: first, the visit of Saint Helena in the fourth century, and then the confirmation of the autonomy of the Cypriot Church in the fifth century.

Indeed, a cursory look at the available, yet scanty, late antique source material shows that this is almost exclusively concerned with the second event related by Kyprianos, namely the discovery of the relic of Barnabas, founder of the Church of Cyprus, by Archbishop Anthemios outside Salamis/Constantia (the island's provincial capital). This led to the much discussed autocephaly of the Cypriot Church, a privilege jealously guarded throughout subsequent centuries.[2] The earlier event upon which Kyprianos dwells persistently, Helena's alleged visit on her way back to Constantinople from the Holy Land where she had discovered the relic of the True Cross, is not recorded until the Medieval period, and Cypriot monasteries like Stavrovouni (near Larnaca) and Saint Nicholas of the Cats (near Cape Gata), whose traditions link their foundation with the Constantinian period and the empress mother, do not preserve any kind of evidence to buttress their claims.[3]

T.B. Mitford's statement that the Roman period, also characterised by the same lack of written sources, was one of "tranquil obscurity" for Cyprus, remains totally valid for most of Late Antiquity as well, in view of the marked dearth of textual material at least until the seventh century.[4] Occasionally we do hear about natural disasters and raids that interrupted the peaceful existence of the islanders, such as the fourth century earthquakes that affected the great urban centres, or the Isaurian attacks of the early fifth century.[5] These events, together with the mid-sixth century plague and its frequent recurrences which, although not documented, must have affected Cyprus too, may have had an impact on the island's economy and demography.[6] The population is estimated to have reached 200,000 in the Roman period,[7] and a similar figure may be assumed, albeit with much caution, for the sixth century before the outbreak of the epidemic; a probably welcome boost was provided by the transfer of captives, presumably Christian Armenians, after a campaign against the Persians in the late 570s.[8]

Late antique Cyprus enjoyed a vigorous urban culture. According to the sixth century geographical list of cities known as the *Synekdemos of Hierokles*, the island boasted 13 *poleis*,[9] all coastal save two: Tamasos on the north-eastern foothills of the Troodos massif was situated in an area renowned for its copper mines, while Chytroi (Kythraia) on the south flank of the Kyrenia range had control of the most important springs on the island, that supplied Salamis on the east coast with water through a long aqueduct.[10] Salamis may have intermittently served as administrative capital in the Roman period (second to third centuries). However, it was not until its mid-fourth century reconstruction (necessitated after serious earthquake damage), when it was renamed Constantia in honour of Constans I, that it became the permanent provincial capital of Cyprus.[11] It was also the seat of the metropolitan of the island, who had eleven or more suffragan bishops.[12] The increasingly important role of the church in urban life towards the end of the period is illustrated by the inscriptions of the first half of the seventh century from the aqueduct of Salamis/Constantia, that commemorate the completion of parts of the work under successive archbishops.[13]

Cyprus emerges somewhat from the dark, as far as the written record is concerned, only in the seventh century. Although this is at least partly due to accidents of survival – we just happen to have several texts, mainly hagiographic, some locally written – it must also be related to developments in the eastern Mediterranean at that time, ushered in by the protracted Persian wars and advance in Syria-Palestine and Egypt, the ascent to the throne of Heraclius, and finally, the beginning of Arab expansion. Cyprus played a key role in all these events: in 609/10 it was used by Heraclius as a base on his way to the throne and the future emperor struck coins there.[14] A few years later, *c.* 619, the island was probably attacked by the Persians: our unique testimony is an ambiguous passage in two short versions of the *Life of Saint John the Almsgiver* (the Cypriot patriarch of Alexandria appointed by Heraclius), which is based on the lost *Life* written by John Moschos and Sophronios. According to these texts, a general named Aspagourios was preparing to lay siege to Salamis/Constantia after having been refused entry into the city. The potentially explosive situation was resolved peacefully with the intervention of the respected prelate who reconciled the parties.[15] A reference to captives escaping from their Persian prison and returning to Cyprus may confirm the occurrence of the attack, while the island, as in so many other periods of its history, also welcomed refugees fleeing trouble on the Syro-Palestinian mainland.[16]

Despite these upheavals, or perhaps because of them, the seventh century sources portray a prosperous island whose inhabitants are involved in trade, often travelling overseas for both professional and spiritual reasons. The story of Philentolos, the wealthy land and ship owner from Salamis/Constantia, whose fate after death the synod of the Church of Cyprus felt compelled to discuss because, although a distinguished philanthropist, he was also a notorious hedonist, is often cited as evidence for the wealth to be found on the island in the years immediately preceding the Arab raids.[17]

Archaeology provides supplementary and tangible evidence. The numerous gold coin hoards buried during this period testify to the amount of money circulating on the island.[18] The two Cyprus treasures (found near the north coast) that include spoons, domestic silver plates, gold jewellery and the set of silverware dated to 629/30 known as the David Plates, also betray an affluent society.[19] The evidence for building activity during the previous centuries leads to the same conclusion for the entire late antique period: some eighty basilicas and smaller churches have been identified or excavated on the island, not only in the cities but also in small and remote rural settlements.[20] Three of the very few late antique apse mosaics preserved in the eastern empire are indeed found in a non-urban setting on Cyprus, at Lythrankomi and Livadia in the Karpas, and at Kiti near the south coast, while floor mosaics from secular buildings have also been found in rural areas, such as the Toilet of Venus from a fifth century bath belonging to a villa at Alassa in the southern foothills of the Troodos, and the hunting panel from a late fourth/early fifth century bath at Mansoura (on the northern coast, halfway between Arsinoe and Soloi).[21]

Archaeological surveys, which are being carried out with increasing frequency, help to nuance the picture significantly, irrespective of their tendency to focus on pre-Roman remains (Fig. 6.1). The area of the Kormakiti peninsula on the north coast near the city of Lapethos, today a rather desolate and sparsely populated region, was densely occupied in the sixth and seventh centuries, before being abandoned in the eighth, although some coastal sites in this zone had been abandoned much earlier.[22] A large survey in the north-eastern Mesaoria and the western Karpas peninsula has produced similar results, with a notable concentration of late antique sites along the north coast, facing Cilicia.[23] The valley of the Yialias river in the central plain shows uninterrupted occupation from Roman into early Christian times, although not as dense as that of the northern coast.[24] According to the results of recent work by the Sydney Cyprus Survey Project (SCSP) around the villages of Politiko and Mitsero in the north-eastern foothills of the Troodos massif, to the west of the ancient city of Tamasos, the intensity of activity in this area during the Hellenistic period was not matched until the fifth and sixth centuries, after which decline set in again.[25] A comparable trend, with a peak in the first century A.D., was observed in the Vasilikos valley on the south coast (the area of Saint Helena's alleged activity on the island in the fourth century), although here the resumption of growth occurred slightly later, in the sixth century, and lasted into the late seventh.[26] A French survey in the territory of Amathus, where the Vasilikos valley lies, has confirmed this.[27]

The Canadian Palaipaphos Survey Project (CPSP), conducted in the region of modern Kouklia, is the largest and most detailed venture of this kind carried out so far on Cyprus. Once more, the meticulously examined ceramic evidence shows peak occupation in the first century, followed by decline that lasts through the fourth, before a reversal in the fortunes of the region culminating in the sixth century.[28] Further to the north, the Akamas peninsula, which like the Kormakiti area is sparsely populated

A comparable picture of frequent sea travel between the island and Cilicia is provided by the fifth century *miracula* of Thekla, whose shrine was situated outside Seleucia.[52] Archaeological evidence from elsewhere along the coast opposite Cyprus proves that contacts were not limited to the world of devout pilgrims eager to save their souls or heal their bodies; this region, after all, was one of the most highly urbanised in late antique Asia Minor.[53] At Anemurium, only 64 km across the sea from Cyprus, the most frequent late antique fine-ware is Cypriot red-slip, in particular during the last phase of occupation at the site in the seventh century.[54] At Tarsus and Antioch, on the other hand, this ware appears mainly from the mid-fifth to the early sixth century.[55] It was surely part of the cargo of ships arriving at Seleucia Pieria, Antioch's port at the mouth of the Orontes, whose duties to be paid to the *curiosi* are stipulated in a sixth century inscription now kept in the museum of Antioch.[56] The tariff due varies according to the ship's tonnage and provenance, and the latter includes what are presumably Antioch's major trading partners in the region, namely Phoenicia, Cilicia, Palestine, Egypt and Cyprus.

Cypriot red-slip ware has been found around the Aegean too, and was being exported quite early on, as the late fourth century finds from the Yassi Ada wreck show. Later on it was sent as far away as Cyrenaica and Constantinople in the sixth and seventh centuries.[57] The development of commercial relations between Cyprus and some of these areas is indicated by a small number of lead seals. A sixth century seal found at Tyre and a seal of 629–31, presumably from Constantinople, belong to *kommerkiarioi* of Cyprus, while a mid-seventh century seal found on the island itself belongs to a *kommerkiarios* of Asia, Caria and Lycia.[58]

Although marine archaeology and the excavation of shipwrecks off the coast of Cyprus have not yet attracted the attention they deserve, a few surveys have been conducted in the recent past: the corpus covering the whole Mediterranean and compiled by A.J. Parker lists fifteen shipwrecks in the island's waters. Six of these are dated to the fifth, sixth and seventh centuries (Cape Kiti, Thalassines Spilies to the north of Paphos, and four near Cape Apostolos Andreas), showing the importance of shipping during that period.[59]

Not surprisingly, the archaeological record amply demonstrates that the sea played a major role in the economy of Cyprus. The same is suggested by our written sources.[60] Several miracles reported to have been performed during Spyridon's lifetime indicate that even the inhabitants of an inland settlement like Tremithus were involved in seafaring. We hear of a local sailor who, having been away for two years, returns to find his wife pregnant, and of a ship-owner who, while borrowing money on a regular basis from the bishop, nevertheless tries to cheat his generous benefactor.[61] Our sources also clarify that contacts between the island's ports and those on the surrounding mainland and beyond were numerous. In the fourth century, Epiphanius of Salamis, intending to undertake the journey from Palestine to Cyprus in order to meet Hilarion of Gaza, had no trouble finding a Paphos-bound ship at the port of Caesarea.[62] In December 655, Archbishop Paul of Crete stopped at Cyprus on his way from Egypt to Constantinople and happened to be at Tremithus on Spyridon's feastday for the first public reading of the recently completed Life of the saint by Theodore of Paphos; at the same time, incidentally, a fair where clothes were being sold was also taking place.[63]

According to another contemporary Cypriot author, Anastasius of Sinai, one of the miracles attributed to Saint Athanasius Pentaschoinites, from an inland village near the south coast of Cyprus, involved saving a ship in peril.[64] The mobility of the island's workforce, using of course the sea, is illustrated by one of John the Almsgiver's servants, who had been employed by a customs official in Africa prior to his engagement with John's household on Cyprus.[65] In the late sixth century, George of Choziba also left his native island in order to seek work overseas, although in this case it was spiritual employment George was looking for: he followed the footsteps of his elder brother, a monk at the *laura* of Kalamon in the Judean desert, and himself became a monk at the monastery of Choziba.[66]

The ships criss-crossing the seas around Cyprus, leaving the island's ports carrying LR1 amphorae in their holds, filled with oil and wine and Cypriot red-slip wares, and on their decks suicidal pilgrims, monks in search of solitude, bishops with a penchant for hagiography, and betrayed sailors, surely did not return to the island empty. The evidence, however, is limited to two main types of import. The CPSP finds indicate that during the third and the first half of the fourth century, after the end of Cypriot sigillata production and before the appearance of Cypriot red-slip ware, the only fine ware available in south-western Cyprus, and presumably all over the island, was African red-slip. In later centuries, when the market was inundated by local products, imports were dominated by Phocean red-slip wares from western Asia Minor (Late Roman C), especially in the later fifth and during the sixth century. The importation of amphorae from Cilicia, North Africa, Palestine, and possibly Egypt, started in the later fourth century, although as in the case of fine wares they gradually gave way to locally produced types.[67]

The second imported commodity, which is adequately documented archaeologically, is marble. Since Cyprus does not have good quality marble of its own, stone was used instead for architectural elements. Although some marble was shipped in during the Classical, Hellenistic and Roman periods, it was not until the late fifth century that imports started in earnest, with the construction of the vast Campanopetra basilica at Salamis/Constantia.[68] Even less important buildings, like the recently excavated beach basilica at Curium and the churches of the settlement at Cape Drepanum, were liberally provided with marble.[69] Indeed, such was the appreciation of its beauty and its availability on the island that mosaic floors in the sixth century had to share their earlier virtual monopoly of floor coverage with marble *opus sectile* and even plain marble slabs, which are found not only along the coast, where access to the imported commodity was of course easier, but on inland sites too.[70] The trade in marble architectural elements, mainly from the quarries of Proconnesus on the Sea of Marmara, is well attested during the late antique period all over the Mediterranean, and Cyprus was no exception in taking advantage of the possibilities offered by this state of affairs.[71]

Rural Settlements

Finally, we shall examine below three rural sites that provide an alternative picture of the island's economy in Late Antiquity to that offered by the evidence from the cities, usually focused on their harbours, imported goods, long-distance trade and lavish architecture.

The extensive survey of the Vasilikos valley, mentioned above, included the partial excavation between 1987 and 1991 of Kalavasos-Kopetra (ancient name unknown), identified as the major late antique settlement in the area. Perched on a hill overlooking the east bank of the river, at a distance of 5 km from the coast, this unfortified rural settlement must have belonged to the territory of the nearest city, Amathus, located less than 16 km to the west on, or very near, the Roman road which followed the island's south coast. Its population is estimated not to have exceeded 1,000 inhabitants during its apogee, dated by the ceramic evidence to the sixth-to-seventh centuries, to which 90% of the finds are attributed. Half of the latter are amphorae, whose presence is surely linked to the olive or wine press identified in Area IV of the excavation. Among the fine wares recovered, slightly more than half were Cypriot red-slip, one third Phocean red-slip, and the remainder Egyptian and African imports. Although the question of the channels through which these reached the village has not been addressed, and despite the markets of nearby Amathus remaining the most likely direct source, the existence of an anchorage at Zygi-Petrini, at the mouth of the valley, would suggest that this was perhaps the entrance for goods imported directly or trans-shipped intra-regionally from other parts of Cyprus. Zygi-Petrini has also produced evidence of late antique activity, including an unpublished kiln discovered nearby in 1996, associated with late Roman amphora sherds.

Apart from the press mentioned above, two residential quarters were identified, as well as a building of uncertain function (public or private?) in Area VI; three basilicas were also excavated. The architecture and decoration of these churches, all rather small timber-roofed three-aisled structures built during the sixth and early seventh century, suggest a prosperous, although not exceedingly wealthy community. The raw materials used for construction were locally available; nevertheless, small quantities of marble were imported for the *opus sectile* floor of the basilica in Area V and for the altar table of another in Area II, whose *bema* had a polychrome geometric floor mosaic. Numerous *tesserae* recovered during the excavation, including glass and gold examples, indicate that the apses of both churches were decorated with wall mosaics. Columns and capitals, however, were made of gypsum, and the floor of the Area I (Sirmata) basilica, standing together with an adjacent complex centred around a courtyard on a low mound at the edge of the settlement – identified as monastic – was paved with gypsum slabs (Fig. 6.2).[72] The same local material was used in the Area II basilica to mould small, but elaborate relief panels, including a unique piece depicting an enthroned Virgin and Child.[73] The precise function of these panels within the basilica's decorative scheme remains uncertain.

The survival of the rural community at Kalavasos-Kopetra was presumably dependent on short-distance trade: a ready market for its agricultural produce was available in the nearby port city of Amathus, easily accessible along a main road. In addition, the village had access to a harbour of its own. The latter's main function, however, was clearly linked to the copper mines situated 6.5 km to the north of the settlement, whose growth is surely at least partly due to the exploitation of the area's mineral resources. The brief flourishing of Kalavasos-Kopetra as a modest provincial

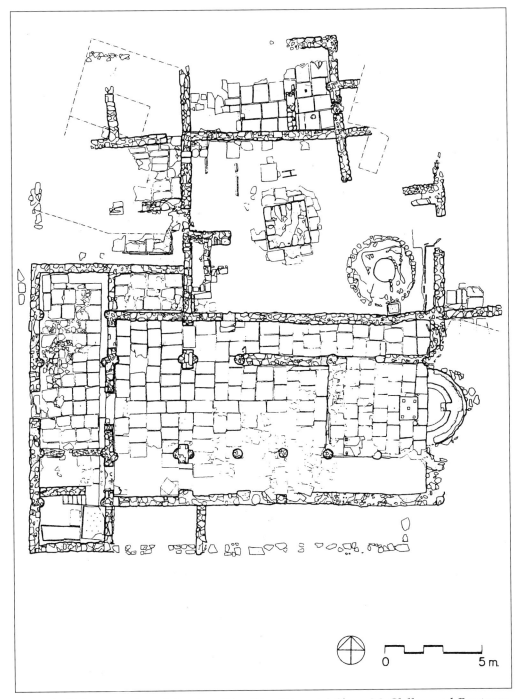

Fig. 6.2: Kalavasos: plan of the Area I basilica (Sirmata) (from McClellan and Rautman, 1991).

Constantinople. When the grain shipments were interrupted in the wake of the Persian occupation of Egypt in 618/19, Cape Drepanum lost its alleged *raison d'être* and declined rapidly and irrevocably. This, at least, is the opinion of the current excavator of the site,[78] which must remain conjectural in view of the lack of firm evidence, either textual or material. That the settlement was indeed to a large extent dependent on the sea is beyond doubt, but whether this dependence took this particular form remains to be seen.

A few miles to the north of Cape Drepanum, the University of Aarhus team, which surveyed part of the Akamas, also excavated a small late antique rural settlement at Ayios Kononas in 1989–91. The site, provided with a perpetual spring, lies about 1.7 km from the west coast of the peninsula on a late Roman road (fourth century?) that connected it with the Cape Drepanum settlement and the main Roman road to Paphos and beyond.[79]

The earliest structure excavated is dated by numismatic evidence to the fourth century and has been tentatively identified as a *villa rustica*. A metal slag deposit nearby, together with traces of furnaces and charcoal (dated by accelerated radiocarbon to the third/fourth century), suggest that some copper smelting activity was conducted on a small scale, presumably covering no more than local demand for metals employed in the manufacture of agricultural implements and household items.[80]

The settlement grew considerably during the fifth/sixth century, when the *villa rustica* was altered and several houses were built. Five have been partly excavated, showing that they sometimes had an upper storey. A church was also added in *c.* 600, built of limestone extracted from a quarry on the site itself, although by this time the settlement was already in decline. The mouldings in the three-aisled structure bear so many similarities to those of the Cape Drepanum basilicas that they have been attributed to the same workshop. The Ayios Kononas basilica is, nevertheless, a much more modest affair, with furnishings and architectural elements made of local materials and employing no imported marble.

Around 90% of the dateable surface finds from the area of Ayios Kononas are attributed to the late Roman/early Byzantine period, and the excavated structures confirm that this was the period of peak activity on the site, which was abandoned in the course of the seventh century. Neither the church, which had collapsed by the eighth century, nor the houses have provided any evidence of violent destruction, the latter having been emptied of their contents before their abandonment.[81] The underwater survey of the region's most important anchorage, however, at Kioni below Ayios Kononas, has yielded mainly Hellenistic and Roman pottery, suggesting that the sea was of no great importance to the early Byzantine settlement's economy. Nevertheless, some fishing implements found in a dump outside one of the excavated houses indicate that it was at least used as a source of food. Agriculture clearly remained the basis of the local, largely self-sufficient economy, shown by extensive terracing around the site.

The variety of regional economic patterns that our three examples of rural settlements illustrate, even within the confines of a relatively small area like Cyprus, cannot be detected by looking at the urban centres alone, for these usually offer a much more uniform picture. The village economy in each of the above cases was conditioned by the locally available resources and, most importantly, by the degree of accessibility to a major urban centre and a harbour. Ayios Kononas provides the most extreme case of isolation, due to its geographical position and despite its access to both the sea and the island's road network. Its inward-looking economy was based on agriculture and on resources available *in situ*. Raw and building materials were locally extracted and processed, and no wish to emulate the opulence of nearby settlements like Cape Drepanum, that would require the import of luxury items and materials, can be detected in the architecture, decoration or contents of its buildings. This contrasts sharply with Cape Drepanum, which appears to have been much more dependent on the sea and contacts beyond the shores of Cyprus, turning its back on its hinterland. Kalavasos, on the other hand, although economically self-contained with its mineral, ceramic and agricultural production, and possessing its own harbour, was clearly integrated within a regional economy centred on the city of Amathus, developing a character far removed from the subsistence economy of Ayios Kononas.

Notes

1   Archimandrite Kyprianos, 1788 (repr. Nicosia 1971) (Venice), 100.
2   Hackett, 1901: 13–32; Hill, 1940–52: vol.1, 273–79.
3   For a discussion of the development of the Helena legend in Cyprus, see Kyrris, 1984: 24–30.
4   Mitford, 1980: 1295.
5   On the earthquakes and their impact, see Papageorgiou, 1993: 27–28 with further bibliography; Isaurian raids: Bidez, 1913: 139.
6   Chrysos, 1993: 8–9.
7   Michaelides, 1996: 143, who quotes as his source T. Potter's forthcoming chapter on Roman Cyprus in vol.2 of the *History of Cyprus*, edited by T. Papadopoullos and published by the Archbishop Makarios III Foundation (Nicosia); an earlier estimate of 500,000 is clearly over-optimistic: Beloch, 1886, 249–50.
8   de Boor, 1887: 143; see also Hill, 1940–52: vol.1, 281, and Kyrris, 1970: 157–81.
9   Constantia, Tamasos, Citium, Amathus, Curium, Paphos, Arsinoe, Soloi, Lapethos, Kyrenia, Kirboia (?), Chytroi, Carpasia: Burckhardt, 1893: 36; see also Hill, 1940–52: vol.1, 261–62.
10   Sodini, 1998.
11   Kyrris, 1984: 21–22.
12   The council of Serdica (343) was attended by twelve bishops from Cyprus whose sees are, however, not given: Mansi, 1901–27: vol.III, 69; according to the fifth century ecclesiastical historian Sozomenos, in Cyprus even rural settlements (*komai*) had bishops: Bidez and Hansen, 1960: 330.
13   Sodini, 1998.
14   The suggestion in Chrysos, 1984 that the section of the Salamis aqueduct financed by Heraclius was built at this time, is refuted in Sodini, 1998: 632–33, where a date in 631 is suggested, based on the reading of the indiction in the surviving inscription.
15   Texts in Delehaye, 1927: 25, and shorter version in Lappa-Zizicas, 1970: 277. Modern scholarship remains divided on the issue of Aspagourios' role and presence in Cyprus: according to some historians a Persian attack is quite likely: Chrysos, 1993: 12–13; Foss, 1975: 724 (attack dated to 617); Mango, 1984: 38–39; and Howard-Johnston, 1999: 33; other scholars, however, remain cautious: Hill, 1940–52: vol.1, 282; Festugière, 1974: 336; Déroche, 1995: 36, n.67; and Sodini, 1998: 622 and 632.
16   For returning captives of the Persians, see Festugière, 1974: 375–76; refugees in the 610s included Bishop Paul of Edessa: Honigmann, 1951: 20, n.5; see also Chrysos, 1999: 207–8 with more examples; for a slightly later reference to a Jewish slave escaping from his Arab masters on the mainland, see Flusin, 1991: 386 and 391.

17   Halkin, 1945: 56–64.

18   Dikigoropoulos, 1961: 24–26; see also *JHS* 71 (1951), 260; *JHS* 72 (1952), 117; *JHS* 73 (1953), 137.

19   Kazhdan, 1991: 570, with bibliography.

20   For late antique architecture in Cyprus, see Delvoye, 1972: 17–21; *idem*, 1980: 313–27; Megaw, 1974; Papageorgiou, 1985: 299–324, and *idem*, 1986: 490–504.

21   Megaw and Hawkins, 1977; Megaw, 1985: 173–98; Michaelides, 1992: 76 no.41, 93 no.51, 115–23 nos.67–71; Michaelides, 1993a: 265–74.

22   Catling, 1972: 1–82; Quilici, 1989: 7–23.

23   Hadjisavvas, 1991; see however Symeonoglou, 1972: 187–98, where it is argued that the late antique period witnessed a marked decline in occupation compared to Hellenistic and Roman times.

24   Catling, 1982: 227–36.

25   Knapp and Given, 1996: 334.

26   McClellan, Rautman, and Todd, 1993: 423; Todd, 1989: 41–50.

27   Aupert, 1996: 178.

28   Sørensen *et al.*, 1987: 277; Rupp, 1987: 32; Lund, 1993: 139–43.

29   Fejfer and Mathiesen, 1991: 222; *idem*, 1992: 72–73; Fejfer, 1995: 24–25.

30   For an earlier general overview of the evidence for both urban and rural sites, see Papageorgiou, 1993.

31   Sources collected in Wallace and Orphanides, 1990: 54–55, 131, 146–50, 160–62, 224–25; see also Michaelides, 1996: 144–45, and Raptou, 1996: 249–54.

32   des Gagniers and Tinh, 1985: xxvii.

33   Knapp and Given, 1996: 302, 332–33.

34   As suggested for the Roman period in Mitford, 1980: 1331; for a reconstruction of the island's Roman road system, based on the evidence of milestones and the *Tabula Peutingeriana*, see Mitford, 1980: 1333–35 and 1340.

35   Childs, 1988: 130.

36   Fox, Zacharias, and Franklin, 1987: 169–84.

37   On Heraclius' Cypriot coinage, see Chrysos, 1984: 53–54, with bibliography. The mint was operating again on Cyprus in 626/627.

38   Muhly, 1996: 46.

39   Paschoud, 1971–89: vol.1, 94; see also Michaelides, 1996: 141–42 and 146 and Raptou, 1996: 254–56; on references to Cypriot timber by ancient authors, see also Thirgood, 1987: 70–76.

40   Wallace and Orphanides, 1990: 71–72, 162–63.

41   *BCH* 94 (1970), 219 [near Platres]; *BCH* 101 (1977), 716 [Ayios Theodoros]; *BCH* 107 (1983), 907 [Kambos Tsakistras]; *RDAC* (1977), 178–201 [Kakopetria]; *RDAC* (1987), 253–57 [Ayios Theodoros]; for a sanctuary dedicated to Zeus Labranios, and attested by an inscription found near Chandria at 1500m a.s.l. below the peak of Mount Adelphi, see Mitford, 1947: 206–8.

42   According to Strabo: Wallace and Orphanides, 1990: 131; the remains of some structures near Lagoudera, no longer visible, have been identified as a church (?) and a bath belonging to a late antique settlement: Winfield, n.d: 4.

43   Wallace and Orphanides, 1990: 131, 144–45. For a discussion of Strabo's remarks, see Thomsen's commentary in Fejfer, 1995: 31–33; for the Piacenza pilgrim's account, see Wilkinson, 1977: 79.

44   Michaelides, 1996: 142 and 146–47; Wallace and Orphanides, 1990: 24.

45   Van den Ven, 1953: 12–13, 53–56, 71–73.

46   Hadjisavvas, 1992.

47   *BCH* 113 (1989), 848; *BCH* 114 (1990), 951; Demestika and Michaelides, forthcoming; Peacock and Williams, 1986: 185–7; van Alfen, 1996: 189–213; Empereur and Picon, 1989: 242–43.

48   Hayes, 1972: 372–85, 420.

49   Festugière, 1974: 345, 362, 408–9.

50   'Sophronii monachi sophistae Narratio miraculorum Ss. Cyri et Joannis sapientium Anargyrorum'. In Migne, J.-P. (ed.) *Patrologiae cursus completus, Series graeca,* vol.87/3, col.3625, 3628, 3652–56; also in Fernandez Marcos, 1975: 370–72, 387–89.

51   Van den Ven, 1953: 81–82.

52　Dagron, 1978: 330–32, 390; the ships arriving from Cyprus carrying pilgrims to Thekla's shrine may have also been involved in trade between the island and Seleucia, according to Vryonis, 1981: 200–201.

53　Foss, 1996.

54　Williams, 1989: 27–28; interestingly, according to a recent study of the art of Anemurium, the mosaic pavements do not betray any particular affinities with Cypriot examples; see Campbell, 1998.

55　Hayes, 1972: 385.

56　Dagron, 1985: 435–51.

57　Hayes, 1972: 372–83; Hayes, 1980: 528.

58　Cheynet, Morrisson and Seibt, 199: no.138 [Tyre seal]; no.255 in this catalogue, also found at Tyre, belongs to the seventh century Bishop, Leo of Citium; Zacos and Veglery, 1972: no.132 [Constantinople seal], and see p.165–66 for a table of late seventh and eighth century seals of the *apotheke* of Asia; the seal from Cyprus, which is earlier than the ten specimens listed, is not included; Dikigoropoulos, 1961: appendix II no.38 [Cyprus seal].

59　Parker, 1992: nos.202, 203, 204, 206, 212 and 1145; the other Cypriot shipwrecks are either of earlier (Hellenistic/Roman) or uncertain date.

60　For a general survey of the evidence on daily life contained in seventh century Cypriot hagiography, see Yannopoulos, 1983: 79–85.

61　Van den Ven, 1953: 65, 92–95.

62　'Vita S. Epiphanii'. In Migne, J.-P. (ed.) *Patrologiae cursus completus, Series graeca*, vol.41, col.65.

63　Van den Ven, 1953: 89.

64　Flusin, 1991: 387.

65　Festugière, 1974: 368.

66　Houze, 1888: 95–144.

67　Lund, 1993: 138–39.

68　Megaw, 1974: 68; Michaelides, 1996: 139; Roux, 1998: 241; I am most grateful to D. Michaelides for comments on marble imports to Cyprus, for drafts of papers, bibliographical references and other suggestions.

69　*BCH* 120 (1996), 1088; on the Cape Drepanum churches, see below.

70　Michaelides, 1992: 8–9; see also Michaelides, 1993b: 69–114.

71　On the marble trade see Kapitän, 1980: 71–136, and Sodini, 1989: 163–86.

72　In addition to the bibliography in n.26 above and in the following footnote, see also *Annual Report to the Director of Antiquities* (1988), 50–51; *Annual Report to the Director of Antiquities* (1989), 55–56; *Annual Report to the Director of Antiquities* (1990), 54; *Annual Report to the Director of Antiquities* (1991), 60–61; *BCH* 113 (1989), 829–30; *BCH* 114 (1990), 967; *BCH* 115 (1991), 816–17; McClellan and Rautman, 1989: 157–66; Rautman and McClellan, 1987: 45–54; *idem*, 1988: 51–63; *idem*, 1991: 10–20.

73　*BCH* 116 (1992), 812–13; Rautman and McClellan, 1989/90: 24; *idem*, 1990: 238; McClellan and Rautman, 1991: 233–35 and fig. 5; *idem*, 1994: at 290.

74　Bekker-Nielsen *et al.*, 1991.

75　Megaw, 1974: 71–72; Michaelides, 1992: 99–107 nos.56–60; Papageorgiou, 1993: 36; *Annual Report to the Director of Antiquities* 1991: 67; *BCH* 116 (1992), 831; *BCH* 121 (1997), 925–26 and 931–32; Bakirtzis, 1999: 35–48.

76　Michaelides, forthcoming; Megaw, 1997: 343–52.

77　Giangrande *et al.*, 1987: 185–98; *idem*, 199–212.

78　Bakirtzis, 1995: 247–54; *idem*, 1997: 327–32; see also the forthcoming paper by the same author on recent excavations at Cape Drepanum, given at the Third International Congress of Cypriot Studies (Nicosia, April 17, 1996).

79　On the area's road system, see Bekker-Nielsen *et al.*, 1991.

80　Fejfer and Mathiesen, 1991 and 1992; Fejfer, 1995; excavation reports in *BCH* 114 (1990), 983; *BCH* 115 (1991), 829–31; *BCH* 116 (1992), 828–30 and *Annual Report to the Director of Antiquities, Cyprus* (1989), *Annual Report to the Director of Antiquities* 63–64; (1990), *Annual Report to the Director of Antiquities* 62–63; (1991), 62.

81　Fejfer, 1995: 24, 86; Fejfer and Hayes, 1995: 62–69.

Bibliography

Aupert, P., 1996. *Guide d'Amathonte* (École Française d'Athènes: Sites et Monuments XV, Paris).

Bakirtzis, C., 1995. 'The Role of Cyprus in the Grain Supply of Constantinople in the Early Christian Period'. In V. Karageorghis and D. Michaelides (ed.) *Proceedings of the International Symposium Cyprus and the Sea, Nicosia 1993* (Nicosia), 247–54.

Bakirtzis, C., 1997. 'A Sea-Route from Cyprus to the Aegean in the Early Christian Period'. In *Proceedings of the International Archaeological Conference Cyprus and the Aegean in Antiquity from the Prehistoric Period to the 7th Century A.D., Nicosia 8–10 December 1995* (Nicosia), 327–32.

Bakirtzis, C., 1999. 'Early Christian Rock-Cut Tombs at Hagios Georgios, Peyia, Cyprus'. In N. Patterson Ševčenko and C. Moss (ed.) *Medieval Cyprus. Studies in Art, Architecture, and History in Memory of Doula Mouriki* (Princeton University Press), 35–48.

Bekker-Nielsen, T., Hannestad, N. and Jensen, M., 1991. 'An Ancient Road on the West Coast of Cyprus. A Preliminary Report', *RDAC*, 203–10.

Beloch, J., 1886. *Die Bevölkerung der griechisch-römischen Welt* (Leipzig).

Bidez, J., 1913 (revised by F. Winkelmann, Berlin 1981). *Philostorgius, Kirchengeschichte* (Leipzig).

Bidez, J. and Hansen, G.C., 1960. *Sozomenus Kirchengeschichte* (Berlin).

Bryer, A. and Georghallides, G.S., 1993 (ed.). *The Sweet Land of Cyprus, Papers Given at the Twenty-Fifth Jubilee Symposium of Byzantine Studies, Birmingham* (Nicosia).

Burckhardt, A., 1893. *Hieroclis Synecdemus* (Leipzig).

Campbell, S., 1998. *The Mosaics of Anemurium* (Pontifical Institute of Mediaeval Studies, Toronto).

Catling, H.W., 1972. 'An Early Byzantine Pottery Factory at Dhiorios in Cyprus', *Levant* 4, 1–82.

Catling, H.W., 1982. 'The Ancient Topography of the Yialias Valley', *RDAC*, 227–36.

Cheynet, J.-C., Morrisson, C. and Seibt, W., 1991. *Sceaux byzantins de la collection Henri Seyrig* (Paris).

Childs, W.A.P., 1988. 'First Preliminary Report on the Excavations at Polis Chrysochous by Princeton University', *RDAC* (part 2), 121–130.

Chrysos, E., 1984. 'O Herakleios stin Kypro'. In C. Constantinides (ed.) *Praktika Symposiou Kypriakis Istorias, Leukosia 2–3 Maiou 1983* (Ioannina), 53–62.

Chrysos, E., 1993. 'Cyprus in Early Byzantine Times'. In A. Bryer and G.S. Georghallides (ed.) *The Sweet Land of Cyprus, Papers given at the Twenty-Fifth Jubilee Symposium of Byzantine Studies, Birmingham* (Nicosia), 3–14.

Chrysos, E., 1999. 'Apo tin istoria tou monachismou stin Kypro ton evdomo aiona', *Epetirida Kentrou Meleton Ieras Monis Kykkou* 4, 205–17.

Constantinides, C., (ed.) 1984. *Praktika Sumposiou Kypriakis Istorias, Leukosia 2–3 Maiou 1983* (Ioannina).

Dagron, G., 1978. *Vie et miracles de sainte Thècle, texte grec, traduction et commentaire* (Subsidia Hagiographica 62, Brussels).

Dagron, G., 1985. 'Un tarif des sportules à payer aux *Curiosi* du port de Séleucie de Piérie (VIe siècle)', *Travaux et Mémoires* 9, 435–51.

Delehaye, H., 1927. 'Une vie inédite de Saint Jean l'Aumônier', *Analecta Bollandiana* 45, 5–74.

de Boor, C., 1887 (revised by P. Wirth, Stuttgart 1972). *Theophylacti Simocattae Historiae* (Leipzig).

Delvoye, C., 1972. 'La place de Chypre dans l'architecture paléochrétienne de la Méditerranée'. In *Praktika tou Protou Diethnous Kyprologikou Synedriou*, vol. 2: Mesaionikon tmima (Nicosia), 17–21.

Delvoye, C., 1980. 'La place des grandes basiliques de Salamine de Chypre dans l'architecture paléochrétienne'. In M. Yon (ed.) *Salamine de Chypre. Histoire et archéologie. Etat des recherches* (Colloques Internationaux du CNRS 578, Paris), 313–27.

Demestika, S. and Michaelides, D., forthcoming. 'The Excavation of a Late Roman 1 Amphora Kiln in Paphos'. In *Actes du colloque La céramique byzantine et proto-islamique en Syrie-Jordanie, Amman 3–5 Décembre 1994*.

Déroche, V., 1995. *Études sur Léontios de Néapolis* (Acta Universitatis Upsaliensis, Studia Byzantina Upsaliensia 3, Uppsala).

des Gagniers, J. and Tinh, T.T., 1985. *Soloi. dix campagnes de fouilles (1964–1974), volume premier* (Sainte-Foy).

Dikigoropoulos, A.I., 1961. *Cyprus "Betwixt Greeks and Saracens" A.D. 647–965* (Thesis submitted for the degree of Doctor of Philosophy in the University of Oxford).

Empereur, J.-Y. and Picon, M., 1989. 'Les régions de production d'amphores impériales en Méditerranée orientale'. In *Amphores romaines et histoire économique: dix ans de recherche, Actes du colloque de Sienne, 22–24 mai 1986* (Collection de l'École Française de Rome 114), 223–48.

Fejfer, J. and Hayes, P.P., 1995. 'Ancient Akamas and the Abandonment of Sites in Seventh-century A.D. Cyprus'. In P.W. Wallace (ed.) *Visitors, Immigrants, and Invaders in Cyprus* (Institute of Cypriot Studies, University at Albany, State University of New York), 62–69.

Fejfer, J. and Mathiesen, H.E., 1991. 'The Danish Akamas-Project. The First Two Seasons of Work (1989 and 1990)', *RDAC*, 211–23.

Fejfer, J. and Mathiesen, H.E., 1992. 'Ayios Kononas. A Late Roman/Early Byzantine Site in the Akamas'. In P. Åström (ed.) *Acta Cypria: Acts of an International Congress on Cypriote Archaeology held in Göteborg on 22–24 August 1991, Part 2* (Göteborg), 67–83.

Fejfer, J., 1995. *Ancient Akamas 1. Settlement and Environment* (Aarhus).

Fernandez Marcos, N., 1975. *Los Thaumata de Sofronio. Contribución al estudio de la 'incubatio' cristiana* (Madrid).

Festugière, A.J., 1974. *Léontios de Néapolis: Vie de Syméon le Fou et Vie de Jean de Chypre* (Paris).

Flusin, B., 1991. 'Démons et Sarrasins. L'auteur et le propos des *Dièghmata stèriktika* d'Anastase le Sinaïte', *Travaux et Mémoires* 11, 381–409.

Foss, C., 1975. 'The Persians in Asia Minor and the End of Antiquity', *English Historical Review* 90, 721–47.

Foss, C., 1996. 'The Cities of Pamphylia in the Byzantine Age'. In C. Foss, *Cities, Fortresses and Villages of Byzantine Asia Minor* (Aldershot).

Fox, W.A., Zacharias, S. and Franklin, U.M., 1987. 'Investigations of Ancient Metallurgical Sites in the Paphos District, Cyprus'. In D.W. Rupp, *Western Cyprus: Connections. An Archaeological Symposium held at Brock University, St. Catharines, Ontario Canada 1986* (Göteborg), 169–84.

Giangrande, C., Richards, G., Kennet, D. and Adams, J., 1987. 'Cyprus Underwater Survey, 1983–84. A Preliminary Report', *RDAC*, 185–98.

Hackett, J., 1901. *A History of the Orthodox Church of Cyprus* (London).

Hadjisavvas, S., 1991. *Katavoles 1: Archaiologiki episkopisi 20 katechomenon simera chorion tis eparchias Ammochostou* (Nicosia).

Hadjisavvas, S., 1992. *Olive Oil Processing in Cyprus, from the Bronze Age to the Byzantine Period* (Nicosia).

Halkin, F., 1945. 'La vision de Kaioumos et le sort éternel de Philentolos Olympiou', *Analecta Bollandiana* 63, 56–64.

Hayes, J.W., 1972. *Late Roman Pottery* (London).

Hayes, J.W., 1980. *Supplement to Late Roman Pottery* (London).

Hill, G., 1940–52. *A History of Cyprus*, 4 vols. (Cambridge).

Honigmann, E., 1951. *Evêques et évêchés monophysites d'Asie antérieure au VIe siècle* (Corpus scriptorum christianorum orientalium 127, Subsidia 2, Louvain).

Houze, C., 1888. 'Vita sancti Georgii Chozibitae auctore Antonio Chozibita', *Analecta Bollandiana* 7, 95–144.

Howard-Johnston, J., 1999. 'Heraclius' Persian Campaigns and the Revival of the East Roman Empire', *War in History* 6, 1–44.

Kapitän, G., 1980. 'Elementi architettonici per una basilica dal relitto navale del VI secolo di Marzamemi', *Corsi di cultura sull'arte ravennate e bizantina* 27, 71–136.

Karageorghis, V. and Michaelides, D., (ed.) 1996. *The Development of the Cypriot Economy from the Prehistoric Period to the Present Day* (Nicosia).

Kazhdan, A.P., (ed.) 1991. *Oxford Dictionary of Byzantium, Vol. 1* (New York-Oxford).

Knapp, A.B. and Given, M., 1996. 'The Sydney Cyprus Survey Project (SCSP) – Third Season (1995)', *RDAC*, 295–366.

Kyrris, C., 1970. 'Military Colonies in Cyprus in the Byzantine Period: their Character, Purpose and Extent', *Byzantinoslavica* 31, 157–81.

Kyrris, C., 1984. 'Charaktiristika tis Kypriakis Istorias kata tin protobyzantini periodo'. In C. Constantinides (ed.) *Praktika Symposiou Kypriakis Istorias, Leukosia 2–3 Maiou 1983* (Ioannina), 18–40.

Lappa-Zizicas, E., 1970. 'Un épitomé de la Vie de S. Jean l'Aumônier par Jean et Sophronius', *Analecta Bollandiana* 88, 265–78.

Lund, J., 1993. 'Pottery of the Classical, Hellenistic and Roman Periods'. In L.W. Sørensen and D.W. Rupp (ed.) *The Land of the Paphian Aphrodite vol.2: the Canadian Palaipaphos Survey Project. Artifact and Ecofactual Studies* (Göteborg), 79–155.

Mango, C., 1984. 'A Byzantine Hagiographer at Work: Leontios of Neapolis'. In I. Hutter (ed.) *Byzanz und der Westen* (Vienna), 25–41.

Mansi, G.D., 1901–27. *Sacrorum conciliorum nova et amplissima collectio* (Paris-Leipzig), vol.III.

McClellan, M.C. and Rautman, M.L., 1989. 'The 1987 and 1988 Field Seasons of the Kalavasos-Kopetra Project', *RDAC* (1989), 157–66.

MClellan, M.C. and Rautman, M.L., 1991. 'The 1990 Field Season at Kalavasos-Kopetra', *RDAC*, 225–36

Morris, C.E. and Peatfield, A.A.D., 1987. 'Pottery from the Cyprus Underwater Survey, 1983', *RDAC*, 199–212.

McClellan, M.C., Rautman, M.L. and Todd, I.A., 1993. 'The Vasilikos Valley in Late Antiquity'. In A. Bryer and G.S. Georghallides (ed.) *The Sweet Land of Cyprus, Papers Given at the Twenty-Fifth Jubilee Symposium of Byzantine Studies, Birmingham* (Nicosia), 423.

Megaw, A.H.S., 1974. 'Byzantine Architecture and Decoration in Cyprus: Metropolitan or Provincial?', *DOP* 28, 57–88.

Megaw, A.H.S., 1985. 'Mosaici parietali paleobizantini di Cipro', *Corsi di cultura sull'arte ravennate e bizantina* 32, 173–98.

Megaw, A.H.S., 1997. 'The Aegean Connections of Cypriot Church-Builders in Late Antiquity'. In *Proceedings of the International Archaeological Conference 'Cyprus and the Aegean in Antiquity from the Prehistoric period to the 7th century A.D.', Nicosia 8–10 December 1995* (Nicosia), 343–52.

Megaw, A.H.S. and Hawkins, E.J.W., 1977. *The Church of the Panagia Kanakariá at Lythrankomi in Cyprus* (Dumbarton Oaks Studies 14, Washington D.C.).

Michaelides, D., 1992. *Cypriot Mosaics* (Cyprus Department of Antiquities, Nicosia).

Michaelides, D., 1993a. 'The Baths of Mansoura', *RDAC*, 265–74.

Michaelides, D., 1993b. 'Opus Sectile in Cyprus'. In A. Bryer and G.S. Georghallides (ed.) *The Sweet Land of Cyprus, Papers Given at the Twenty-Fifth Jubilee Symposium of Byzantine Studies, Birmingham* (Nicosia), 69–114.

Michaelides, D., 1996. 'The Economy of Cyprus during the Hellenistic and Roman periods'. In V. Karageorghis and D. Michaelides (ed.). *The Development of the Cypriot Economy from the Prehistoric Period to the Present Day* (Nicosia), 139–52.

Michaelides, D., forthcoming. 'The Ambo of Basilica A at Cape Drepanon'. In J. Herrin, M. Mullett and C. Otten-Froux (ed.) *A Mosaic of Byzantine and Cypriot Studies in Honour of A.H.S. Megaw.*

Mitford, T.B., 1947. 'Notes on some Published Inscriptions from Roman Cyprus', *Annual of the British School at Athens* 42, 201–30.

Mitford, T.B., 1980. 'Roman Cyprus'. In H. Temporini (ed.) *Aufstieg und Niedergang der römischen Welt* II. Principat vol.7.2 (Berlin-New York), 1285–1384.

Muhly, J.D., 1996. 'The Significance of Metals in the Late Bronze Age Economy of Cyprus'. In V. Karageorghis and D. Michaelides (ed.) *The Development of the Cypriot Economy from the Prehistoric Period to the Present Day* (Nicosia), 45–59.

Paschoud, F., 1971–89. *Zosime, Histoire Nouvelle*, 3 vols. (Paris).

Papageorgiou, A., 1985. 'L'architecture paléochrétienne de Chypre', *Corsi di cultura sull'arte ravennate e bizantina* 32, 299–324.

Papageorgiou, A., 1986. 'Foreign Influences on the Early Christian Architecture of Cyprus'. In V. Karageorghis (ed.) *Acts of the International Archaeological Symposium Cyprus between the Orient and the Occident'* (Nicosia), 490–504.

Papageorgiou, A., 1993. 'Cities and Countryside at the End of Antiquity and the Beginning of the Middle Ages in Cyprus'. In A. Bryer and G.S. Georghallides (ed.) *The Sweet Land of Cyprus, Papers Given at the Twenty-Fifth Jubilee Symposium of Byzantine Studies, Birmingham* (Nicosia), 27–51.

Parker, A.J., 1992. *Ancient Shipwrecks of the Mediterranean and the Roman Provinces* (Oxford).

Peacock, D.P.S. and Williams, D.F., 1986. *Amphorae and the Roman Economy* (London-New York).

Quilici, L., 1989. 'Poleografia e popolamento della penisola di Kormakiti a Cipro', *Felix Ravenna* 137–38/1–2, 7–23.

Raptou, E., 1996. 'Contribution to the Study of the Economy of Ancient Cyprus: Copper-Timber'. In V. Karageorghis and D. Michaelides (ed.) *The Development of the Cypriot Economy from the Prehistoric Period to the Present Day* (Nicosia), 249–59.

Rautman, M.L. and McClellan, M.C., 1987. 'Cyprus at the End of Antiquity: Investigations at Kalavasos-Kopetra', *Muse* 21, 45–54.

Rautman, M.L. and McClellan, M.C, 1988. 'Kalavasos-Kopetra 1988', *Muse* 22, 51–63.

Rautman, M.L. and McClellan, M.C., 1989/90. 'Kalavasos-Kopetra 1989–90', *Muse* 23/24, 14–29.

Rautman, M.L. and McClellan, M.C., 1990. 'The 1989 Field Season at Kalavasos-Kopetra', *RDAC*, 231–38.

Rautman, M.L. and McClellan, M.C, 1991. 'Kalavasos-Kopetra 1991', *Muse* 25, 10–20.

Rautman, M.L. and McClellan, M.C. 1994. 'The 1991–1993 Field Seasons at Kalavasos-Kopetra', *RDAC*, 289–307.

Roux, G., 1998. *La basilique de la Campanopétra* (Salamine de Chypre XV, Paris).

Rupp, D.W., 1987. *Western Cyprus: Connections. An Archaeological Symposium held at Brock University, St. Catharines, Ontario Canada 1986* (Göteborg).

Sodini, J.-P., 1989. 'Le commerce des marbres à l'époque protobyzantine'. In J. Lefort and C. Morrisson (ed.) *Hommes et richesses dans l'empire byzantin I (IVe-VIIe siècle)* (Paris), 163–86.

Sodini, J.-P., 1998. 'Les inscriptions de l'aqueduc de Kythrea à Salamine de Chypre'. In *Ehuyucía. Mélanges offerts à Hélène Ahrweiler* (Byzantina Sorbonensia 16, Paris), 619–34.

Sørensen, L.W., Guldager, P., Korsholm, M., Lund, J. and Gregory, T.E., 1987. 'Canadian Palaepaphos Survey Project: Second Preliminary Report of Ceramic Finds 1982–1983', *RDAC*, 259–78.

Symeonoglou, S., 1972. 'Archaeological Survey in the Area of Phlamoudhi, Cyprus', *RDAC*, 187–98.

Thirgood, J.V., 1987. *Cyprus. A Chronicle of its Forests, Land, and People* (Vancouver).

Todd, I.A., 1989. 'The 1988 Field Survey in the Vasilikos Valley', *RDAC*, 41–50.

van Alfen, P.G., 1996. 'New Light on the Seventh-Century Yassi Ada Shipwreck: Capacities and Standard Sizes of LRA1 Amphoras', *JRA* 9, 189–213.

Van den Ven, P., 1953. *La légende de Saint Spyridon évêque de Trimithonte* (Bibliothèque du Muséon 33, Louvain).

Vryonis, S., 1981. 'The Panêgyris of the Byzantine Saint: a Study of the Nature of a Medieval Institution, its Origins and Fate'. In S. Hackel (ed.) *The Byzantine Saint. University of Birmingham Fourteenth Spring Symposium of Byzantine Studies* (London), 196–227.

Wallace, P.W. and Orphanides, A.G., 1990. *Sources for the History of Cyprus Vol.1: Greek and Latin Texts to the Third Century A.D.* (Nicosia – New York).

Williams, C., 1989. *Anemurium. The Roman and Early Byzantine Pottery* (Toronto).

Wilkinson, J., 1977. *Jerusalem Pilgrims before the Crusades* (Warminster).

Winfield, D., n.d. *Panagia tou Arakos, Lagoudera. A Guide* (Nicosia).

Yannopoulos, P.A., 1983. 'Les couches populaires de la société chypriote au VIIe siècle selon les sources locales et contemporaines', *Epetiris tou Kentrou Epistimonikon Ereunon* 12, 79–85.

Zacos, G. and Veglery, A., 1972. *Byzantine Lead Seals I* (Basel).

Chapter 7

LR2: a Container for the Military *annona* on the Danubian Border?[1]

Olga Karagiorgou

Στους γονείς μου, Ευάγγελο και Ελευθερία

Introduction: LR2 Typology, Distribution and Quantification

Scholarly research on amphora studies during the last three decades has emphasised the pivotal importance of distribution maps, quantified data, and the use of scientific methods for determining provenance and content in drawing conclusions about various aspects of the ancient economy. It is evident that all such conclusions are subject to constant revision and refinement, as the number of publications on amphora studies from various sites grows and scientific methodologies are improved.

Bearing these initial remarks in mind, sufficient old and new data are now available to warrant revisiting the available archaeological evidence for a particular late Roman amphora, which, while present across the Mediterranean, seems to have been remarkably popular in the Balkan and Aegean world. This is the LR2 (as defined in excavations at Carthage), one of six Roman amphorae that Riley termed "a standard 'package' of amphora types from diverse origins...common throughout the Roman Mediterranean during the later fifth and sixth centuries."[2] Due to editorial restrictions, this reappraisal of LR2 is restricted here to the Aegean and North Balkans (its wider circulation within the Mediterranean is treated at length in my forthcoming thesis[3]). This choice over the north-east Mediterranean is justified by two main reasons. Firstly, LR2 is an amphora of particular importance for the Aegean and North Balkans, since it occurs here much earlier (already in the fourth century) and in much larger quantities than in the rest of the Mediterranean world.[4] Secondly, important pottery publications from Balkan and Aegean sites that have appeared during the last two decades have significantly enriched the evidence available about the 'history' of this amphora type; it is necessary, therefore, to summarise this new evidence, in order to reassess the profile of this amphora and update our knowledge about its distribution, quantification and provenance. Particular emphasis will be given to quantified amphora assemblages, since they offer a numerical indication of the frequency of LR2 occurrences, and enable us to compare its popularity with similar data relating to the five other amphorae in Riley's 'package'. It is hoped that to a certain extent this process will enhance our "limited and fragmentary" knowledge of one major East Mediterranean amphora type[5] and will lead to some interesting observations regarding economic activity in the north-eastern Mediterranean during Late Antiquity.

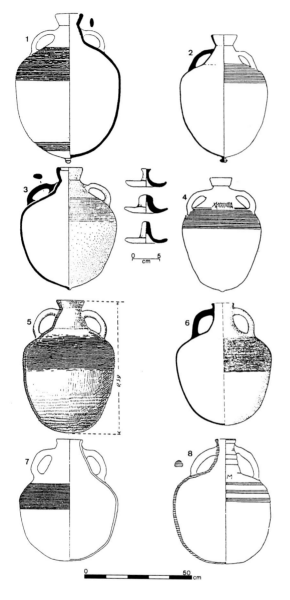

Fig. 7.1: LR2 amphorae.

1. Torone, used for an infant burial (from Papadopoulos, 1989: fig. 11a);
2. Sucidava, fourth century (from Opait, 1984: tafel II.I);
3. Iatrus, amphora and three lids of the first half of the fifth century (from Böttger, 1982: tafel 17, no. 220 and tafel 250, nos. 309–311);
4. Tomis, last quarter of the fifth or beginning of sixth century (from Opait, 1984: tafel II.4);
5. Histria, sixth century (from *Histria Monografie Archeologica Vol. 1*, 1954: 459, fig. 383);
6. Yassi Ada, A.D. 625/626 (from Bass and van Doorninck, 1982: fig. 8–5, no. CA14);
7. Chios, from the northwest fortress tower at Emporio, A.D. 641–673/4 (from Boardman *et al.*, 1989: fig. 36, no. 236);
8. Samos, from a seventh century context in the cisterns near the Efpalinos tunnel (after Hautumm, 1981: abb. 23).

LR2 is a broad-bellied, wheel-made container with a wide shoulder, tapered neck, and conical or cup-shaped mouth (Fig. 7.1). The body is usually globular and the base generally incorporates a small protrusion in the centre (at least in the case of early variants). The maximum diameter of the vessel occurs at the shoulder, usually at three-fifths of the total height. Handles are crudely crafted, flattened, and oval in cross section. They are asymmetrically placed, sloping obliquely from neck to shoulder. The vessel is decorated with a series of parallel, closely-aligned ridges extending across the upper shoulders, which were made with a single-pointed instrument that was slowly raised in a continuous spiral, while the vessel was turned on the wheel.[6] The application of the decoration preceded the handle attachment.

In the existing amphora typologies, scholars have identified sub-types of LR2 (Fig. 7.1).[7] It is not easy in all cases to decide whether these formal variations reflect locally produced variants imitating imported (proto)types,[8] or whether they are expressions of the chronological evolution of the type. Scholars, however, who have worked on well-stratified LR2 samples have traced the chronological evolution of some of the type's formal characteristics between the fourth and seventh centuries and have suggested that a certain transformation occurs around the second half of the sixth century:[9] from a vessel with cup-shaped mouth, thick flaring rim, conical neck, large globular body and rounded base with projecting toe, LR2 turns into a vessel with a somewhat more cylindrical neck, narrower mouth, shorter lip, more elongated body and completely rounded base. In the following discussion, LR2 of both the earlier and the later forms will be included and clear distinctions between them will be drawn only in those cases where this can serve as an important dating criterion.

Modern scholarship rightly stresses that "a type can only be properly defined on the basis of *both* form and fabric",[10] a remark that is increasingly being acted on in pottery publications.[11] However, the study of fabrics is far from simplistic, as secure identification of wares ideally presupposes the existence of an extensive database which enables stratified sherds to be linked scientifically with the petrographic characteristics of quarried clay. Since the study of fabrics is generally relatively undeveloped and neglected in most old and modern published reports, adopting a traditional approach in this paper, which principally emphasises vessel form, has been unavoidable.

A final observation should be made about quantification, arguably one of the most controversial tools used within amphora studies. On the one hand, it has been praised as a necessary supplement to typological studies and distribution maps, allowing individual amphora types to be numerically assessed within a site's excavated amphora assemblage and providing insights into the relative quantities exchanged over long-distances. On the other hand, it has been contemplated with suspicion – and sometimes even dismissed – due to a number of potential problems, particularly concerning the subjectivity of identification and dating,[12] the spatial variability and relative size of the amphora deposits sampled (excavated material represents only a part, and not always the most representative one, of an entire ancient site), and the methodological differentiation used to quantify sherds.[13] These warnings are indeed pertinent, but instead of causing mistrust, or the abandonment of quantification as a primary tool for investigating trade, they should lead to a more rigorous analysis of pottery assemblages as a means of improving the present situation. *Ideally*, quantified data should rely on a refined and widely accepted typological model (where sub-types are based on form and/or fabric variations) and should be accompanied by detailed information about the following four points: the size of the excavated area where the sample originates in relation to the total size of the ancient site; the function of the excavated context (public, domestic, commercial, religious); other contextual data (stratigraphy, coins, fine wares), which can contribute to the secure dating of the stratum from which the amphorae derive; and the method of quantification implemented (analysis by weight, count, estimated vessel-equivalents).

Not all of the amphora studies discussed below adhere to this 'ideal' style of presentation, either because they were products of their time (e.g. quantification is absent in pre-1970s amphora studies), because they reflect the judgment and fieldwork methods of the individual researcher, or simply because information on the four points enumerated above was not available at the time the site report was written. These studies present amphora assemblages from various types of site and contexts and they use a variety of classification and quantification systems. Despite the variance in standards, I believe that the presentation of this evidence together still indicates general trends regarding communication and economic activity.

In order to present the evidence in a clear way and to facilitate conclusions, I have tried to 'homogenise' these studies according to the 'ideal style of presentation' commented on above: the various classification systems used in these studies have been translated into the classification system adopted in this volume of papers, and issues like the function of the excavated area, its date (on coin finds or other historical evidence), the volume of the amphora finds, and the quantification method used are discussed specifically when this information is available. If quantified data are absent, then any information on the popularity of a certain type, albeit of more or less subjective nature, is taken into account (e.g. the personal impression of the excavator(s) about type frequency).

This study attempts to discuss sites within the Balkan peninsula and the Aegean world, where LR2 finds have been recorded, as comprehensively as possible. In order to handle the material in a coherent way, the presentation of the sites follows a specific geographical route. Starting from the capital of the Byzantine Empire, I then turn immediately to the North Balkans following a roughly west-east route (via the Former Yugoslav Republic of Macedonia, Serbia, Bulgaria, Rumania), and subsequently address the Aegean evidence, from the Yassi Ada shipwreck to the south-east, anticlockwise to sites and islands in the eastern, northern and western Aegean respectively.[14]

Distribution and Quantification of LR2 on North Balkan and Aegean Sites

A. Constantinople

At Saraçhane,[15] the only site in the Byzantine capital where pottery from well stratified deposits has been published, Riley's entire amphora 'package' is present. LR1, representing about 15–20% of sixth and seventh century deposits, has precedence over all other types. Despite the fact that LR2 had been manufactured since the fourth century, it appears surprisingly late at Saraçhane (early sixth century deposits) and continues to keep a low profile during the seventh century (only 2–3% of all amphorae).

North Balkans (Fig. 7.2)

LR2 seems to be very popular in the North Balkans (especially in Bulgaria and the Dobroudja region in Rumania), but a lack of final publications on well-stratified and quantified pottery finds for most sites impedes full appreciation of the importance of this type in the area.

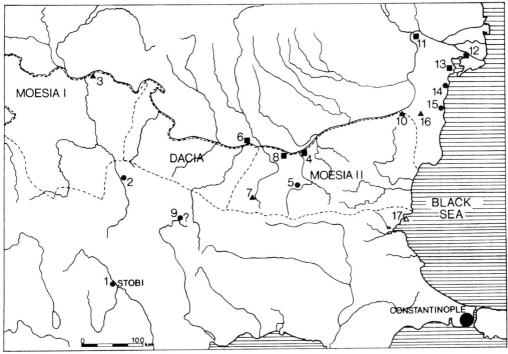

▲MILITARY ●CIVILIAN ■BOTH △SHIPWRECK

FYROM**	Serbia	Bulgaria	Rumania
1. Stobi*	2. Justiniana Prima* 3. Viminacium*	4. Iatrus* 5. Nikopolis* 7. Golemanovo Kale* 8. Novae 9. Pernik 18. Neseber	6. Sucidava 10. Sacidava 11. Dinogetia 12. Independenta* 13. Topraichioi* 14. Histria 15. Tomis 16. Tropaeum Traiani 17. Neseber

* Quantified data available
** Former Yugoslav Republic of Macedonia

Fig. 7.2: Map of archaeological sites in the North Balkans discussed in the text. (Drawing: S. Kingsley).

The pottery finds from Stobi cover the period from the earliest documented occupation of the site in the third century B.C. until its abandonment in the sixth century A.D.[16] All of Riley's amphora 'package' is present, except LR5.[17] LR1 was found in deposits dated between the fourth and the sixth centuries and LR2 in contexts of the early to middle fifth centuries. The nature of the pottery publication from Stobi does not allow conclusions about the relative frequency of individual amphorae types from the site to be drawn; only LR3's rarity is noted specifically.

At Justiniana Prima, some LR2 were found among the transport vessels from the 1978–1983 excavations in the south-west quarter of the Upper City, where a number of buildings of military character (*principia*?) were identified.[18] No quantified data were included in the site publication, but it is clearly stated that "les amphores était particulièrement rares dans le quartier sud-ouest de la Ville Haute: chaque type, sauf le type V/3 (i.e. LR8) n'est représenté que par un petit nombre d'exemplaires".[19] The assemblage does, however, include LR1 and LR2.

Archaeological research at the late antique fort on the site of Svetinja (about 1,200 m east of Viminacium) brought to light a substantial pottery assemblage, which the excavators dated from A.D. 567 to 596.[20] The pottery, retrieved from seven houses built along the rampart, consisted mainly (88%) of sherds belonging to seven amphora types. Only four types from Riley's 'package' were represented: the overwhelming majority of sherds belonged to LR1 (54%) and LR2 (42%), while LR4 and LR8 were poorly represented.

A positive development for future pottery studies on Bulgarian sites is exemplified by the work of Böttger on the pottery from Iatrus, and Falkner on the pottery from Nicopolis ad Istrum. The 1992 publication of pottery from Golemanovo Kale provides a useful source of comparative material, while the anticipated publication of the settlement of Dichin (about 10 km west of Nicopolis ad Istrum), where research was initiated in 1996 under the direction of Dr. A. Poulter, will further complete the regional picture.

Iatrus (near the modern Bulgarian village of Krivina) was founded in the early fourth century as a military station, and acquired the character of a civilian settlement, with more diverse types of structures and ceramic types, during its peak period of occupation (*c.* 370–420). The Hunnic invasion of 422 destroyed the site, and after its recovery at the end of the fifth century the settlement was smaller and simpler. Nevertheless, a basilica was built during the sixth century, before the site was abandoned by the Byzantines soon after A.D. 600. Contexts of the eighth and ninth centuries suggest that the Slavic infiltration was slow and peaceful (typical Slavic ceramics co-existing with provincial Byzantine types), while eleventh century coins and other finds attest to the reappearence of Byzantines in the area.[21] Excavations on the site between 1958 and 1981 covered an area of about 0.6 ha, (equating to 25% of the settlement's total occupied area)[22] and brought to light a variety of amphorae, spanning the period from the fourth to the tenth/eleventh centuries.[23] The late antique amphora types included five of Riley's amphora 'package' (Böttger's typology in brackets): LR1 (type II.1), LR2 (type I.1), LR8 (type III.1), LR3 and LR4 (both listed as 'Typ II Varia'). The tabulated results on the amphora finds[24] indicate that LR1 and LR2 were the most popular amphorae on the site, with LR2 numerically dominant, especially during the first half of the fifth century when the volume of amphora imports reaching the site seems to have peaked. However, both types seem to slowly disappear towards the end of the seventh century, at which date they most probably only represent residual material.[25] LR8, LR3 and LR4 are poorly represented.

The early Byzantine city of Nicopolis ad Istrum was established *c.* A.D. 450 to the south of its Roman forerunner after the latter had been destroyed by fire, probably when sacked by the Huns in 447. The new city was, in turn, abandoned at the end of the sixth or at the beginning of the seventh century, when Byzantine hegemony over the lower Danube was finally lost to the Slavs and Bulgars.[26] The main body of ceramic material, excavated in fourteen separate areas of the city (including fortification areas, towers and churches), covered the general period of occupation from *c.* A.D. 450 to 600, but earlier material was also recorded.[27] Out of a total of approximately 100,000 sherds found in well-stratified levels, an estimated 4,000 belong to amphorae.[28] Falkner, the site pottery specialist, distinguished thirty-two different amphora wares. Amongst these, a long cylindrical-bodied amphora of North African origin (Falkner's ware no. 37: P/W Class 33) was numerically dominant. LR2 (Falkner's ware no. 94) was the best represented type of Riley's amphora 'package'. Other well-known Roman amphora types from the site include Benghazi Type MRA 7 of probable Aegean origin (Falkner's ware no. 96), LR1 (Falkner's ware no. 164) and Palestinian types (Falkner's ware no. 76, which includes both barrel-shaped and elongated LR4 variants). The majority of the remaining material mainly comprises unfamiliar wares and forms (but ware no. 19 is assigned a Tunisian provenance, and ware no. 167 is probably related to LR3).[29] A series of graphs in the site publication show that in the period spanning A.D. 350–450 MRA 7 was dominant, followed by P/W Class 33 and then LR2 (30%, 28% and 18%, respectively); between A.D. 450 and 600, LR2 decreases in volume (14% of all amphorae), while the other two main imports increase, to each comprise 34% of the total amphora assemblage.[30] Data for ware no. 164 (LR1) are not available in a graph format, but according to Appendix 2 in the site publication, where pottery from twenty dated contexts is presented by type and ware, LR1 does seem to co-exist with LR2 at Nicopolis from A.D. 350–600 (although it is far less common than the other three amphora types).[31]

Systematic excavations from 1936 to 1964 at the site of Sucidava (*Sykibida* in Procopius), situated 3 km west of modern Corabia on the north bank of the Danube, have brought to light the remains of a fortified civilian settlement of 25 ha and, at a distance of only 100 m to the south-east, the remains of a separate citadel measuring about 2 ha.[32] The civilian settlement evolved on the site of a Roman garrison at the end of the second century, or the beginning of the third century A.D., while the citadel was built by Constantine the Great (324–337); a stone bridge connecting the citadel with Palatiolon (ancient Oescus), on the other side of the Danube, was constructed simultaneously. The coins found at Sucidava show an uninterrupted series from Aurelian (270–275) to Theodosios II (408–450). In the mid-fifth century (A.D. 442 or 447), the site suffered from attacks by the Huns, but was again restored, probably under Justin I (518–527) or by Justinian I (527–565). On the basis of the numismatic profile, the Byzantine garrison seems to have departed from Sucidava around A.D. 600. Scorpan briefly refers to the amphorae found at Sucidava in his monograph on the site, where the illustrated examples include well-known types (LR1–4).[33] Although no quantified data are available, Scorpan classified the amphorae into two groups. The first contains the slender LR8, and the second amphorae with 'ribbed' bodies (i.e. LR1, LR5 and a peculiar amphora, which looks like a squat offspring of LR1). Scorpan notes that the amphorae from the second group are more numerous at Sucidava. Taking into account that LR5 are generally rare in the Danubian provinces, Scorpan's observation must, most probably, refer to LR1. Scorpan also observed that the amphorae with *dipinti* (and we may assume from the context of his manuscript that these are LR1 and LR8) are imports and, even more noteworthy, that their distribution is very limited and does not extend beyond the walls of the citadel (i.e. the quarters of the military garrison). By contrast, neither the civilian settlement, nor its surrounding area have yielded any amphorae bearing *dipinti*.

A significant number of late antique amphorae were discovered during the 1936–1937 excavations at the fortified hill-top site of Golemanovo Kale, in the area of Sadovec in North Bulgaria. By the time of its publication, two-thirds of the original material had been lost.[34] Among the preserved amphora from the site LR1, LR2 and LR8 are best represented (six, seven and twenty-one diagnostic fragments respectively are included in the published catalogue).[35] The only *terminus ante quem* for these amphorae is supplied by the coin evidence, which indicates that occupation at Golemanovo Kale came to an end in, or soon after, A.D. 584.[36]

LR2 have been also recorded at Novae (modern Svishtov, 50 km north of Nicopolis ad Istrum),[37] and at Pernik;[38] no quantified data, however, are yet available for either site.

Although LR2 are particularly frequent on Rumanian sites, especially in the Dobroudja region,[39] our understanding of amphora consumption patterns in the area is impeded by the near-absence of quantified data and evidence about local kilns and their output.[40] A systematic study of late antique kilns in Dobrudja, as well as of quantified pottery assemblages like the results that have emerged in the 1990s at sites such as Tropaichoi and Independenta, are needed before late antique exchange patterns in this region can be assessed more formally.

Sacidava (*Skedevà* in Procopius, modern Musait in south-west Dobrudja) was a Roman fort erected at the end of the third century on the south bank of the Danube, between Dorostolon and Axiopolis. Excavations on the hill above Musait have revealed a modest-sized fortress reinforced with rectangular towers. Coins from between the reigns of Aurelian (A.D. 270–275) and Theodosius II (408–450) are numerous (over 150 examples), whereas none from the second half of the fifth century have been recorded, and only ten from between the reigns of Anastasius I (491–518) and Maurice (582–602).[41] In the 1969–1971 excavation report Scorpan suggested that life on the site continued, albeit in a limited form, during the first half of the seventh century and that Sacidava was gradually abandoned in the course of the second half of the seventh century. The same report includes a brief list and a few illustrations of typical pottery finds from the site, including an LR1 and an LR2, both dated by Scorpan to the sixth century.[42] Scorpan dealt with the pottery from Sacidava in greater depth in a subsequent article in 1975,[43] where he classified the site's amphorae into thirteen types, compared them (when possible) with similar finds from other sites in the Dobroudja area, and commented on how common each type was in each century. Unfortunately, Scorpan's quantitative methods leave much to be desired. However, in view of the absence of superior information, we must attach some value to his firm observation that LR1 examples are well-represented and that LR2 are most numerous among the thirteen amphora types excavated.

Dinogetia (modern Garvan), a city and stronghold along the *limes* in Scythia Minor, is located on a small island in the Danube. Excavation results have identified two main phases of occupation: a late antique one (fourth-to-sixth century), when a rectangular fortress was built on a rocky outcrop (excavations have revealed a main street 4–5 m wide and official buildings such as the *praetorium,* baths, and a basilica), and a middle Byzantine one (tenth-to-twelfth centuries).[44] The late antique fortress was partly burnt down, probably during the Cotrigur attack of 559,[45] and was deserted *c.* 600. Unfortunately, no study of the site's late antique pottery has been published, and our only information about amphorae occurs in the 1966 report, which summarises the excavation results from the east part of the north-west sector of the fortress.[46] The eleven excavated rooms served as storehouses for cereals and other provisions, as the numerous *pithoi,* amphora fragments and millstones found indicate. No quantitative data are available, but one is left with the impression that LR2 sherds were common: one fragmentary example was found between Towers 9 and 10 next to fragments of a millstone, and more LR2 sherds came from Room IIIA, Room VII (which also housed four large *pithoi,* and two millstones – one unfinished), Room IX (sherds from three vessels), and from the road running past the *praetorium* in front of room VII. Apart from LR2, LR3 seems to be the only other late antique amphora type from Riley's 'package' present at Dinogetia. The year A.D. 559, when almost the entire city was reduced to ashes, provides a *terminus ante quem* for these finds.

The ancient name of a site which lies 2.5 km east of the modern village of Independenta (Murighiol) in Dobrudja, on the south bank of the lower Danube, is not known, but both Halmyris (*It. Ant.* 226.4) and Gratiana (Proc. *De aed.* 4.11) have been suggested.[47] Of the three phases identified during the 1981–83 and 1985–6 excavations (dating from the fourth century B.C. to the third decade of the seventh century A.D.), amphorae proved most numerous and varied in the late antique phase when the site was occupied by a fort (48% of all pottery and about thirty-three types). Well-known amphorae include types LR1–LR4. Amongst these, LR1 and LR2 were consistently most highly represented.[48] LR2 appears on the site for the first time in the first half of the fourth century, which is slightly earlier than when LR1 appears in smaller quantities in the second half of the fourth century. From then, until the beginning of the seventh century, the two types are constantly present, with LR2 generally numerically dominant.

The 1979–1983 excavations at the late Roman fort at Topraichoi (the first one of its type to be systematically investigated in Dobrudja), uncovered an abundance of archaeological material, including about 2,000 coins, which enabled a firm site chronology to be established.[49] The fort was built between A.D 369 and 372, as part of a more extensive effort to strengthen the frontiers along the Danube and Rhine. Archaeological evidence has shown that during the first fifty years of its existence (roughly from 370–420) the *burgus* of Topraichioi was predominantly military in nature: the small garrison apparently fulfilled the task of guarding and supervising a natural cross-roads for terrestrial communication (the pottery from this phase was un-impressive, both in quantity and diversity, although it is striking that weaponry was numerous). During the next fifty years or so, roughly from 420 until its destruction at some point in the second half of the fifth century, it seems that the *burgus* no longer sheltered a garrison and that occupation acquired an exclusively civilian nature. The majority of the pottery and tools from the site (millstones, fishing-net weights, reaping hooks, scythes), as well as a large storehouse, relate to this second phase, when weaponry was less numerous. Based on the above evidence, the site's excavators suggested that from about A.D. 420 onwards, as it gradually lost its exclusive military character, the *burgus* served as a storehouse for the local military *annona*, and its purpose was to guarantee the availability of supplies for troops. Although I am not aware of a specific publication on amphora finds from Tropaichioi, a useful impression of the excavated quantities of LR1 and LR2 (which seem to be the predominant types), is provided by a histogram of comparative assemblages published by Opait in his article on the pottery from Independenta.[50] This shows both types co-existing at Topraichioi from the second half of the fourth century up to the end of the *burgus'* life. During the second half of the fourth century LR2 significantly outnumbers LR1 (about 17.5% compared to 4.5%), but during the next fifty years LR1 levels increase and take a slight precedence over LR2 (17% and 15% respectively).

Histria was a Greek colony on Lake Sinoe, north of Constanza. The city prospered between the fourth and sixth centuries, when its ramparts were rebuilt three times (some bricks in the fortifications bear stamps of Anastasius I). Excavations have uncovered a commercial district containing various workshops, private dwellings, and several public buildings, including a sixth century basilica. The settlement's prosperity had come to an end by *c.* 580, as the very humble houses from the latest phase indicate. The numerous coins of Maurice (582–602) on the site can be related to this emperor's attempt to protect the area against Avar attacks; the number of Byzantine coins decreases thereafter and cease to be deposited after the reign of Heraclius.[51] I am unaware of any publication devoted to the systematic presentation and analysis of pottery from Histria. For the purposes of this paper, we can mention the illustrated examples of LR1, LR2 and LR4 (one example each) in the 1961 report of the excavation of the sixth-to-seventh century layers in two rooms of unidentified function in the central sector of the city (Building D6: Rooms C and D),[52] and two probable fragments of LR2 mouths (one dated to the fifth century) illustrated amongst the finds from the excavation of the two Roman baths.[53] The catalogue of amphora finds from the latter consists of a simple list of diagnostic fragments, which are neither identified, nor quantified. Thus, no safe conclusions can be drawn about the types and frequency of late antique amphorae from this excavation.

A large group of LR2 (the second largest concentration of these amphorae after the Yassi Ada shipwreck discussed below) were discovered at Tomis, modern Constanza, on the west coast of the Black Sea. During Late Antiquity Tomis was the civil and ecclesiastical metropolis of the province of Scythia Minor and two large fifth-to-sixth century basilicas have been excavated in the city. Justinian I rebuilt the fortifications and the city withstood a siege by the Avars in 599. Thereafter, its history is obscure for some centuries, but in the tenth century Konstantia is referred to as a station on the shipping route of Rus' to Constantinople.[54] The LR2 were discovered during the 1965–1968 excavation of the substructure of the so-called 'Edifice with Floor Mosaics', situated to the west of the modern port. The substructure consists of eleven vaulted rooms. Room nos. 3 and 4 contained iron anchors, lamps, weights, and amphorae (mainly about 120 LR2), which according to the results of chemical analysis were filled with Somalian olibanum, turpentine, Arabian myrrh, pine-resins, mastic from Chios, and pigments. Additional recycled LR4 amphorae contained iron nails.[55] These finds, today stored at the Constanza museum, indicate that the vaulted rooms served as a chandlery. All the LR2 found in the 'Edifice' bear *graffiti*, which combine the Latin numbers X and I, and *dipinti* in Greek letters. Radulescu has suggested that the former numbers refer to the conventional capacity of the vessel, while the Greek ones reflect the real quantity within each vessel. The *dipinti* are interpreted as control marks placed on the vessels when they passed through customs. The diversity and peculiarity of the LR2 contents at Tomis, as well as the fact that they bear more than one Greek *dipinti*, makes it almost certain that these amphorae had been reused.

The last site within the North Balkans where LR2 have also been recorded is Tropaeum Traiani (modern Cetatea). At least one LR2 (together with an LR1) is illustrated in the excavation report, but is not identified as such in the pottery catalogue.[56] No other well-known amphora types are included in this publication, and no quantified data are presented.

C. The Aegean (Fig. 7.3)
The LR2 seems to be equally important in the Aegean Sea region, and the quantified pottery data that have started to appear within the archaeological literature during the last twenty or so years enables the importance of this amphora type in the area to be re-evaluated.

The largest concentration of LR2 so far recorded comes from the Yassi Ada shipwreck, located near one of several islands bordering the Chuka Channel in the south-eastern Aegean Sea. After the 1961–1964 excavation and the additional 1980 investigation, the total number of transport vessels found on the shipwreck amounted to 822, of which 103 (16%) were LR1 and 719 (85%) LR2.[57] The importance of the Yassi Ada shipwreck is that it constitutes a 'closed' archaeological site, which can be dated accurately thanks to the coins on-board. The dates and the mint distribution of these coins (fifty-four copper and sixteen gold ones) provide a *terminus post quem* of the sixteenth year of Heraclius' reign in 625/6 for the date when the ship sunk, and indicate that its main area of operation was the North Aegean.[58]

The detailed study of a much larger sample of LR2 from the Yassi Ada shipwreck in 1989 (460 vessels in total) led to significant new conclusions. First of all, it was observed that 80% of them shared very similar fabrics and thus formed a relatively homogenous group, which, on the basis of variations in dimensions and decoration, could be divided into four major sub-types (I-IV).[59] The 130 vessels of sub-type I, in particular, were remarkably uniform in form and dimension,[60] indicating a certain standardisation that proved that the previously stated "lack of standard sizes among the amphorae of the Yassi Ada", had been distorted by a lumping together of different amphora forms. The remaining 20% of the LR2 belonged to about forty secondary sub-types, mostly only represented by one example. The amphorae in roughly half of these secondary sub-types and those of the four major sub-types (I-IV), all had very similar fabrics, which was seen as an indication of derivation from a single primary production region. At the same time, however, about twelve to fourteen distinctly different fabrics were observed amongst the remaining amphorae from the secondary sub-types, and this was regarded as evidence that the LR2 under transport were manufactured in a number of other production centres as well.

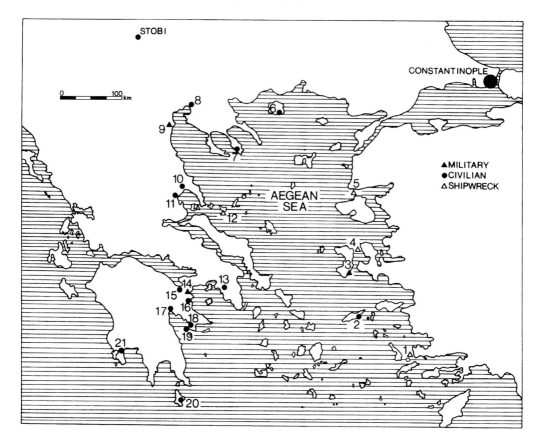

East Aegean Coast	North Aegean Coast	West Aegean Coast
1. Yassi Ada*	6. Thasos*	9. Louloudies*
2. Samos*	7. Torone*	10. Demetrias
3. Chios-Emporio	8. Thessalonica	11. Thebes
4. Prasso Islets		12. Skopelos
5. Methymna		13. Athens
		14. Isthmia
		15. Corinth
		16. Kenchreai
		17. Argos*
		18. Halieis
		19. Chinitsa Island
		20. Kythera
		21. Nichoria

* Quantified data available

Fig. 7.3: Map of archaeological sites in the Aegean discussed in the text. (Drawing: S. Kingsley).

Should we accept the theory that the varied collection of secondary LR2 sub-types originated from kilns of limited output? Not quite. We believe, on the basis of morphological characteristics, that some of the secondary sub-types are much earlier in date than those of the four major sub-types;[61] it is unfortunate that none of the illustrated examples preserve their bases, as the presence or absence of a basal knob would help date these amphorae more firmly to before, or after, the middle of the sixth century. On the other hand, all of the illustrated amphorae of the four major subtypes (thought to be of a later date and coming from a single production centre) do indeed have rounded bases. Thus, it may also be possible that the earlier LR2 examples on the Yassi Ada ship were simply the remnant of former cargoes, most of which had broken or been dispersed during their lengthy period of reuse. As a result, their presence on the Yassi Ada ship does not necessarily imply that numerous LR2 workshops were in operation at the time when the ship sunk.

Many LR2 amphorae were found during the 1980s excavations of the German Archaeological Institute in the ancient city of Samos. They were recovered from the tunnel of Efpalinos, from two cisterns situated about 30 m east of the south entrance of the tunnel, and from the ecclesiastical complex that was built during the second half of the sixth century over the ruins of the Roman baths. More LR2 vessels were found in a pit deposit situated to the east of the ecclesiastical complex, which was excavated in 1982 by the Greek Archaeological Service.

The Efpalinos tunnel, a construction of the second half of the sixth century B.C., was used twice as a refuge by the inhabitants of Samos: once during the Persian presence in the Aegean in the 620s, and then in the third quarter of the seventh century, when the island may have been briefly occupied by the Arabs. Use of the tunnel as a hiding-place during those years is confirmed by coin finds, mainly issues of Heraclius and Constans II, and by the discovery of an immense quantity of pottery (5–6 tons of amphorae, *stamnoi*, *pithoi*, etc.) apparently used by the frightened people of Samos for the storage of essential foodstuffs such as oil, wheat, and salt. Hautumm studied the amphorae from the Efpalinos tunnel and published a lengthy study of five of the types present.[62] These consisted of (with Hautumm's identification of provenance and content in brackets): LR1 (an Egyptian wheat amphora), LR2 (an olive oil amphora), LR3 (an Egyptian vessel for liquids), P/W Class 35 (cylindrical wheat amphorae from North Africa), and LR8 (the *spatheion*). In his study, Hautumm attached particular emphasis to the form, origin, content, distribution and date range of each type. Little attention was paid to quantification, but in certain instances some useful comments were included.[63] It is clearly stated, for example, that LR2 are "am häufigsten vertreten" and that about 430 examples could be reconstructed, although the original total number within both the Efpalinos tunnel and the cisterns must have comprised at least 500–600 vessels. Quantities of P/W Class 35 amphorae in the Efpalinos tunnel were estimated at a couple of hundred, while only three to four dozen LR8 were apparently present. No hint is offered about the frequency of LR1 and LR3.

After the Roman baths collapsed during an earthquake in the mid-fourth century, an ecclesiastical complex was constructed over them during the reign of Justin II (565–578).[64] The excavations indicate that this was comprehensively destroyed in the first quarter of the seventh century, then rebuilt shortly afterwards, before suffering final destruction during the Arab invasion in the third quarter of the seventh century. The complex consisted of two distinct areas. To the north, occupying what was originally the north portico of the Roman baths, was a three-aisled basilica with an ambo, atrium and baptistery. To the south was a domestic complex comprising a treading area, alongside a lever-and-weights press and collecting basins to the west; warehouses used to store agricultural produce were located to the east. One of these storerooms contained twenty LR2, each of 30 lt capacity (and as at Iatrus, a millstone was found next to this concentration). In the adjoining room were 120 LR1 amphorae, each of 8 lt capacity.

Amongst other finds, the pit deposit to the east of the ecclesiastical complex contained an abundance of pottery (transport vessels, kitchen- and table-wares). Amphorae comprised the most numerous group and included two LR1, six LR2, ten of the so-called 'Samos Cistern Type' vessel, and two LR8.[65] The latest dated coin amongst the fifteen bronze coins found in the pit is a half-*follis* of the Emperor Heraclius from A.D. 615–629. The coin evidence, and the proximity of the pit to the ecclesiastical complex, suggested that the artifacts were thrown into it when the ecclesiastical complex was cleared and repaired after its destruction in the first quarter of the seventh century.

Another interesting amphora assemblage was uncovered during the 1952–1955 British excavation of the fortress on the acropolis at Emporio, on Chios. The fortress was constructed during the reign of Heraclius (A.D. 640–641), or more likely under Constans II (641–668), in response to the Arab threat in the Aegean. By the end of the third quarter of the seventh century (most probably before 673/4), however, the Arabs had managed to destroy it.[66] Quantified data on the fort's amphorae are not available, but the excavators state specifically that LR2 was "the commonest type from the fortress floor". Four examples are illustrated in the site report; other well-known types illustrated include P/W Class 35 (two examples), LR1, LR4 and LR5 (one example each). An isolated and fragmentary LR2, probably belonging to the earlier variant (as indicated by the mouth profile) has been found in the sea near the Prasso islets to the north-east of Chios.[67]

The pottery assemblage from Thasos published in 1992 includes material excavated from the Double Basilica at Aliki (between 1969 and 1977), a villa (1972), as well as material uncovered during the old École Française d'Athènes excavations mainly from the Agora area. The quantified amphora statistics clearly shows that LR1 has a distinct precedence over all other types (56%). LR2 comprises 27% of the assemblage, followed by LR3, and Palestinian imports (10% and 7%).[68]

Torone is situated on the west coast of the Sithonia peninsula in Chalkidike and is one of the few all-weather anchorages along the entire Thracian coastline. Excavations conducted there since 1975 have concentrated on the Isthmus and Lower City, and a late antique cemetery has been investigated on Terrace IV between Promontories 1 and 2.[69] Coins of Constantine I indicate that the latter was first used in the first half of the fourth century. Some burials, almost exclusively of infants, had been placed in amphorae, a fact that proved instrumental in establishing an on-site typology. The first published pottery report illustrates the seven types of amphorae – all imported – present at Torone.[70] Quantified data, however, are only available for material from the

Isthmus and Lower City[71] (the cemetery will be discussed in a forthcoming volume). The range of amphora types currently identified include LR1–LR4, and P/W Class 34, of which LR2 has an overall precedence (53% compared to LR1 37%, LR3 6%, LR4 4% and P/W Class 34 less than 1%). The morphological characteristics of the two illustrated LR2 examples suggest a date preceding the mid-sixth century.

It is most frustrating that the amphora-based study of economic trends in the late antique North Aegean is limited to Thasos and Torone. The obvious void created by the absence of comparable information from Thessalonica, the most important regional port city and the second most important city in the Empire from the seventh century onwards, is hard to ignore. Amphora sherds have been recorded sporadically during rescue excavations,[72] but an extensive study of all material from the city is urgently needed to further illuminate the crucial role that Thessalonica undoubtedly played in the late antique Balkan economy.

LR2 amphorae were relatively abundant within the pottery assemblage retrieved during the 1995 field survey of an area of about 17 ha at the site of Louloudies, situated 10 km north-east of Katerini and 3 km north of the village of Korinos in Pieria. Rescue excavations have uncovered a small sixth century fortress (*quadriburgium*) enclosing a Christian basilica, a house (*megaron*), and ancillary structures, while the 1995 geophysical survey identified another sixth century fort about 160 m to the south.[73] A total of 76 kg of pottery was collected during field-walking. Four of Riley's amphora 'package' were present within the survey assemblage, which was dominated by LR1 and LR2 vessels in almost equal percentages.[74] Without complementary excavation, the validity of this information may be questionable.

LR2 seem to have been highly popular in the two Thessalian port cities of Demetrias and Thebes. Rim fragments were retrieved during the excavation of the atrium in the Basilica of Damokratia at the former city.[75] None of the amphorae have been classified or quantified, although associated coins date the deposit to the second half of the fourth century. Two well-preserved LR2 vessels are illustrated in the 1976 report on rescue excavations at the late antique city of Thessalian Thebes (modern Nea Anchialos),[76] and A. Ntina, the current excavations' supervisor, has kindly informed me that this type is very common. The examples published in 1976 came from an unidentified late antique building complex situated very close to the city Cathedral (Basilica C), which, based on the coin evidence, seems to have been abandoned towards the end of the sixth century.

The only other LR2 amphora from Thessaly, as far as I am aware, is an unpublished example which today stands in isolation in the yard of the Episkopi church on the island of Skopelos.[77] The shell encrusted surface of the vessel indicates that it was once part of a ship's cargo, which must have sunk nearby. Indeed, the maritime sea-lane leading through the Sporades islands (south of Skiathos and Skopelos, and then through the pass between Alonnesos and Peristera) was well-used by sea-craft travelling between the eastern coast of Thessaly and either Constantinople or the western coast of Asia Minor, as is confirmed by the numerous shipwrecks in the area.[78]

In Athens, LR2 (together with LR3, LR5, and P/W Class 47) have been recorded in the Agora,[79] but the nature of their publication prevents conclusions being drawn about relative quantities. An LR2 amphora is illustrated in the report of the 1957–1958

University of Chicago excavations at Isthmia.[80] This was one of several transport and storage vessels which were reconstructed from the prodigious quantities of coarse pottery found in Tower 7 of the Justinianic fortress. A well-preserved group of unpublished LR2 (probably from the site's excavations) are stored in the museum of Isthmia.[81]

Corinth, the late antique capital of the province of Achaia, is situated on the isthmus of Corinth in the north-east Peloponnese in a location of strategic and commercial importance. The city undoubtedly enjoyed a leading role in the economy of the Aegean world, due to the volume of trade that took place within its two harbours: Lechaion on the gulf of Corinth, and Kenchreai on the Saronic gulf. Without a synthesis of the amphorae uncovered during the systematic and extensive excavations of the city, its cosmopolitan and enterprising character must remain undefined. We can simply refer to a couple of LR2 vessels recorded by the Americal School of Classical Studies at Athens in the area south-west of the forum and east of the city's theatre,[82] and note the absence of the type in the publication of the Roman pottery excavated between 1961–1975 from the Sanctuary of Demetre and Kore on the slopes of the Acrocorinth.[83] This absence, however, is explicable by the fact that the pottery does not post-date the early fourth century. LR2 finds were also recovered recently during the rescue excavation of a late Roman bath south-west of the Roman Forum, in the Panayia Field.[84] The bath was built at the end of the fifth century, or during the first half of the sixth century, and seems to have been abandoned by the end of the sixth or early seventh century. The publication of this site is exemplary inasmuch as a detailed description and quantification of stratified pottery is provided. The amphora sample, albeit small, includes four well-known late antique types: LR1 (ten fragments), LR2 (twenty-seven sherds), LR4 (twenty-four fragments), and LR5 (three sherds).

Material relevant to our discussion was also found during the 1963–66 and 1968 excavations of Kenchreai, the eastern port of Corinth. The objective of this project was to investigate the city's late harbour, which was developed after the re-founding of Corinth in 44/3 B.C. in a cove to the east of the original harbour mouth. This anchorage was artificially developed by the construction of moles, warehouses, a stoa, and other storage and shop facilities, and by the redevelopment of the sanctuary of Aphrodite and the construction of a sanctuary of Isis. All these facilities continued to be adapted and used throughout the Roman period and into the fourth century. A rapid decline occurred soon after, except in the sanctuary of Isis which was succeeded by a church used into the sixth century. Adamsheck, who published Kenchreai's pottery,[85] observed that it primarily reflects the harbour area's Roman occupation and is a problematic sample because most of the site's strata had been greatly disturbed; (only a few deposits, like the destruction debris in the Temple of Isis, formed during the earthquake of A.D. 375, showed coherence). Thus, the Kenchreai pottery report can only be used as a broad index of representative, but mainly poorly dated, amphora types. Well-known types present included LR1, LR2 and P/W Class 47. An almost intact LR2 example with a tall, conical neck, thick and outwardly-flaring rim, and a basal knob was recovered from the destruction debris of the Isis sanctuary and thus pre-dates A.D. 375.[86]

Abadie has made interesting observations on amphora types and quantities at Argos in her "esquisse d'un travail qui n'est pas terminé et qui est donc susceptible d'être affiné par la suite", where she studied amphora material from about thirty trenches.[87] All of Riley's 'package' is present at Argos (LR1–LR5 and LR8). LR2 first appears cautiously in the fifth century, but dominates in the following century, when it accounts for 28% of all amphorae, as compared to 21% for LR1 (the second most popular amphora type at sixth century Argos). None of the remaining types from Riley's 'package' exceeds 10% in the sixth century.

A remarkable concentration of LR2 fragments was discovered at ancient Halieis (opposite the modern village of Porto Cheli in southern Argolis), at the mouth of the Argolic gulf. Excavations conducted in the 1960s and 1970s revealed extensive architectural remains of the Classical and Early Hellenistic city (including at least five, and perhaps eight, olive oil press installations in fourth century B.C. houses), which was probably abandoned in the early third century B.C.[88] During Late Antiquity the central area of the Classical town was reoccupied, and the settlement's prosperity peaked during the second half of the sixth century. The name of this new settlement is unknown from historical sources. Other than a bath and about twenty graves scattered around the site's nucleus (dug inside rooms of Classical houses), no other architecture has been uncovered.[89]

The settlement is characterised by a striking abundance of pottery, especially amphorae. All vessels, except one probable late Roman North African P/W Class 35 amphora – used for a child's burial – belonged to the LR2 type (twelve out of the thirteen fragments published by Rudolf).[90] Both principal forms of this amphora type were attested, although the later form with a plain or short base was more common. No *dipinti* or other inscriptions were recorded. Three amphora stands were recovered, used either during the production process or perhaps when the vessels were filled before transport. The large quantity of material dumped around the site, and the discovery of a large heap of what appears to be refined clay near a furnace, indicate that a main occupation of the inhabitants of late antique Halieis was pottery production, with a certain specialisation of amphorae, apparently of LR2 type.

The area surrounding Halieis is rich in clay, which would have been suitable as raw material, and two late antique kilns were briefly reported from the vicinity by the Argolid Exploration Project in 1979 (Site B19) opposite Kounoupi island, between Ermioni and Porto Cheli.[91] In 1985, the Stanford Southern Argolid Survey reported wasters and at least one pottery kiln from the same site and identified the sherds produced there as belonging to LR2 amphorae.[92] The discovery of an unpublished shipwreck containing LR2 at a depth of 4–7 m in the vicinity of Porto Cheli (Cheliou port) furnishes complementary evidence that this local product was linked into wider inter-regional exchange.[93] Finally, three fragments of LR2 were found with early seventh century coins on the island of Chinitsa, located about 1 km opposite Porto Cheli. Optical emission spectroscopy conducted by the Fitch Laboratory confirmed that they most probably originated from the Halieis kilns.[94]

Finally, in the east of the Peloponnese, isolated examples of LR2 have been reported on the island of Kythera[95] and on the site of Nichoria in Messenia (south-west Peloponnese).[96]

Conclusions

A. LR2 Frequency and Content

One key observation requires emphasis following the present overview of the amphora evidence presented from the Balkan and Aegean sites: LR2, which "is widespread throughout the Mediterranean [but] does not appear to have been the predominant amphora on any site so far published",[97] has now been identified as the predominant transport vessel for the first time on a number of sites, which, apart from the much discussed Yassi Ada shipwreck, include Iatrus, Independenta, Sacidava, Samos, Chios, Torone, Argos, and Halieis. The same is probably also true for Dinogetia, Topraichioi and perhaps Nea Anchialos. Alongside these sites, LR2 also follows closely behind LR1 numerically at Viminacium and Louloudies. Both types are closely related on most sites (Iatrus, Independenta, Sacidava, the Yassi Ada shipwreck, Torone, Samos and Argos). The abundance of LR2, and relative dominance of LR1 and LR2 in similar percentages on most Balkan and Aegean sites, seems to reflect agricultural special-isation and a distinct market orientation.

Both wine and olive oil have been suggested as the main products transported in both vessels, without definitively linking either type to one specific product (but see Decker, Chapter 4). Hautumm has drawn attention to the greasy interior surface of numerous LR2 jars found near the Efpalinos tunnel on Samos, which he interpreted as the residue of the olive oil they originally carried.[98] A strong piece of evidence in favour of olive oil as the prime content of LR2 is provided by the *dipinti* written on a group of eight published amphorae from North Balkan sites (two from Sucidava, two from Novae and four from Histria). These amphorae have been broadly dated, on paleographic grounds, to the sixth century and all *dipinti* on them contain the word *elaiou* (olive oil) or *glykelaiou* (sweet olive oil).[99] At the ecclesiastical complex at Samos, however, LR1 and LR2 were found in an area associated with both the production of wine and olive oil, which may suggest that these types were used for transporting both commodities (although the presence of the LR1 in a room directly connected to the wine press may be significant). Finally, inscriptions referring to the identity or quality of their contents were recorded on a number of LR2 from the Yassi Ada wreck.[100] Five amphorae bear the *graffito* ELE, which may be an abbreviation for *elaiai* (olives) or *elaion* (olive oil), and three other bear the *graffito* GLY, which is possibly an abbreviation for *glykys* (sweet [wine]). It is noteworthy that two amphorae with the *graffito* ELE did indeed contain eroded olive stones; regrettably, no organic contents were preserved in the amphorae inscribed with the *graffito* GLY. The hypothesis that wine and olives, or olive oil, were carried within the Yassi Ada LR2 cargo was further supported by the chemical analysis of the content of some sealed amphorae: a total of 1,380 grape seeds was found in sixty-nine vessels, some clearly pitched, while eroded olive stones were found in thirty-one examples, some also pitched. If nothing else, this evidence demonstrates that the clear-cut assumption that unlined amphorae carried olive oil, while pitch-lined ones carried wine, does not always reflect reality.[101] Crucially though, the relevance of this set of data is questionable, because the cargo amphorae had evidently been re-used and filled with various produce several times before the fateful voyage.

Hautumm's argument, which in my view strongly favours olive oil or olives as the primary content of LR2, emphasises that while this amphora type is very common in the olive oil producing Aegean area and turns up in areas with limited or no olive cultivation (North Balkans, British Isles), it is uncommon in other olive oil producing areas of the Empire (Syria, North Africa, Spain), where the import of Aegean olive oil would have been superfluous.[102] Indeed, the LR2 kilns identified in the vicinity of Halieis in the north-east Peloponnese occur in an area with a long tradition in olive cultivation throughout the centuries (the late antique evidence, in particular, includes numerous *mortaria* and *orbes* from *trapeta*).[103] One factor underlying such a concerted investment in olive cultivation and oil processing was the rich soils on the hillsides and valleys surrounding Halieis, which are ideal for olives but less suited to wheat cultivation.[104] Textual evidence, which clearly underlines the role of the Peloponnese as one of the main (but certainly not the only) olive oil producers in the Aegean, is of slightly later date: it is found in the works of Constantine Porphyrogenitus (who usually repeats information from earlier centuries), in tenth century hagiographical texts, and in the memoirs of an English traveller at the end of the twelfth or the early thirteenth century, who stated that no place in the whole world produced as much olive oil as the southern Peloponnese.[105]

If we now turn to the areas which received LR2, for example Danubian sites, which are of special interest to this paper, we will observe that olive oil must have been a greatly demanded foodstuff, since it could not be supplied by local production. In the period between *c.* A.D. 250 and 450, Nicopolis ad Istrum seems to have been self-sufficient in wheat, barley, rye, pulses and partly in grapes.[106] At Iatrus, two *horrea*, dated to the second half of the fourth century, and a large processing installation containing at least twelve millstones, dated to the first half of the fifth century,[107] seem to imply that Iatrus was a major centre for the collection, processing and storage of grain during this period. Comparable evidence is known from the fourth century *quadriburgium* at Moesia, built at a strategic point where the river Porechka joins the Danube and located alongside granaries which were too large to have only supplied this small garrison.[108] Since both Iatrus and the *quadriburgium* on Porechka were situated at river mouths, we may assume that they both served as storage centres redistributing agricultural produce by ship to other garrisons along the Danubian *limes*. The development of local specialisation in agricultural goods has been linked with the personal initiative of the emperor Valens to improve the supply system to forts along the frontier lines; this phenomenon can be perceived in the *Codex Theodosianus*, which includes an edict of Valens relating specifically to the supply of wheat to the frontier forts (*C. Th.* VII.4.15).[109] Wine supplies may also have been partially procured from local sources in the Danube: its production, albeit of low quality, is proven by the discovery of calcinated grape pips and scales from Iatrus[110] and Nicopolis ad Istrum, where vineyards were most probably introduced when the city was founded *c.* A.D. 110.[111] Further to the south, however, the one grape pip encountered at Stobi during botanical analysis is hardly indicative of widespread local viticulture (modern grape cultivation in the Vardar valley has only proved possible by using sophisticated irrigation). Finally, climatic factors, particularly cold winters, prevented olive cultivation and forced oil to be imported. Today, the olive-growing areas are located much further south in Macedonia and on the Adriatic.

Fig. 7.4: Nea Achialos (Thessalian Thebes). LR2 from a sixth century context (with lid) (from Iatridou, 1976: pl. 139c).

Archaeological evidence, in the form of amphora finds of Hellenistic, Roman and late Roman date, indicate that even Stobi relied on trade with the West and the Aegean in order to provide its olive oil and (to a lesser extent) wine consumption needs.[112]

Finally, I believe that some morphological attributes of the LR2 amphora support the theory that olive oil was its prime content. LR2 seems to be the only known amphora type manufactured with matching lids: these have small rims, protruding handles, and were fired in the typical LR2 fabric. Complete examples have been found at Saraçhane, Stobi, Iatrus and Nea Anchialos (Fig. 7.4),[113] and in all cases seem to be associated with the earlier form with a pronounced conical neck and funnel-shaped mouth. Since the long-distance transport of vessels with protruding, breakable lids would have been functionally inefficient, their purpose is puzzling. Böttger ingeniously attempted to resolve this issue by arguing that the lids were inserted *inside* the amphora's mouth; the 'handle' projected downwards and was held in place with wax, resin or some other perishable material. This idea may be supported by the unusually rough surface of the handle and the correspondingly deliberately smoothed flat under-side of the lid (which would have been visible, according to Böttger). Although possibly valid, this idea surely requires confirmation by the discovery of complete LR2 examples sealed in this manner.[114] However, the lids could easily have been used conventionally if we accept that they rested on the narrowest point of the funnel-shaped mouth; this system would have enabled the protruding handle to be 'guarded' by the tall mouth. Another possibility is that these lids travelled separately alongside the amphorae, and were only used once the amphora had been unsealed.

Most significantly, the association of LR2 amphorae with lids may indicate that their prime content was a substance not affected by the absence of air-tight conditions. This almost certainly excludes wine, which had to be consumed relatively quickly after the amphora's seal was broken. This fact may also explain the difference in capacity between LR1 and LR2 containers: the capacity of the latter is mainly about 40 litres, while the former holds about 15 litres on average.[115] This basic difference is clearly evident within the ecclesiastical complex on Samos where the twenty LR2 each had a capacity of 30 litres and the 120 LR1 each contained 8 litres. The detrimental impact of oxygen on the flavour and body of the wine, and conversely olive oil's relative long 'shelf-life', may have conditioned differences in metrology. Thus, while the wine-carrying LR1 had to be emptied fairly soon once opened, the olive oil carrying LR2 (with lids facilitating multiple takings of olive oil) could serve longer as storage vessels.

Another characteristic of the LR2, which is perhaps related to content, is the shape of its mouth. At least in its earlier form the mouth is wide, tall and funnel-shaped. These features may have been designed specifically to accommodate a funnel required to drain a greasy and relatively slow moving viscous commodity (filling a vessel with an easily manipulated liquid, such as wine, requires neither a wide mouth, nor a funnel).[116] If correct, then the evolution of the LR2 shape, especially the mouth (as described in the introduction), may be indicative of content. Thus, the earlier LR2 form may have been used exclusively for olive oil, while the later development (with a more cylindrical neck and narrower mouth) carried both olive oil and wine. In this respect it is significant to recall that evidence that LR2 was a versatile container comes almost exclusively from late archaeological contexts of the seventh century (amphorae from the ecclesiastical complex on Samos and the Yassi Ada shipwreck).

B. *LR2 Distribution and the* annona militaris

If, on the basis of the afore-mentioned arguments, our view that the LR2 was *originally* used exclusively as an olive oil container is correct, then it follows that this amphora type circulated within a well-organised economic structure. Was the State the protagonist behind inter-regional exchange or was the private entrepreneur respons-ible, choosing to sell commodities to economically dependent areas where comparable produce was absent or scarce? In order to answer this question one should take into account the function of the sites where LR1 and LR2 are found in large quantities.

Particularly significant is that the majority of sites where LR2 has a high profile (either most popular, or second most common following closely behind LR1) are military establishments along the Danubian *limes*: Viminacium, Iatrus, Topraichioi, Independenta, Dinogetia, Sacidava, and possibly also Sucidava. It is even more revealing that outside the Danubian border some Aegean sites with a similarly high LR2 visibility (excluding the LR2 production centres, like Halieis or possibly Argos) also have a distinct military character: the fortress at Emporio on Chios, and the double fort at Louloudies. In my view, these observations justify the assumption that LR2, as well as LR1, were particularly important in the late antique Balkan area first and foremost because they were the main receptacles of the military *annona* in olive oil (LR2) and wine (LR1) transported to the region's military establishments.

Indirect evidence for the role of these two containers in a well-organised system of foodstuff distribution is provided by their inscriptions. These are either *dipinti* or *graffiti* in Greek letters, interpreted either as inscriptions of theological meaning,[117] or as numbers indicating vessel capacity;[118] sometimes the name (presumably of the owner?) is also added.[119] Such *dipinti* and/or *graffiti* appear on LR1 and LR2 types more often than on any other contemporary amphora. At Iatrus, for example, only six out of a total of seventeen different amphora types attested incorporate *dipinti*; LR1 and especially *LR2* are associated with the overwhelming majority.[120] Among the amphorae from

Yassi Ada, *graffiti* (not *dipinti*) scratched into the clay after firing have been reported from ninety-five of the 460 LR2 vessels, and from only three of the sixty LR1 vessels examined. If part of the inscriptions on individual amphorae were indeed indications of capacities, then their frequency mainly on LR1 and LR2 vessels indicates that the production and distribution of these two vessel types were under the control of a well-organised central authority, which felt the need to carefully identify and measure transported commodities. This kind of control would have been most necessary for foodstuffs intended either for the military or the civilian *annona*. However, the apparent scarcity of LR2 in Constantinople (although perhaps a result of limited excavation), may indicate that the olive oil destined for the civilian *annona* in Constantinople reached the capital in different containers. Furthermore, it would have been more efficient to gather the latter from neighbouring Bithynia,[121] rather than from the Aegean.

It may be argued that the closest parallel to the distribution of Aegean olive oil in Late Antiquity to military sites in the Balkans (especially the Danube) and Aegean forts is Roman Baetica in modern Spain, which was the main supplier of olive oil (and even wine and garum) to the *limes* forts of north-west Imperium Romanum.[122] The impressive control exercised over the production and distribution of Baetican olive oil is evident from the control stamps on Dressel 20 amphorae (which name their town of origin, net vessel weight, type of oil carried, and producer's name) and by a number of inscriptions mentioning officials who supervised the production, transport, and payment of freight to private *navicularii*. The State's involvement in this market, aimed at guaranteeing olive oil supply to the city of Rome and for the *annona militaris*, becomes very clear by the reign of Severus, when amphorae bearing stamps with full or abbreviated imperial titles appear. Baetica remained the main supplier of olive oil to Rome during the first and second centuries A.D., but during the third century its mass production was undercut by N. Africa. However, it has been suggested that during the later third to early fourth century, Baetica concentrated export to fort sites along the *limes*. By the fourth and fifth centuries the industry produced even smaller quantities of olive oil, and exchange was restricted to fewer markets in the West Mediterranean.[123]

If Baetican oil was thus restricted and N. African produce was mainly destined for Rome, it would be natural to assume that the substantial demands for olive oil by garrisons along the Danubian frontier and in the Balkan forts would have had to be fulfilled by another olive oil producing area, presumably close by. The Aegean fitted this role perfectly and it is no coincidence that the rapid development of olive culture during the fourth century has been perceived not just in the Southern Argolid in the Peloponnese, but also on the Aegean islands of Lesbos and Thera (future research will most probably enrich this list).[124] This investment does not seem to be an isolated example of localised imperially blessed, or even instigated, concern. The radical change observed in amphora distribution during the fourth century, when much of the diversity notable amongst Roman Imperial types is superseded by a few, completely new large containers, mostly produced in the Levant (these are all six of Riley's amphora 'package'), has also been regarded as another officially-initiated act to promote agricultural productivity in the Eastern Mediterranean.[125] All these changes should be viewed against historical developments in the Eastern Roman Empire in the fourth century, when Constantinople became a capital and soon the largest of many cities in the Eastern Empire. The dislocation from the West, where barbarian incursions had interrupted agricultural production and trade, necessitated systematic agricultural exploitation in the East, where new opportunities for products arose. Throughout the fourth centuries, emperors like Diocletian, Constantine and Valens had reorganised and strengthened the Empire, paying particular attention to a seriously threatened imperial border, and the one closest to the new capital, the Danubian frontier. It is clear that the efficient supply of the imperial armies in this zone was also one of the greatest imperial worries.

Calculating the scale of demand for olive oil in provisioning the North Balkans is an issue directly related to estimating the size of the military presence in this area, itself fraught with difficulties due to the nature of our sources.[126] The late Roman army of the Danubian border would have comprised three main groups: firstly, the *limitanei* (the infantry and cavalry troops of the frontier divisions and the permanent garrisons, together with their attached auxiliaries, which provided local static and mobile reserves); secondly, large parts of the *comitatenses*, i.e. the field armies of the *Magister militum per Illyricum* (responsible for the defense of the Danubian provinces of Moesia I and Dacia Ripensis) and the field armies of the field army of the *Magister militum per Thracias* (responsible for the defense of the Danubian provinces of Moesia II and Scythia); and thirdly, a series of small flotillas, maintained along the Danube and in the ports along the west coast of the Black Sea, which included both warships and transport vessels of various capacities. During the reign of Justinian, a new field command, the *questura excercitus*, was added (see below), which included a further fleet of transport vessels.[127] Furthermore, a substantial number of federate or allied forces must have existed; the Empire usually employed them next to the regular field armies and the frontier divisions, either permanently or on a short-term mercenary basis.

This army manned two main lines of defense: the first was a linear frontier consisting of fortified posts, major fortresses and a connecting network of minor fortified positions; the second one, made up of a reserve of mobile field units, was scattered in garrison towns and fortresses across the provinces behind the frontier.[128] In his *Buildings* (IV.v.-vii, xi), Procopius enumerates about 130 forts (at least twenty-three of them newly built by Justinian and the rest restored by him) within the territory of the four Danubian provinces of the Eastern Empire: Moesia I, Dacia, Moesia II and Scythia. Even if the obviously panegyric tone of Procopius's work casts some suspicion on the extent and effect of Justinian's building and restoration programme on the military establishments in the area, we have no substantial grounds to doubt their number. It is worth noting that eight of Procopius's forts, Sycibida, Nicopolis, Novae, Halmyris (Independenta), Tomis, Iatron, Scedeba and Viminacium (if we make an allowance for the site of Svetinja, situated 1,200 m east of Viminacium),[129] are among the sites where a strong presence of LR2 has been archaeologically attested.

Next to these 130 or so forts, we should also take into account the stations of the legionary troops. According to the *Notitia Dignitatum* (dated between A.D. 395 and 413), the eight legions of the four Danubian provinces (two for each province) were accommodated in the following twenty-one stations: Singidunum, Viminacium and Cuppi (in Moesia I), Variana, Cebrus, Oescus, Sucidava, Aegeta, Transdrobeta, Burgus Novus, Zernae and Ratiaria (in Dacia), Novae, Sexagintaprista, Durostorum and

Transmarisca (in Moesia II) and Noviodunum, Aegissus, Platypegiae, Troesmis and Axiupolis (in Scythia).[130] Three observations are important at this stage. Firstly, two of the afore-mentioned stations (Sucidava in Dacia and Novae in Moesia II), and possibly a third one (Viminacium in Moesia I, see above), are among the enumerated sites with a possible strong LR2 profile; secondly, eleven of these stations (Singidunum, Viminacium, Oescus, Ratiaria, Durostorum, Nikopolis, Novae, Aegissus, Axiupolis, Noviodunum and Troesmis) have the status of a city (they are mentioned in the *Synekdemos* of Hierokles);[131] finally, according to the conclusions of modern scholarship, which estimates that during the fourth and fifth centuries the strength of a legion was around 1,000 men,[132] the total legionary manpower in the Danubian stations mentioned above, should have been around 8,000 men. Next to them, Treadgold estimates another 36,000 men for auxiliary units and cavalry, bringing the total of the *limitanei* in the four Danubian provinces up to 44,000 men.[133] This is well below Jones' estimate of 64,000 men.[134] A compromising average between these two figures would give 54,000 as the strength of the *limitanei* in the four Danubian provinces around the beginning of the fourth century.

The total number of the *comitatenses*, the mobile field forces in the Balkans in the fourth century, is estimated at 42,000 by Treadgold (17,500 for the *Magister militum per Illyricum*, plus 24,500 for the *Magister militum per Thracias*),[135] or at 41,000 by Haldon (who proposes 23,500 for the *Magister militum per Thracias*). These mobile troops must have been dispersed in numerous forts all over the Balkans, but it is only reasonable to assume that a large part of them (half of their total manpower, if not more) was in – or very near – the four Danubian provinces. Haldon has suggested that by the end of Justinian's reign up to three-quarters of these field army units became permanently garrisoned in, or near, frontier towns and cities, where they served as reinforcements to the frontier garrisons in many cases, rather than as a mobile reserve.[136] This would imply that about 13,125 men (three-quarters of the *Magister militum per Illyricum*) were added to the *limitanei* of Moesia I and Dacia Ripensis, while about 17,625 or 18,375 men (three-quarters of the *Magister militum per Thracias*, according to the estimates of Haldon and Treadgold respectively) were added to the *limitanei* of Moesia II and Scythia.

It does not, however, necessarily follow that the army force on the Danubian frontier increased dramatically during Justinian's reign from 54,000 (number of *limitanei* in the four Danubian provinces; see above) to 84,750 or 85,500 (number of *limitanei*, plus three-quarters of the combined manpower of the *Magistri militum per Illyricum et Thracias*).[137] The permanent shift of these large units of *comitatenses* to nearer the Danubian frontier was meant to fill the gaps created amongst the ranks of the Danubian *limitanei* during their long battles against the invading barbarians, which must have also claimed their toll amongst the original ranks of the Balkan *comitatenses*. Further losses may also have occurred through desertions, while the demands of the Justinianic campaigns in the West must have put additional strain on the Danubian legions. Under these conditions, it seems more probable that the military presence in the Danubian provinces was somewhat weaker in Justinian's reign than when the *Notitia Dignitatum* was composed in the early fifth century, for example, when the total manpower in the four Danubian provinces must have numbered – in my view – at least 75,000 (54,000 *limitanei*, plus at least another 21,000 troops: half of the combined manpower of the *Magistri militum per Illyricum et Thracias*).

Military requirements would have affected both the immediate hinterland and the cities in the northern Balkans. Regarding imports in particular, it is reasonable to assume that the Danubian cities (the *Synekdemos* enumerates thirty-two cities in the four Danubian provinces) received similar imports to those dispatched to the region's forts. These could have reached the cities as either direct imports, or as objects exchanged between the local inhabitants and the soldiers at the forts.[138] Because of the relatively greater prosperity in cities, one would presumably expect to find a greater diversity of imported goods there, than in the stagnated life of a fort. This means that a city should possess a broader variety of imported transport vessels, while the forts should contain a more limited range of imported types, reflecting the arrival of standardised and pre-ordered foodstuffs. This point is well illustrated when one compares the variety of amphora types at Nicolopis ad Istrum and the Bulgarian fort of Golemanovo Kale, for example. While there are only three types of amphora at the fort (LR1, LR2 and LR8),[139] a broader variety of types (LR3, LR4, LR5 and the N. African P/W Class 33) are attested at Nicopolis and other civilian settlements.

Unfortunately, the Imperial concern over the supply of wine and olive oil to the Danubian or Balkan forts is not illustrated in the inscriptional record of LR1 and LR2 as vividly as in the case of the carefully stamped Dressel 20 amphorae and other Baetican olive oil containers. This fact may suggest that the State was not so directly involved in this kind of specific trade in the Eastern Roman Empire. An impression, however, of direct imperial concern over the adequate provisioning of the Danubian provinces in general can be obtained through the archaeological record and, in fewer cases, through the written sources. The excavation results from Iatrus and Nicopolis ad Istrum suggest that despite difficulties caused by the Gothic and Hunnic invasions, and by the consequences of the defeat of Valens at Adrianople, the Danubian provinces continued to enjoy a high level of prosperity until the mid-fifth century, based upon local, large-scale grain production on one hand, and imports of olive oil and (to a lesser extent) wine and other products on the other.[140] However, this picture seems to change after the mid-fifth century, when barbarian in-roads became more frequent and disrupted crop sowing and harvesting. Evidence from Nicopolis ad Istrum indicates that imported amphorae from a variety of sources (Africa, Aegean, Cilicia and even Gaza) became far more popular in the city during the period from *c.* 450 to 600. This has been interpreted as an imperial initiative introduced in order to meet the deficiencies in local agricultural supply, caused by the enemy or even perhaps climatic change (although the latter is hard to prove).[141] Consequently, instead of a settlement depending on its economic hinterland, the city became a military and ecclesiastical stronghold maintained and supplied directly by the imperial government whose interests it served.[142]

A similar picture emerges for the fort at Independenta,[143] where the high quantities of LR1 and LR2, particularly towards the end of the sixth and the beginning of the seventh century, can only be explained by the central administration's conscious efforts to maintain an efficient and constant supply of necessary foodstuffs to the *limes* forts. The continuous import of these two amphora types to Independenta during such troubled times must surely indicate that their content was of primary importance to the fort's occupants.

The imperial initiative towards the maintenance of an efficient supply system for the Danubian provinces is best demonstrated by the Justinianic creation of the new administrative unit of the *Quaestura Exercitus* in 536, which included the peculiar combination of two Danubian (Moesia II and Scythia) and three Aegean provinces (Caria, the Cyclades and Cyprus). Texts inform us that the main purpose of this reorganisation was to ensure that the forces in the Danube residing in Moesia II and Scythia received their *annona* supplies from the Aegean provinces. The *questor exercitus* had to cater for both the *comitatenses* (mobile troops) and the *limitanei* (border troops) and the law creating the office contained a schedule of the *annonae* of both army bodies of Mysia and Scythia. Unfortunately this section in Justinian's novels is lost.[144]

Commodities from the Aegean and more distant regions, intended for the forts and cities within the southern Danubian plain, would have been easily transported by ship through the Black Sea and then west up the Danube, possibly on shallow-draft boats. This route is confirmed by the upper part of the body of an LR2 amphora discovered with other amphora sherds underwater near Neseber in Bulgaria (Fig. 7.2), that most probably originates from a shipwreck dated *c.* A.D. 500–625.[145]

Aegean imports destined for the inland cities of the North Balkans, like Stobi and Garicin Grad, must in all probability have passed up the Vardar valley through Thessalonica over a distance of 160 km. The alternative route, however, from the Adriatic across the Via Egnatia to Heraclea and then up to Stobi was far longer (about 325 km) and thus less favourable.

Although no concrete evidence exists about the kind of ships that transported these supplies to the Danubian troops, or about vessel ownership, a hypothesis can be put forward concerning the origin of these ships. The present overview of amphora assemblages from Balkan and Aegean sites clearly demonstrates the close relationship between LR1 (produced on a number of sites along the Cilician coast near Antioch, and also on Cyprus) and LR2 (an Aegean product). A similar picture emerges when one considers a wider sample of amphora finds from the Mediterranean, which demonstrates that not only are LR1 and LR2 usually found together, but also that the presence of LR2 presupposes the presence of LR1, while the opposite is not always the case.[146] On the basis of this economic juxtaposition, the assumption that ships coming from Syria and Cilicia with LR1 cargoes stopped in the Aegean to take on LR2 consignments seems reasonable.

In this respect, it is worth noting the reference to Cilician merchants in the so-called 'Tariff of Abydos', dated to the reign of Anastasius (*c.* A.D. 492), which specifies the import, export and control taxes that merchants bringing foodstuff to Constantinople paid to state officials at the customs of Abydos.[147] The text mentions four different groups of merchants: firstly wine merchants, secondly merchants of olive oil, dried vegetables and lard, thirdly the wheat merchants, and fourthly the Cilicians. While all other merchants are defined according to the commodity in which they traded, the Cilicians are defined by their place of origin. This may imply that in contrast to other merchants, the Cilicians were associated with a highly specific form of exchange. Furthermore, the tariff clarifies that they paid 1 carat less import tax than the merchants involved in the transport of wine, olive oil, dried vegetables and lard. The special privilege accorded to the Cilicians is hard to explain. Durliat and Guillou have dismissed, rightly in my view, Antoniadis-Bibicou's argument that this privilege was due to Anastasius's personal favouratism towards the Isaurians; in the opinion of the two French scholars, the Cilicians' privilege was possibly due to the fact that they used smaller ships than those of Egyptian or Syrian merchants and, therefore, paid less tax proportionately. They also noted, however, that if this was true, then a similar privilege should have been bestowed on other small ships. The exception made to the Cilicians still remains puzzling.

I find it difficult to accept that the Cilician merchants, coming from a particularly rich and fertile area with a long tradition in sea-trade,[148] would have confined their movements to ships of limited tonnage. Bearing in mind that the Cilicians originated from the main production area of LR1,[149] and that they had to sail through the Aegean *en route* to Constantinople, where they probably had numerous supply depots, I would prefer to explain their privilege in terms of their special status as the main transporters of the military *annona* to the Danubian provinces. It is possible that portions of their cargo were commercial and intended for the capital, which compelled them to pay some tax at the Abydos customs-house. The largest consignment amongst the Cilician ships' cargo, however, may well have comprised LR1 and LR2 intended for delivery to the ports on the west coast of the Black Sea.

Undoubtedly, taxes levied in kind, which proved to be surplus to seasonal military requirements, would have subsequently entered the trade chain as commercial produce, and it is thus that LR2 containing olive oil were diffused more broadly across the Mediterranean basin in Late Antiquity, reaching as far as the British Isles. This well-organised exchange system, which designed and produced LR2 intentionally to package olive oil destined as *annona militaris*, but also allowed the surplus to enter the free market, was bound to lose its equilibrium when its main market, the Danubian frontier, gradually slipped away from Byzantine control and hostilities extended across most of the Balkan peninsula. These problems certainly must have affected the strong chain of demand and supply that existed between the North Balkans and the Aegean, and most probably caused a certain decline in the agricultural production, as well as in the production of LR2 containers. I believe that it is within this context that we should explain the increased tendency from the second half of the sixth and through the seventh century of LR2 recycling and their indiscriminate use to transport both olive oil, wine, and perhaps also other commodities. (We may assume that the Arab raids throughout the seventh centuries caused similar problems to the main production areas of LR1). It is this gradual disassociation of LR2 from the exclusive transport of olive oil that led, in my view, to the alteration of its formal characteristics that can be perceived from the second half of the sixth century onwards.

The ideas expressed above, should be viewed as a working hypothesis, which may well be modified or revised in the light of future excavations; as with all archaeological data any conclusions remain dependent upon the interpretation of what is inevitably a slender body of evidence. It is obvious, for example, that the amphora evidence from the first ten or so excavated Danubian military establishments (discussed above) represents less than one-tenth (according to Procopius's testimony) of the original total – mostly unexcavated and not yet surveyed – and that a wider sample of civilian settlements from the area needs to be studied in order to compare our conclusions regarding military trade and settlement.

Nevertheless, I hope to have demonstrated clearly the crucial importance of future quantification of well-stratified pottery assemblages from the areas under discussion and, furthermore, the great potential they can contribute to our study of the late antique Balkan and Aegean economy. I conclude by wishing that such studies will appear shortly, in order to complement, revise or completely overthrow the tentative conclusions presented here.

Notes

1 I would like to express my thanks to Dr. Marlia Mango for initiating my interest in amphora studies, and to Dr. B. Ward-Perkins, Dr. N. Pollard, Dr. J. Howard-Johnston, and the editors of this volume, for their useful comments on the first draft of this paper especially Sean Kingsley who kindly prepared the maps for this paper; none of the above are responsible for its shortcomings.

2 Riley, 1989: 151. The other five amphorae in this 'package' are LR1 (see Decker, Chapter 4), LR3 from western Asia Minor, the Palestinian LR4 and LR5 (see Kingsley Chapter 3), and the North African LR8 (*spatheia*).

3 'The Archaeology of Late Antique Thessaly', under the supervision of Dr. Marlia Mango, St. John's College, Oxford (expected date of submission, end of 2000).

4 For a quick reference on this point, which is more extensively discussed in my thesis, cf. Riley, 1975: 33 (on Caesarea), Pollard, 1998: 158 (on Karanis, Egypt), Riley, 1979: 217–8 (on Berenice), Riley, 1982: 117 (on Carthage: American mission), Peacock, 1984: 119 (on Carthage: British mission), Keay, 1989: 47–8 (on Sabratha), Wilson, 1990: 267–8 (on Sicily), Bonifay and Piéri, 1995: 109–11 (on Marseille), Keay, 1984: 352–7 (on Spanish Catalania), Thomas, 1959: 91–2 and *idem.*, 1981: 9–11, 26–7 (on British Isles).

5 Opait, 1984: 311.

6 Ballance *et al.*, 1989: 106; Thomas, 1959: 91–92.

7 Cf. Scorpan, 1975: 311, pls. II.8–9, IX.5, 7 (subtype A1), pls. II.10, IX.8, 9 (subtype A2), pls. III.1, 2, IX.9 (subtype A3); *idem.*, 1976: 177, pl. VII and *idem.*, 1976: 274, fig. 10; Riley, 1975: 33, distinguishing between earlier (fifth century) and later (early sixth century) examples; Böttger, 1982: 38–41; Bass and van Doorninck, 1982: 157–60, figs. 8–5: nos. CA 13–17 (subtype 2a) and nos. CA 18–20 (subtype 2b); van Doorninck, 1989: 248 (four major and forty secondary subtypes); Hayes, 1992: 66 (subtypes 9A and 9B); Bonifay and Piéri, 1995: 109–10, fig. 53–5 (earlier form) and 8.55 (later form).

8 Such a study requires extensive fieldwork on LR2 kilns found outside its main production areas.

9 The main work on this issue is that of Opait, 1984: 312–6, tafeln II, XII. Similar observations have been made by Bonifay and Piéri, 1995: 109–10.

10 Peacock and Williams, 1986: 7–8.

11 For example, Falkner defines types in his report on the pottery from early Byzantine Nicopolis ad Istrum by studying the appearance of wares visible at x10 magnification; Falkner, 1999: 58, 274.

12 Amphorae are notoriously bad indicators of short-term chronology, as they seem to have been less susceptible to regular stylistic changes than other pottery forms such as fine-wares.

13 For warnings against the inappropriate dependence on quantified data based on unrepresentative pottery, see Bonifay,1986: 295–6, and Tomber, 1989: 506.

14 A more extensive commentary (with quantified data in tabulated form) on the amphora evidence from many of these sites is found in my thesis.

15 Hayes, 1968: 215; *idem.*, 1992: 62–71, esp. 66 and fig. 22.8, 10–11.

16 The latest coins in the final destruction levels of the site date to the fifth year of the reign of Justin II, A.D. 569–570; cf. Wiseman, 1973: 19.

17 Anderson-Stojanovic, 1992: 96–97, pls. 82–3 and 184, esp. 96, pl. 82.700–701 and pl. 184: C-71–359 (LR2).

18 Bjelajac, 1990: 160, 175–6 (on amphorae), esp. 176 (type V/5), pl. XXI/7 (LR2).

19 Bjelajac, 1990: 175.

20   Popovic, 1987, 35–7, fig. 13–14.

21   Kazhdan, 1991c: 970.

22   Bartosiewicz *et al.*, 1995: 5. The results of the excavations, carried out by members of the Bulgarian and East Germany Academy of Sciences, have been published in a series of five monographs; cf. Dimova *et al.*, 1979; Böttger *et al.*, 1982; Wendel *et al.*, 1986; Hermann *et al.*, 1991 and Bartosiewicz *et al.*, 1995.

23   The pottery from Iatrus was published in Böttger, 1982: 33–148 (1966–1973 seasons) and in Böttger, 1991: 157–66 (1975–1981 seasons). Conclusions on the economy of Iatrus, based on the combined pottery evidence, were discussed in Böttger, 1995: 67–80. Böttger's dating of the excavation layers at Iatrus has received criticism (Mackensen, 1991) and his amphora typology is not free of serious weaknesses either. This issue is extensively discussed in my thesis.

24   Böttger, 1982: 70, tabelle 1 and Böttger, 1991: 157, tabelle 1.

25   Herrmann, 1986: 12; Wendel, 1986: 115–6, tafel 19.2, 19.4–8, 19.10–11, 38a (LR2) and 19.12–16 (LR1).

26   Poulter, 1999: 3–27 (on the history of the excavations and a description of the site).

27   Poulter, 1999: 6–7, 11–3.

28   Poulter, 1999: 28; Falkner, 1999: 115.

29   Falkner, 1999: 114 (table 8.1) and 274–80 (Appendix: the Wares). On Falkner's ware no. 94 (LR2), cf. *idem.*: 252 and fig. 9.52: 1056–62.

30   Falkner, 1999: 117, fig. 8.4.

31   Falkner, 1999: 281–96.

32   Tudor, 1965: 13–20, 28–34, 79–101, figs. 4 and 16. Cf. also Kazhdan, 1991e: 1974.

33   Tudor, 1965: 88, 114, 119–22, figs. 32–33 (*dipinti*), pls. IV.4 (LR8) and XXV.6 (LR2), 9 (LR1), 10 (LR4).

34   Mackensen, 1992a: 239.

35   Mackensen, 1992a: 239–54, esp. 239–42, tafel 51.1–7 (LR2).

36   Mackensen, 1992b: 354.

37   36 For a brief presentation of the site and the excavation results until 1990, cf. Press and Sarnowski, 1990. Articles on the excavation's progress, and on various finds from Novae, have been published mainly in the following journals: *Archeologia* (from 1973), *Latomus* (from 1974), *Klio* (from 1976), *Meander* (from 1979) and *Eos* (from 1980). Information on the amphora finds is expected to be included in Sarnowski, T. (ed.), *Novae. Das Stabsgebäude. Architektur und Funde* (Limesforschungen. Römisch-Germanische Komission), Frankfurt (forthcoming).

38   Cangova et *al.*, 1981: 142, fig. 61.

39   Radulescu, 1976: 114: "Birneförmoge Amphoren mit Streifen (LR2) [sind] in der Dobrudscha sehr verbreitet"; Scorpan, 1975: 311: "Le type A (i.e. LRA 2). La plus répandue (et caractéristique) forme d'amphore de la Dobroudja romano-byzantine". Cf. also, *idem.*, 1976: 177 and 1977: 274, where the same statement is repeated.

40   Riley, 1979: 218–9. The only kiln studies in the area, as far as I know, are the works of Coja and Dupont, 1979 (on archaic, classical and Hellenistic kilns at Histria), and of Irimia, 1968 (on three late antique kilns excavated at Oltina). The latter kilns were used primarily for firing bricks and roof-tiles; on the basis of petrological analysis (Williams, 1982: 102), the numerous amphora sherds with "combed surface" (probably LR2), which were also discovered during their excavation, were not produced locally.

41   Kazhdan, 1991d: 1825.

42   Scorpan, 1973: 328–31 (English summary of the excavation results regarding the site stratigraphy), 320 (on pottery finds), and figs. 34 (LR1) and 36.3 (LR2).

43   Scorpan, 1975: 311–2, pls. II.8–10, III.1–2, IX.5, 7, 8, 10, X.1–2 (LR2).

44   Kazhdan, 1991a: 625.

45   The width of the ash layer recorded during the excavations was 1.5 m; cf. Barnea, 1966: 237. The date of the destruction of Dinogetia is also confirmed by coin finds in the east part of the north-west sector of the fortress: twelve coins found in rooms I, VI, VIII and XI dated from the fourth to sixth century, the latest being a Justinianic issue from Constantinople of A.D. 552–3; cf. Barnea, 1966: 240, 249, 253, 257.

46   Barnea, 1966. Excavations in the north-west sector of the fortress were specifically intended to shed light on the late antique phase of the settlement pre-dating the great fire of 559 (until then more

attention had been given to the upper layers of the tenth to twelfth century houses). For a plan of the fortress, cf. Barnea, 1980: pl. IX. For a detailed plan of the eleven rooms excavated in 1966, cf. Barnea, 1966: figs. 1–2; on amphorae from the site, cf. *idem*, p. 244–5, 250, 254 and figs. 5.7, 8.7 and 12.7 (LR2).

47 On the excavations conducted by the Archaeological Institute of Bucharest and the Danube Delta Museum of Tulcea, see Zahariade *et al.*, 1987.

48 Opait, 1991: 139–40 (nos. 52–63) and pls. 8–9 (LR2; Opait, Amfore piriforme, Tip II); 145–6 (nos. 101–5) and pl. 17 (LR1; Opait, Amfore ovoidale, Tip I.1); 214, pls. 50–51 (histograms on the relative proportions of the two types at Independenta, Topraichioi, Iatrus, Berenice, Carthage and Istanbul); 215, pl. 52 (graph showing the fluctuations of the two types at Independenta between the first half of the fourth century and the second decade of the seventh century).

49 Zahariade and Opait, 1986: 565–71.

50 Opait, 1991: 214.

51 Kazhdan, 1991b: 939. Cf. also Preda and Nubar, 1973: 174–233, esp. 241.

52 Condurachi, 1961: 269, pl. IV and fig. 11.

53 Suceveanu *et al.*, 1982: 99, 120 and pls. 4: III.4 and 18: 61. The sector containing the two second century A.D. baths became a commercial region in the fourth century, and was later occupied by a basilica and a cemetery before being abandoned in the seventh century; cf. Suceveanu *et al.*, 1982: 75–92.

54 Browning and Kazhdan, 1991: 2092.

55 Radulescu, 1973: 197–198 (on the amphora contents), 202–3 (on the *graffiti* and *dipinti*) and figs. 6–7. Cf. also, Scorpan, 1976: 170, 180, 182 (on LR4 containing nails), and *idem*, 1977: 276.

56 Barnea *et al.*, 1979: 190, figs. 167–8, 170; 3.5 (LR1), and 167–170: 3.2 (LR2).

57 On the 1961–1964 excavation results, cf. Bass and van Doorninck, 1982, where a representative sample of thirty LR1 and eighty LR2 is discussed. On the larger sample of LR1 and LR2 that was raised from the seabed later, cf. van Doornick, 1989. The re-examination of the Yassi Ada amphorae, in the light of the far larger 1989 sample led to new conclusions regarding the typology of these vessels, enriched the collection of *graffiti* available, and enabled the organic contents of intact amphorae to be examined. It is evident that the 'final' Yassi Ada shipwreck publication of 1982 must always be appreciated against the background of these later observations.

58 Fagerlie, 1982: 144–54. The absence of weapons on-board may also imply that the voyage occurred following the withdrawal of the Persian fleet from the Aegean in 626; cf. van Doorninck, 1989: 247.

59 van Doornick, 1989: 248.

60 Their maximum diameter (averaging 43 cm) occurs at one-half and equals three-fourths of the total height; the height of the neck plus its maximum diametre equals 1/4 of the total height of the vessel; all maximum diametres for necks fall within 1.5 cm, and capacity variance within the group is minimal.

61 van Doornick, 1989, fig. 1.1, 1.4 and 1.7.

62 Hautumm, 1981: 9, 174.

63 Hautumm, 1981: 21 (on LR2), 77 (on P/W class 35), 116 (on LR8).

64 Steckner, 1989.

65 Gerousi, 1992–3: 252–7, figs. 1–4.

66 Ballance *et al.*, 1989: 3, 7–8 (on the history of the fortress), 106–7, figs. 37–38 and pls. 24–25 (on the amphora finds). LR2: nos. 236, 237, 238 and 240.

67 Garnett and Boardman, 1961: 113, fig. 13.38.

68 Abadie-Reynal and Sodini, 1992: 7–8 (on the provenance of the material), 53–62 (on amphorae), 56–7, nos. CC284–319, figs. 23–24 and pl. Va-c, e (LR2). Our quantified data are based on the numbers of the separately counted bases, body fragments, handles and complete or upper bodies of vessels for each amphora type, as listed in the site publication.

69 Papadopoulos, 1989: 67–78, figs. 2–3.

70 Papadopoulos, 1989: 83–102, esp. 83–7, 100 and fig. 11 (on type I, i.e. LR2); cf. also *idem.*, figs. 8c and 9a-b: LR2 used for burials.

71 Our quantified data are based on Papadopoulos, 1989: 82, table 3.

72 For example, sherds retrieved during the 1965 excavation of rooms next to the Octagonon in the Palace of Galerius include LR2 and LR4. Cf. Petsas, 1966: 334 and figs. 343b, 343d.

73 Poulter *et al.*, 1998: 463–4, 483–5 and fig. 14.
74 Beckmann, 1998: 503, 505–6 (on amphorae), fig. 25: nos. 23, 25 (LR2 thick, flared rims) and fig.25: no. 24 (LR2 knobbed base).
75 Einwanger, 1981: 21ff and esp. 23ff (on the date), 48 and tafel 60: III511–3, 517, 519 (LR2 rim fragments).
76 Iatridou, 1976: 190–2, pl. 139c-d.
77 Personal observation made during fieldwork in summer 1996. On the middle Byzantine church of Episkopi on Skopelos, cf. Andreas Xyngopoulos, 1956, 181–98.
78 On these shipwrecks, including at least four wrecks of the fourth century B.C. and five of the middle Byzantine period, cf. Mavrikis, 1997: 286–320. No late antique shipwrecks have so far come to light in the area.
79 Robinson, 1959: 109, M272, pl. 29 for a late fourth century example. Cf. also M235, pl. 28 and P4129, P16074, pl. 40.
80 Broneer, 1959: 321, 336–337 (no. 16), and pl. 72b.
81 Pers. comm., Dr. J. Hayes 1999.
82 Williams and Fischer, 1976: 133 and pl. 23.79; Williams and Zervos, 1983: 26 and pl. 10.72.
83 Warner Slane, 1990.
84 Sanders, 1999: 459–63.
85 Adamsheck, 1979: 108–24, pls. 26–27; esp. 114–7: RC 14 (LR2) and RC 16 (a probable LR2 of later date).
86 Adamsheck, 1979: 114–5, pl. 26: RC14.
87 Abadie, 1989.
88 Ault, 1999: 55, fn. 5, 559–64, figs. 11–15. Evidence *ex silentio* (finds from the third century B.C. to the fourth century A.D. are virtually absent at Halieis) indicate that the site remained uninhabited until the fourth century: cf. Rudolph, 1979: 304, fn. 22.
89 No signs of late antique fortifications have been discovered on the site. It appears likely – although not yet corroborated by any archaeological evidence – that the harbour was still in use during Late Antiquity. The date when the site was abandoned, caused by Arab pirates and/or Slav attackers, is placed in the early decades of the seventh century; cf. Rudolf, 1979: 296, 303–5.
90 Rudolph, 1979: 305–9, figs. 3–5. Numerous fragments of LR2 from the harbour area, decorated with spiral-grooving, were also recorded during the 1962–68 excavations: cf. Jameson, 1969: 339–340, fig. 9, and more generally Jameson *et al.*, 1994: 402.
91 Rudolph, 1979: 304, fn. 23.
92 Zimmermann Munn, 1985. It is possible that the LR2 kiln on site B-19, identified in 1985, was one of the two kilns already reported in 1979 by the Argolid Exploration Project.
93 Parker, 1992: 335.
94 Megaw and Jones, 1983: 246.
95 Goldstream and Huxley, 1972: 172 (no. 47), fig. 52, pl. 49 (probably a late example).
96 McDonald *et al.*, 1983: 353, 384 and pl. 10–10 (P1756).
97 Riley, 1982: 118.
98 Hautumm, 1981: 47.
99 Derda, 1992: 139, 146–51 (nos. 1–2 from Bulgaria and 2–7 from Rumania). For this reference I am grateful to Dr. Sean Kingsley.
100 van Doornick, 1989: 252, fig. 2.
101 On the issue of pitch-lining, see in particular Opait, 1998, where amphora types found during dredging operations of the Circular Harbour in Carthage were seperated in the report into pitched and plain examples. The LR2 were in the category of non-lined amphorae and were thus assumed to have carried olive oil. LR2 fragments lined with resin were discovered at Marseille; cf. Bonifay and Piéri, 1995: 111.
102 Hautumm, 1981: 46–8.
103 Jameson et al., 1994: 268–76 (on the history of olive cultivation in the area) and 385 (table 6.6), 400–4 (table 6.9) on evidence of olive cultivation during the Roman and late Roman period. Press apparatus from the Southern Argolid Survey is discussed in Runnels *et al.*, 1995: 128–33.

104 van Andel and Runnels, 1987: 105–9, 20–21 (maps); Jameson *et al.*, 1994: 383–94, figs. 6.17–18, back-pocket map 8.

105 Anagnostakis, 1996: 125, 127 and fns. 18, 34–6.

106 Poulter *et al.*,1999: 41.

107 On these installations, see Böttger, 1995: 69, esp. fn. 8, with further bibliography.

108 Poulter *et al.*, 1999: 46.

109 Böttger, 1995: 69, fn. 8.

110 Böttger, 1995: 70 and 293.

111 Poulter *et al.*, 1999: 34.

112 Anderson-Stojanovic, 1992: 192–3.

113 Hayes, 1992: 66, fig. 22.12; Anderson-Stojanovic, 1992: 97, pls. 83.712–3; Böttger, 1982: 41–2, tafel 25; Iatridou, 1976: pl. 139c-f.

114 The LR2 from the Yassi Ada wreck did not illuminate this problem: the 165 stoppers from the shipwreck were all roughly rounded amphora sherds (av. dm. 5–7 cm) shaped to loosely fit the mouths of both the LR1 and LR2; cf. Bass, 1982: 160–161, fig. 8–7. The discrepancy between the number of estimated cargo vessels and the number of stoppers retrieved (900 compared to 165) may be explained by the excavation collection strategy, or because most stoppers were perishable, or (less likely) because many amphorae were empty during the ship's final voyage.

115 Hautumm, 1981: 51–2, 63. The small dimensions of LR2, as opposed to LR1, are also noted by Böttger, 1982: 87 and by Popovic, 1987: 13.

116 For possible such funnels, although of earlier date, cf. Robinson, 1959: 17 and pls. 2, 19: F64 (first century B.C. to first century A.D.), 85 and pl. 18: M9 (mid-first century A.D.), 95 and pl. 18: M119 (early third century A.D.).

117 For example, abbreviations of 'Virgin Mary is giving birth to Christ' and the Christian symbol A+Y ('Christ is the A and Y of life'). For an interesting group of LR2 from Rumania and Bulgaria bearing such inscriptions, cf. Derda, 1992: 136 and esp. 146–51.

118 For example, the most popular combinations of Greek letters on LR2 from Iatrus indicating numbers are NB (52), Ns (56) or nr (83), and are usually preceded by certain symbols, which have been interpreted as the alexandrino-italian *sextarius* (0.543 lt) or the heavy Roman *libra* (0.326 kg); cf. Böttger, 1982: 87–9. At Tomis, the most common letters painted on LR2 are N (50) and n (60), also interpreted as capacity indications in *sextarii*; cf. Radulescu, 1973: 202–203.

119 For example, the name *Baleriou Poritou* on a LR2 from Thasos; cf. Abadie-Reynal and Sodini, 1992: 56, fig. 24 and pl. Vc, e.

120 Amphora types with *dipinti* at Iatrus are Böttger's Forms I.1 (LR2), I.2 (PW35?), I.5, I.6, II.1 (LR1) and III.1 (LR1a?); however, Böttger states clearly that the *dipinti* "besonders häufig auf Amphoren der Form I1 (LR2) begegnen"; cf. Böttger, 1982: 87.

121 According to Constantine Porphyrogenitus, who oftens repeats information from earlier centuries, the olive oil from Nicaea was provided for the imperial household service during expeditions; cf. C. Porphyrogenitus, 1990. *Three Treatises on Imperial Military Expeditions* (ed. J. Haldon, Vienna), 132.601.

122 On the organisation of production and transport of Baetican olive oil in general, cf. Keay, 1984: 402–5; in particular for the *limes*, cf. Rodríguez, 1986: 765–6. Hautumm (1981: 48–51) has proposed that Dresel 20, an exclusive container of Baetican olive oil, became the prototype on which the LR2 was modelled because of its wide distribution and strong association with olive oil. A different view, which links the formal characteristics of LR2 to earlier Aegean amphorae, is discussed in my thesis.

123 Keay, 1984: 404.

124 Jameson *et al.*, 1994: 404.

125 Slane Warner, 1990: 109; Hayes, 1997: 32–3.

126 On the difficulties presented by the issue, cf. Jones, 1964: 679–86; MacMullen, 1980 and Treadgold, 1995: 43–64.

127 *Wars*, III, xi.13–16.

128 *Buildings*, IV.i.33–35.

129 *Buildings*, IV.vi.34–35 (Sycibida), xi.20 (Nicopolis), vi.1–3, 5 (Novae), vii. 20 (Halmyris, i.e. Independenta), xi.20 (Tomis), vii.6 (Iatron), xi.20 (Scedeba) and v.17 and vi.1 (Viminacium).

130 Jones, 1964: III, 370–1 (Appendix II).

131 *Synekdemos* 13 (636.1–8, on Moesia II), 20 (655.1–6, on Dacia), 21 (657.1–6, on Moesia I) and 13–14 (637.1–15, on Scythia).

132 MacMullen, 1980: 457.

133 Treadgold, 1995: 52.

134 Jones, 1964: 682.

135 Treadgold, 1995: 50 and fig. 6 on p. 48; Haldon, 1999: 100.

136 Haldon, 1999: 69.

137 Haldon (1997: 251) believes that "the main field armies of the empire in the mid-sixth century were maintained at approximately the same strength as in the early fifth century".

138 For literary references to the engagement of soldiers in trans-Dunabian trade, cf. Poulter, 1999: 43.

139 With the exception of just one North African *spatheion*, type Keay XXVI G; cf. Mackensen, 1992: 251–2.

140 The ceramic evidence from Iatrus does not reflect any disruptions in the supply system to the Danubian forts during the last quarter of the fourth century caused by the Gothic invasions, or in the first half of the fifth century, caused by the incursions of the Huns; cf. Böttger, 1982: 83. The quality of workmanship and finish of the LR2 at Iatrus, in particular, remains almost equal throughout the site's occupation according to Böttger, which may indicate that the city was supplied by the same production centres throughout its history; cf. Böttger, 1982: 38. Imported wares at Iatrus (amphorae, table- and kitchen-wares) remained constant throughout the city's history (fourth to sixth century), at about 40% of the assemblage; amphorae represent no less than 30% of the total imported pottery during this period; cf. Böttger, 1995: 69, 71, 80. A similar picture of stable economic life emerges for Nicopolis ad Istrum for the period between the middle of the fourth through to the middle of the fifth century; cf. Poulter *et al.*, 1999: 45.

141 Poulter, 1999: 47.

142 If this officially sponsored supply of food and materials also constitutes payment for the Danubian army (instead of coin), then this might explain the low rate of coin loss at Iatrus and Nicopolis during the sixth century; cf. Poulter, 1999: 48.

143 Opait, 1991: 182.

144 Just. *Nov.* 41 (A.D. 536). Cf. also Jones, 1964: 280, 661. The separate mention of *comitatenses* and *limitanei* in the Justinianic novels may go back to the fifth century, since Justinian used large sections from the constitution of 443.

145 Bouzek and Kordac, 1963: 257, pl. I (below) and Parker, 1992: 287.

146 This point is amply demonstrated in my thesis.

147 Durliat and Guillou, 1984; esp. 596.

148 The compilation of the *Expositio totius mundi et gentium*, an exemplary sea merchants' handbook written in the mid-fourth century – possible at Tyre (cf. Rougé, 1966: 9, 19, 32) – must have been influenced by the strong tradition of sea-trade along the whole of the East Mediterranean coast, from Cilicia to Palestine.

149 On the location of LR1 production centres, cf. Williams, 1979 and esp. Empereur and Picon, 1989: 33, fig. 21. For a LR1 kiln discovered in Paphos, Cyprus, see Demesticha and Michaelidis

Bibliography

Abadie, C., 1989. 'Les amphores protobyzantines d'Argos (IVe-VIe siècles)'. In V. Déroche and J.-M. Spieser (ed.) *Recherches sur la céramique byzantine* (BCH Suppl. XVIII, Paris)), 47–57.

Abadie-Reynal, C. and Sodini, J.-P., 1992. *La céramique Paléochrétienne de Thasos (Aliki, Delkos, Fouilles Anciennes)* (Études Thasiennes XIII, Athens).

Adamsheck, B., 1979. *Kenchreai: Eastern Port of Corinth, Vol IV. The Pottery* (Leiden).

Anagnostakis, H., 1996. 'Elladika paramythia kai eladikí paramythia sto Byzantio tou 10ou aiona'. In *Proceedings of a Conference on 'Elia kai Ladi'* (Kalamata, 7–9 May 1993, Athens), 121–50.

Anderson-Stojanovic, V.R., 1992. 'Stobi: the Hellenistic and Roman Pottery'. In J. Wiseman (ed.) *Stobi: Results of the Joint American-Yugoslav Archaeological Investigations, 1970–1981* (Princeton).

Ault, B.A., 1999. 'Koprones and Oil Presses at Halieis: Interaction of Town and Country and the Integration of Domestic and Regional Economies', *Hesperia* 68, 549–73.

Ballance, M., Boardman, J., Corbett, S. and Hood, S., 1989. *Excavations in Chios 1952–1955: Byzantine Emporio* (Oxford).

Barnea, I., 1966. 'L' incendie de la cité de Dinogetia au VIe siècle', *Dacia* 10, 237–59.

Barnea, I., 1980. 'Dinogetia-ville byzantine du bas-Danube', *Byzantina* 10, 237–87.

Barnea, I., Cataniciu, I.B., Margineanu-Carstoiu, M. and Papuc, G., 1979. *Tropaeum Traiani I, Cetatea* (Biblioteca de archeologie 35, Bucharest).

Bartosiewicz, L. *et al.*, 1995. *Iatrus-Krivina: Spätantike Befestigung und Frühmittelalterliche Siedlung an der unteren Donau, Vol. V: Studien zur Geschichte des Kastells Iatrus* (Berlin).

Bass, G.F. and van Doorninck, F.H., 1982. *Yassi Ada, a Seventh-Century Byzantine Shipwreck* (Texas).

Beckmann, M., 1998. 'Field Survey at Louloudies: a New Late Roman Fortification in Pieria', *ABSA* 93, 503–511.

Bjelajac, L., 1990. 'La céramique et les lampes'. In B. Bavant, V. Kondic and J.-M. Spieser (ed.) *Caricin Grad II* (Collection de l'École Française de Rome-75, Belgrade-Rome), 161–90.

Bonifay, M., 1986. 'Observations sur les amphores tardives à Marseille d'après les fouilles de la Bourse (1980–1984)', *RAN* 19, 269–305.

Bonifay, M. and Piéri, D., 1995. 'Amphores du Ve au VIIe s. à Marseille: nouvelles données sur la typologie et le contenu', *JRA* 8, 94–120.

Böttger, B., 1991. 'Die Gefässkeramischen Funde (1975–1981)'. In J. Herrmann *et al.*, *Iatrus-Krivina: Spätantike Befestigung und Frühmittelalterliche Siedlung an der unteren Donau, Vol. IV: Ergebnisse der Ausgrabungen 1975–1981* (Berlin), 157–66.

Böttger, B., 1995. 'Die Gefässkeramischen aus Iatrus und ihre Wirtschaftlischen Aussagen'. In L Bartosiewicz *et al.*, 1995. *Iatrus-Krivina: Spätantike Befestigung und Frühmittelalterliche Siedlung an der unteren Donau, Vol. V: Studien zur Geschichte des Kastells Iatrus* (Berlin), 67–80.

Böttger, B. *et al.*, 1982. Iatrus-Krivina: Spätantike Befestigung und Frühmittelalterliche Siedlung an der unteren Donau, Vol. II. Ergebnisse der Ausgrabungen 1966–1973 (Berlin).

Böttger, B., 1982. 'Die Gefässkeramik aus dem Kastell Iatrus'. In B. Böttger et al., Iatrus-Krivina: Spätantike Befestigung und Frühmittelalterliche Siedlung an der unteren Donau, vol. 2. Ergebnisse der Ausgrabungen 1966–1973 (Berlin), 33–148.

Bouzek, J. and Kordac, K., 1963. 'Examination of Amphora Fragments from an Early Medieval Shipwreck from the Black Sea', *Listy Filologicke* 11, 256–8.

Broneer, O., 1959. 'Excavations at Isthmia; Fourth Campaign, 1957–1958', *Hesperia* XXVIII, 298–343.

Browning, R. and Kazhdan, A., 1991. 'Tomis'. In A. Kazhdan, A-M. Talbot, A. Cutler, T.E. Gregory and N.P. Ševcenko, *The Oxford Dictionary of Byzantium, Vol. I* (Oxford), 2092.

Cangova, J. *et al.*, 1981. Pernik. Poselišcen zivot na Chelma Krakra ot V Chil n.e. do VI v. na n.e. Band I. (Editions Acad. Bulgare des Sciences, Sofia).

Coja, M. and Dupont, P., 1979. *Histria V: ateliers céramiques* (Bucarest-Paris).

Condurachi, E. *et al.* 1961. 'Santierul arheologic Histria', *Materiale si Cercetàri Arheologice* 7, 227–71.

Demesticha, S. and Michaelides, D. (forthcoming). 'The Excavation of a Late Roman 1 Amphora Kiln in Paphos'. In *Actes du colloque: la céramique byzantine et proto-islam en Syrie-Jordanie* (Amman 3–5 decembre 1994).

Derda, T., 1992. 'Inscriptions with the Formula "Theo charis kerdos" in Late Roman Amphorae', *ZPE* 94, 135–52.

Dimova, V. *et al.*, 1979. *Iatrus-Krivina: Spätantike Befestigung und Frühmittelalterliche Siedlung an der unteren Donau, Vol. I. Ergebnisse der Ausgrabungen 1966–1973* (Berlin).

Durliat, J. and Guillou, A., 1984. 'Le tarif d'Abydos (vers 492)', *BCH* 108, 581–98.

Einwanger, J., 1981. *Demetrias IV: Keramik und Kleinfunde aus der Damokratia – Basilica in Demetrias, Vols. 1–2* (Bonn).

Empereur, J.-Y. and Picon, M., 1989. 'Les régions de production d'amphores imperiales en Mediterranée orientale'. In *Amphores romaines et histoire économique* (Rome).

Fagerlie, J., 1982. 'The Coins'. In G.F. Bass and F.H. van Doorninck., 1982. *Yassi Ada, a Seventh-Century Byzantine Shipwreck* (Texas), 145–54.

Falkner, R., 1999. 'The Pottery'. In A. Poulter *et al.*, *Nicopolis ad Istrum: the Finds* (Society of Antiquaries of London, Leicester University Press), 55–296.

Garnett, R. and Boardman, J., 1961. 'Underwater Reconnaissance off the Island of Chios, 1954', *ABSA* 56, 102–11.

Gerousi, E., 1992–3. 'Kerameika palaiochristianikon chronon apo tin periochi tou Episkopeiou tis Samou' *Archaiologiko Deltio* 47/48, vol. A, 251–68.

Goldstream, J.N. and Huxley, G.L., 1972 (ed.). *Kythera: Excavations and Studies Conducted by the University of Pennsylvania Museum and the British School at Athens* (London).

Haldon, J.F., 1997. *Byzantium in the Seventh Century* (Cambridge University Press, 4th ed.).

Haldon, J.F., 1999. *Welfare, State and Society in the Byzantine World, 565–1204* (London).

Hautumm, W., 1981. *Studien zu Amphoren der spätrömischen und byzantinischen Zeit* (Fulda).

Hayes, J.W., 1968. 'A Seventh-Century Pottery Group', *DOP* 22, 203.

Hayes, J.W., 1992. *Excavations at Saraçhane in Istanbul, Vol. II* (Princeton University Press).

Hayes, J.W., 1997. *Handbook of Mediterranean Roman Pottery* (London).

Herrmann, J., 1986. 'Die Altbulgarische Siedlung über dem Antiken Kastell Iatrus/Krivina bei Ruse, VR Bulgarien. Zum Abschlus der Ausgrabungen'. In M. Wendel *et al.*, *Iatrus-Krivina: Spätantike Befestigung und Frühmittelalterliche Siedlung an der unteren Donau, vol. III: Die Mittelalterliche Siedlungen* (Berlin), 5–16.

Herrmann, J. *et al.*, 1991. *Iatrus-Krivina: Spätantike Befestigung und Frühmittelalterliche Siedlung an der unteren Donau, Vol. IV: Ergebnisse der Ausgrabungen 1975–1981* (Berlin).

Iatridou, E., 1976. 'Anaskaphes. Nea Anchialos', *Archaiologiko Deltio* 31, vol. B1, 190–2.

Irimia, M., 1968. 'Cuptoarele Romano-Bizantine de ars ceramica de la Oltina (Jud. Constanta)', *Pontica* 1, 379–408.

Jameson, M.H., 1969. 'Excavations at Porto Cheli and Vicinity. Preliminary Report I: Halieis, 1962–1968', *Hesperia* 38, 311–42.

Jameson, M.H., Runnels, C.N. and van Andel, T., 1994. *The Southern Argolid from Prehistory to the Present Day* (Stanford).

Jones, A.H.M., 1964. *The Late Roman Empire, 284–602: a Social and Administrative Survey, Vols. I-III* (Oxford).

Kazhdan, A., 1991a. 'Dinogetia'. In A. Kazhdan, A-M. Talbot, A. Cutler, T.E. Gregory and N.P. Ševcenko, *The Oxford Dictionary of Byzantium, Vol. I* (Oxford), 625.

Kazhdan, A., 1991b. 'Histria'. In A. Kazhdan, A-M. Talbot, A. Cutler, T.E. Gregory and N.P. Ševcenko, *The Oxford Dictionary of Byzantium, Vol. 2* (Oxford), 939.

Kazhdan, A., 1991c. 'Iatrus'. In A. Kazhdan, A-M. Talbot, A. Cutler, T.E. Gregory and N.P. Ševcenko, *The Oxford Dictionary of Byzantium, Vol. 2* (Oxford), 970.

Kazhdan, A., 1991d. 'Sacidava'. In A. Kazhdan, A-M. Talbot, A. Cutler, T.E. Gregory and N.P. Ševcenko, *The Oxford Dictionary of Byzantium, Vol. 3* (Oxford), 1825.

Kazhdan, A., 1991e. 'Sucidava'. In A. Kazhdan, A-M. Talbot, A. Cutler, T.E. Gregory and N.P. Ševcenko, *The Oxford Dictionary of Byzantium, Vol. 3* (Oxford), 1974.

van Doorninck JR., F.H., 1989. 'The Cargo Amphoras on the 7th century Yassi Ada and 11th Century Serçe Limani Shipwrecks: Two Examples of a Reuse of Byzantine Amphoras as Transport Jars'. In V. Déroche and J.-M. Spieser (ed.) *Recherches sur la céramique byzantine* (BCH Suppl. XVIII, Paris), 247–57.

Warner Slane, K., 1990. *Corinth XVIII.ii. The Sanctuary of Demeter and Kore: the Roman Pottery and Lamps* (Princeton).

Wendel, M., 1986. 'Die Mittelaltedichen Siedlungen'. In M. Wendel *et al.*, *Iatrus-Krivina: Spätantike Befestigung und Frühmittelalterliche Siedlung an der unteren Donau, vol. III. Die Mittelalterliche Siedlungen* (Berlin), 27–207.

Wendel, M., *et al.*, 1986. *Iatrus-Krivina: Spätantike Befestigung und Frühmittelalterliche Siedlung an der unteren Donau, vol. III. Die Mittelalterliche Siedlungen* (Berlin).

Williams, C.K. and Fischer, J.E., 1976. 'Corinth, 1975: Forum Southwest', *Hesperia 45*, 99–162.

Williams, C.K. and Zervos, O., 1983. 'Corinth 1982: East of the Theatre', *Hesperia 52*, 1–47.

Williams, D.F., 1979. 'The Heavy Mineral Separation of Ancient Ceramics by Centrifugation; a Preliminary Report', *Archaeometry 21–22*, 177–82.

Williams, D.F., 1982. 'The Petrology of Certain Byzantine Amphorae: some Suggestions as to Origins'. In *Actes du colloque sur la céramique antique, Carthage 23–24 June 1980* (CEDAC, Carthage), 99–110.

Wilson, R.J.A., 1990. *Sicily under the Roman Empire: the Archaeology of a Roman Province, 36 BC – AD 535* (London).

Wiseman, I., 1973. *Stobi: a Guide to the Excavations* (Beograd).

Zahariade, M. and Opait, A, 1986. 'A New Late Roman Fortification on the Territory of Romania: the Burgus at Topraichioi, Tulcea County'. In *Studien zu den Militärgrenzen Roms III: 13. Internationaler Limeskongress* (Aalen 1983, Stuttgart), 565–72.

Zahariade, M., *et al.*, 1987. 'Early and Late Roman Fortification at Independenta, Tulcea County', *Dacia* N.S. 31, 97–106.

Zimmermann Munn, M.L., 1985. 'A Late Roman Kiln Site in the Hermionid, Greece', *AJA 89*, 342–43.

Chapter 8

Specialisation, Trade, and Prosperity: an Overview of the Economy of the Late Antique Eastern Mediterranean[1]

Bryan Ward-Perkins

Prosperity and the Late Antique East

In 1964 A.H.M. Jones published his remarkable survey of the later Roman Empire.[2] His vision of the period was imposing, but undeniably bleak, dominated by a mighty State that weighed heavily upon its subjects. More recent research, by both historians and archaeologists, has painted the period in much lighter tones, emphasising in particular dynamic change rather than suffocating rigidity. A generation of English-speaking historians, charmed by that wizard of words Peter Brown has peopled the cities and villages of Late Antiquity, not with Jones' soldiers and bureaucrats, but with saints and ascetics, and with their more fallible human followers. At the same time – but at quite the other end of the scholarly spectrum – the arrival in the Mediterranean of techniques of stratigraphic excavation, of systematic rural survey, and of detailed pottery analysis, brought about an archaeological revolution. It was now possible to chart accurately, both a remarkable spread of late antique settlement within the eastern Mediterranean, and the equally impressive diffusion of pot-sherds from their place of production.

It is on this archaeological revolution that this collection of essays focuses, and specifically on the evidence for prosperity, production and exchange in the eastern Mediterranean. As the Editors make clear in their introduction (Chapter 1), this is an area of research well developed for the late antique western Mediterranean, but for which studies of synthesis of the eastern material are still scarce.[3] And yet in the entire Roman world it is in the East that fifth and sixth century economic complexity and prosperity can most readily be identified. When Jones wrote his chapter on 'The Land' – which is a sad tale of harsh social and legal restrictions, over-taxation, and consequent abandonment of the soil and depopulation – he already had to make exception for the flourishing late antique villages of the north Syrian limestone massif, studied and published in the 1950s by Georges Tchalenko.[4]

Subsequent research has shown that north Syria was no exception, but was instead typical of much of the late antique East. This research has taken different forms, according to the traditions of scholarship of the various archaeologists involved and to the nature of the local remains: in modern Greece, Cyprus, Israel and Jordan, field-survey; in upland and semi-desert regions of southern Turkey, Syria, Jordan and Israel, the examination, recording and excavation of impressive stone-built standing remains;

and, in both Israel and Jordan, the excavation of a remarkable series of mosaic pavements in rural churches and synagogues.[5] But, diverse though it is in its nature, all the evidence points to the same conclusion: that in much of the eastern Empire the fifth and sixth centuries saw not only a remarkable rise in the density and geographical spread of settlement, but also a rise in prosperity and in conspicuous expenditure.[6] For the eastern Empire, our view of the late antique economy has moved a very long way from Jones' grim assessment of 1964.

What is also striking, and very clear from the papers presented in this volume, is that the rise in the density and prosperity of rural settlements in a particular area is frequently paralleled by a spread of one or more archaeologically documented products from that same area, often over long distances and in large quantities. Table-wares from Cyprus, LR1 amphorae from Cyprus, Cilicia and northern Syria, and LR4 and LR5 amphorae from Palestine were distributed widely through the Mediterranean, and sometimes even beyond it, at more-or-less the same time as rural settlement boomed in their areas of production.[7] It is very hard to avoid the conclusion that these two phenomena are closely connected, in other words that the prosperity of much of the eastern empire was made possible by a rise in specialised production and exchange.

It is, however, too early to conclude that all parts of the eastern Empire benefited equally from late antique economic growth. For some areas, for instance central and eastern Asia Minor, we simply do not yet have reliable information. For others, such as Cyrenaica (Chapter 2) and the north Balkans in the fifth century, the evidence already suggests a late antique economy that was stagnant or even declining, rather than one that was flourishing.[8] Similarly, although it is very striking how small exotic objects, like imported items of table-ware, reached even inland rural sites in the late antique East (Chapter 3, p. 58), it is nonetheless obvious, and indeed demonstrated here through the varied quantities of imported marble on three Cypriot sites (Chapter 6, pp. 115–120), that settlements of high social status with good access to major transport routes enjoyed a much higher proportion of imported goods than other sites. In other words, rhythms of change and standards of prosperity were far from even and constant throughout the East.

Measuring Economic Activity

There is no doubt that, ideally, economic activity needs to be quantified. As is well-known, the documentary evidence is extremely disappointing when it comes to hard figures (to put it mildly); so we rely on archaeological data, particularly from the study of pottery, since this is a product which survives in sufficient quantities to be susceptible to statistical analysis. At present, quantified studies of eastern pottery are very rare indeed, whereas in the West a considerable body of quantified data has been collected over the last thirty years or so. Thus, when studying Aegean and Balkan trade (Chapter 7) we are still almost entirely dependent on pottery reports (when they exist at all), which provide only vague indications of the relative presence of different wares; whereas, in the West, in cities like Carthage, Rome and Marseille, an impressive number of different deposits have been excavated, carefully quantified, and published.

Of course, even where the percentage presence of a particular type of pottery has been published, this figure cannot immediately be translated into absolute quantities. It is perfectly possible for a high percentage presence of a particular type of amphora to represent in reality only a small total quantity of goods (as, for instance, is certainly the case with the imported Mediterranean wares excavated on fifth and sixth century sites in Britain).[9] A new approach to this problem is presented here for Palestinian amphorae (Chapter 3, p. 55). The proportion of Palestinian wine amphorae documented on two well-published western sites, Carthage and Rome, has been multiplied by the likely total annual consumption of wine in those cities in Late Antiquity (calculated from estimates of total population and estimates of probable per capita annual consumption of wine). The figures produced depend on so many uncertain variables that they can only be the very roughest of approximations. But, rough though they are, they do get us to estimates of absolute consumption, and thus begin to flesh out the bald percentages of the pottery reports. A 5.9% presence of Palestinian amphorae in fifth century Rome may, according to these calculations, have represented a consumption rate within the city of approximately 1.5 million litres of Palestinian wine a year, the equivalent of about 65,500 fifth-century amphorae or fifty-nine full ship-loads per annum. These figures are impressive (and, of course, do not include amphorae passing through Rome on the way to its hinterland), but not implausible; they certainly help to fill the fifth century Mediterranean with shipping (much of it eastern), rather than with just percentages.

Evidence of specialised production and exchange is at present most readily documented for goods distributed overseas, in particular amphorae and table-wares.[10] However, it would almost certainly be a mistake to see overseas distribution as the prime mover within the late antique economy. For every amphora that travelled across the Mediterranean, dozens almost certainly circulated only within a regional economy, and yet more only entirely locally. Flourishing overseas networks of distribution are what we can most readily document; but they almost certainly could not exist without parallel and interlocked regional and local networks of even greater economic significance. Without such overland systems of distribution, imported goods would have got no further than the major ports, and agricultural produce for export would never have reached them; whereas, in reality, we know that wine and oil for export did travel overland to ports and that imported goods often reached considerable distances from the sea (Chapter 1, p. 4; Chapter 3, pp. 51–55; Chapter 4, pp. 76–77). The well-documented evidence for overseas distribution should probably be seen not as an entirely separate phenomenon, but as *indicative* of much more extensive economic activity, of which it is only the most spectacular manifestation.

It is indeed important to maintain a degree of humility in the face of our own ignorance, and to realise that our data are so fragmentary that they will always provide only indications of levels of economic activity, rather than hard and fast information such as would satisfy a modern economist. For instance, there is no way yet that we can reliably place the entirely hypothetical figure of 65,500 fifth-century amphorae of Palestinian wine consumed in Rome each year in the context of consumption within Palestine itself and within neighbouring regions. What percentage of Palestinian production did Rome consume? Further work on levels of population and of production in Palestine and neighbouring regions (as in Chapter 3, pp. 49–50), may eventually provide some very hypothetical answers to this question. But it will certainly never be possible to set the production of those few products, which are archaeologically 'visible', within a reliable context of *total* production and exchange, both visible and invisible. For example, a chance reference in a saint's life happens to suggest that 'Antiochene' cloth was commonly used for clothing the poor in fourth century Rome.[11] It is possible that a vast industry existed, producing cloth in Antioch for the supply of Rome (and indeed perhaps for many other regions as well), and it is even possible that this industry dwarfed the production and exchange of the wine or oil from the same region, that we know to have been distributed widely and in large quantities in LR1 amphorae. But there will probably never be a way of knowing whether this was the case.

Pot-sherds are wonderful pieces of evidence, because they are so breakable, and yet so durable (and hence so common in excavation), and because they contain within themselves so much information. They are relatively easy to date and provenance, as a result of their varied form and fabric (which have already been the subject of extensive typological and mineralogical research). They represent low-value, high bulk goods that, furthermore, in the Roman period carried within them two of the principal cash-crops of the Mediterranean (wine and oil). One could scarcely envisage a more helpful category of evidence to provide an indication of the levels of specialisation and exchange within an economy. There is no doubt at all that pottery will continue to produce a mass of important new evidence. Indeed, these papers reveal that even some fundamental questions about major pot-types still remain to be resolved: for instance, what liquid(s) were most often carried in the Eastern Mediterranean's most popular amphora, the LR1 (Chapter 4, pp. 78–80)?

Beyond the Amphora

On the other hand, one of the most innovative and successful elements of this collection of essays, is that it does very successfully go 'beyond the amphora' (as suggested by the title of Chapter 5), and indeed beyond all varieties of pot-sherd. It is a real breath of fresh air to find within this volume so much discussion of goods other than pottery, particularly from the evidence of written sources – not only for regions where we have no very clear archaeological data for many of their exports (e.g. Egypt and Cyrenaica: Chapter 1, p. 5, notes 31–32; Chapter 2); but also for provinces where there is very useful information in literary texts to supplement and enhance the archaeological data (e.g. for Palestine and Cyprus: Chapter 3, pp. 45–46; Chapter 6: pp. 111–115). The evidence for the specialised production and bulk transportation, even over very long distances, of pottery (whether table-ware or amphora) is now so considerable, that this is a good moment to bring into play written evidence for other, archaeologically invisible, products. Since it is now beyond dispute that amphorae and table-wares were produced by specialised artisans, and were circulated very widely, it is now also much more likely than not that famous products of a region (known only from passing references in texts) were similarly produced and diffused.

Chapter 5 shows that it is not only through written texts, but also through under-exploited but available archaeological data that we can extend the range of goods for which significant evidence survives.[12] The information on the production and diffusion of copper-ware is striking. Obviously, this is a product several notches up, in both value and status, from pottery; but, at least within a local context, it would be at the cheaper end of the luxury market. Even within the Empire, there are occasional finds that suggest the large-scale production and diffusion of copper-ware (e.g. from the excavations at Sardis; from a dispersed hoard perhaps from Syria; and from shipwreck evidence: Chapter 5, pp. 88–95). But perhaps most impressive and indicative of all is the evidence of some 120 Byzantine copper items recovered from Germanic burials in northern Europe (including southern Britain), and of 122 similar pieces excavated in Nubian burials at Ballana and Qustul (Chapter 5, pp. 89–92). These two clusters of material survived here – outside the Empire, at the edge of the known world – because the peoples of these regions still had the helpful habit of burying their dead with grave-goods. Inside the Empire, almost all copper-ware will have disappeared without trace, because copper was always recycled, unless accidentally and irretrievably lost. The finds in Germanic Europe and Nubia are surely only the tiny, but impressive, tip of a gigantic iceberg of production and exchange in metal goods within the Mediterranean, where almost all the evidence has long since disappeared into the melting-pot.[13]

Furthermore, several of these papers demonstrate yet another way of circumventing, or rather supplementing, the evidence of pottery: by the detailed analysis of production sites. Some of the evidence produced is still rather obscure – what precisely were the various vats discovered in Cyrenaica really used for (Chapter 2)? Do they document specialisation, and perhaps also exports, otherwise invisible in the archaeological record? Also, it must be admitted that research in this field still lags far behind that in some regions of the western Mediterranean. It is, for instance, very striking that so few kiln sites producing LR2 amphorae have been discovered, so that we cannot yet confirm the probable Peloponnesian origin of this product (Chapter 7, p. 145), let alone speculate about the contexts in which it was produced. Even for LR1, the most common eastern amphora of Late Antiquity, the discovery of any kiln-sites is a very recent development, and only a handful are so far known, all of them as yet lacking any detailed archaeological context (Chapter 4, p. 77 ; Chapter 6, p. 113).[14]

However, in the few areas where good data do exist, as they do for rural installations in northern Syria (where many oil and wine presses still stand above ground) and in Israel (where a large number of wine presses have been excavated, or have been discovered cut into the natural rock), it is already possible to turn production sites into useable (if necessarily hypothetical) economic data. However accurate or not the details might be, it is quite clear that the huge number of presses documented in Israel and in northern Syria had at least the potential to produce massive surpluses, far above the needs of their local communities (Chapter 3, pp. 49–50; Chapter 4, pp. 80–82). This is a welcome approach, examining surplus at the point of production, rather than solely through amphora finds at the point of consumption (as in the case of Palestinian wine exported to Rome, mentioned above).[15]

Not only has work on production sites produced some very interesting data about possible output, it is also beginning to suggest a very interesting contrast between the economic expansion of the fourth-sixth century East and earlier expansion in the western Mediterranean. Specialised production and production for export in the western Mediterranean was often (though not invariably) associated with large-scale estate-production, sometimes with massive press installations, such as the triple wine presses of the Settefinestre villa in Latium, or the gigantic nine and seventeen olive press complexes of Henschir Sidi Hamdan and Senam Semana in Tripolitania.[16] In the East, despite extensive archaeological fieldwork, very large installations are rare: typical of the Syrian limestone massif and of Palaestina Prima and Secunda, for instance, is a scatter of single presses around a village (Chapter 4, p. 73, 81; Chapter 3, p. 49). If this contrast is borne out by future work, it does lend support to the traditional view that the landscape of the eastern Mediterranean was much less dominated by large estates than that of the West. Interestingly, despite this apparent difference in social structure, both regions (though each in a rather different period) seem to have been able to develop a high degree of specialisation in production and a secure place in networks of long-distance distribution.

In time, the excavation and analysis of production sites should also clarify the relationship between urban and rural crafts, and the location of artisan activity within both villages and towns. There are already important hints of patterns that may emerge: for instance, of primary glass-making on rural sites in Palestine, followed perhaps by the blowing of vessels outside towns, and their sale within them (Chapter 3, pp. 45–46, with Chapter 5, pp. 93–94). One important point, which is not yet clear, is when precisely Roman 'order' and the careful zoning of industrial activity outside and within towns gave way to the essentially unregulated Islamic and medieval town (Chapter 5, p. 94). There are clear indications of this change in the archaeological record – for instance, in the siting of a possible dying industry on top of the ruined *propylaeum* at Scythopolis and of a lime-kiln blocking a street near the forum of Cyrene (Chapter 3, p. 45; Chapter 2, p. 38), and in the placing of industrial installations inside former rich dwelling houses in several cities of Cyrenaica (Chapter 2 *passim*). But close dating for these changes is rarely available, and there may have been very considerable regional variation. The Cyrenaican evidence suggests an early change, indeed in many cases one that occurred already in the third century (e.g. Chapter 2); but the regular row of shops at Sardis (with only very light industrial activity within them), which were maintained in good order until destroyed by fire in the early seventh century, suggests a very different picture in western Asia Minor, almost four centuries later.[17]

Patterns and Mechanisms of Distribution

The pattern of the diffusion of goods in the eastern Mediterranean documented in these articles is a complex one – much more complex than that which has been charted in the late antique West, where the majority of table-wares and amphorae documented in excavation originated in Africa and then moved northwards (Chapter 1, pp. 3–4). For the western Mediterranean, it is still possible to argue that the diffusion of goods was primarily 'state-led': with most of this African production either travelling to Rome as requisitioned goods; or starting off as such (and then being sold on); or travelling, at least for the first stage of its journey, pick-a-back in the grain ships of Rome's *annona*. Even in the West, this model can only be applied to the period before the Vandal capture of Carthage in 439, whereas a diminishing but still impressive flow of African amphorae and red-slip ware continued to reach sites like Rome and Marseille through the fifth, sixth, and even into the seventh century.

In the East, a simple 'state-led' model for distribution cannot begin to fit the evidence for any period in Late Antiquity (Chapter 1, pp. 4–5; Chapter 3, pp. 58–59). Goods in the eastern Mediterranean seem to have travelled in all directions, and not just along the supply routes of the State, in particular the *annona*-axis between Egypt and Constantinople. Greek LR2 amphorae, for instance, are found not just in Constantinople and in the military forts of the Danube, but also in large quantities throughout the Aegean region (Chapter 7, pp. 139–145). Indeed, as is well-known from excavations in the western Mediterranean (at Carthage, Rome, Marseille and elsewhere) and as we have seen above in the case of Palestinian amphorae, a great many eastern amphorae even travelled outside the boundaries of the eastern empire into the barbarian West. These goods cannot by any stretch of the imagination have been part of some state-led diffusion of produce. They must, quite simply, have been traded for profit.

This is not to say that the state played no part in the diffusion of goods within the eastern Mediterranean. Indeed, Chapter 7 argues that provisioning for the army on the Danube is likely to have been one reason for the initial diffusion of Greek LR2 amphorae in the region, and perhaps also of LR1 amphorae from further away.[18] Similarly, the huge state-created market of Constantinople is likely to have been a major stimulus to specialised production and supply (Chapter 3, pp. 56–57). However, no-one would now argue for a monolithic state distribution machine, entirely supplanting private enterprise. As is argued above (Chapter 1, p. 13), even Constantinople relied, for most of its needs, on the market, rather than directly on the State. Similarly, the presence of LR2 amphorae on non-military sites in the Danube region must show that, as well as a state-system of military supply, there were also merchants importing amphorae for profit (or, at the very least, that some military supplies were subsequently sold into the market) (Chapter 7, p. 153). This picture finds support in a chance reference in the *Life of Saint Severinus*, set in the second half of the fifth century in the Danubian province of Noricum, a long way upriver from the area of Byzantine military control. From this source, we learn that merchants were still supplying the inhabitants of Noricum with some olive oil, although now in insufficient quantities to meet demand (presumably because of the disruption caused by marauding Rugi, Thuringians, Alamanni and others).[19] If merchants could reach Noricum in the later fifth century, they could reach almost anywhere.

Unfortunately, it is generally impossible to prove from objects alone the precise mechanisms of exchange that transported them over long distances. Both Phocaean red-slip ware (from north-west Turkey) and Cypriot red-slip ware reached south (as far as Egypt) in considerable quantities in Late Antiquity (Chapter 1, n. 30; Chapter 6, pp. 113–115); and Proconnesian marble from the Sea of Marmara has an equally impressive southward distribution (being present even in the churches of the Negev 'desert-cities').[20] It is entirely possible that these distributions (broadly along the axis that linked Constantinople and Alexandria) were facilitated by transport in grain-ships returning from the capital. On the other hand, both Proconnesian marble and the two red-slip wares also reached mainland Greece in quantity (and even some of the barbarian kingdoms). This diffusion westwards, out of the main axis of state supply, shows that by no means all distribution was state-led, and indeed raises the question of whether the State was needed to encourage distribution, even within the shipping routes that linked Constantinople and Alexandria. If goods could travel quite happily across the main axis of state supply, presumably through private enterprise, do we need to involve the State to explain distribution, even where it could have played a role?

The contrast between the patterns of distribution in the West and those in the East certainly show that models that may work for one region, will not necessarily work for a different one. It has been argued, for the western Mediterranean, that African red-slip ware often travelled north from the grain-producing areas, pick-a-back and as a profitable space-filler, within the full grain ships.[21] In the East something quite different happened: Egyptian red-slip ware, although an important local industry, never took off as an international product (Chapter 1, p. 4). Instead, Egypt and the provinces immediately to its north imported table-wares from Phocaea and Cyprus. In the eastern Mediterranean, if the grain-ships played any significant role in the diffusion of table-wares, it was after the grain had been delivered and when the empty hulls were filled with commercial goods to take home.

A picture of conflict between state-led and private/commercial diffusion of goods, that seems to underlie much discussion of the late antique economy, is probably a false one. The State did undoubtedly requisition goods, but it also encouraged commercial exchange: for instance, as we have seen, the vast majority of the goods needed to support the numerous and often rich inhabitants of Constantinople will have entered the city as goods for sale, not as an element of state taxation. It is indeed very unlikely that a complex and large-scale system of taxation in kind and coin could have existed in an economic vacuum – it is much easier to envisage it operating within a much richer and broader economic context, within which it was closely embedded. Rather than argue about the relative roles and scale of state exchange and private enterprise, it is likely that future research will concentrate more closely on identifying and describing the economic diversity that existed in the late antique East, whatever its precise origins, accepting that the latter often cannot be satisfactorily identified.

Late Antiquity and its End

One very important question does not receive full treatment in these articles: when did all this complexity and prosperity come to an end? Did decline set in with the plague of 541/2, or with the Persian invasions of the very early seventh century, or with the Arab conquest of the Levant in the 630s and 40s and the subsequent raids deep into Byzantine territory? Or did some privileged regions, in particular the Levantine heartlands of the Umayyad empire, continue to flourish into the eighth century, and perhaps even beyond?[22] There are hints within this volume of some answers to these questions, but no more than hints – for instance, of copper-ware production and export to the barbarian north continuing beyond the early seventh century (Chapter 5, p. 93); and of a varied picture in Cyprus, with prosperity lasting into the seventh century, but to different ends of the century in different parts of the island (Chapter 6, pp. 115–120). A fuller set of answers will have to await a subsequent volume; and, probably, much more archaeological research focused specifically on this difficult problem.

It is quite enough of an achievement that this volume of papers documents so fully and clearly the complexity and prosperity of the late antique East. Indeed it does so effectively enough to raise interesting questions about periodisation and about the relationship between 'History' and 'Archaeology.' As I made clear in my opening paragraph, both historians and archaeologists have, over the last thirty years, 'rescued' Late Antiquity from Jones' magisterial but suffocating vision of a 'Later Roman Empire'; but they have done so in very different directions. It is as though, in order to escape a middle ground dominated by Jones' late Roman State, historians have decided to move up into the stratosphere of religious sensibility, while archaeologists have taken the opposite path, down into the world of economic production and exchange. At first sight, very little unites these two approaches, besides a common wish to breathe more life into the period.

There may, however, be more that connects these two approaches than at first meets the eye. The current historical view, of a 'long' and culturally dynamic Late Antiquity, reaching to the end of the sixth century and beyond, was born in the eastern Mediterranean (the main focus, for instance, of Peter Brown's highly influential *World of Late Antiquity*), and has remained most at home there.[23] The eastern provinces are, without question, the true heartlands of today's 'Late Antiquity'. These are, of course, the same provinces, in precisely the same period, that archaeology has shown to have been economically prosperous and sophisticated in the fourth to sixth centuries.[24] It is therefore more than likely that the current heroes of late antique History (whether Fathers of the Church, founders of monasteries, pilgrims, or ascetics), were just as much products of the economic prosperity and complexity of the late antique East, although at the luxury end of the market, as the amphorae, table-wares and metalwork, so fully documented by Archaeology.[25] Both shared common roots in the hard labour and ingenuity of the peasants, artisans and merchants of the eastern Empire, who are the chief protagonists of this volume and who proved capable of transforming subsistence into a remarkable level of prosperity, and thereby of social and cultural complexity. It is only when the archaeological and intellectual maps are brought together, that the current shape of Late Antiquity makes complete sense.

Notes

1   This article is written as an extended comment on the other papers presented in this Volume, rather than as a free-standing piece (hence the frequent references to the other chapters). I have written on the late antique economy, at greater length and more generally (East and West), in Cameron, Ward-Perkins and Whitby, 2000: 315–91. I would like to thank Michael Decker and Sean Kingsley for their invitation, both to participate in the symposium and to provide some concluding remarks to the collection of published papers; and I am also very grateful to Sean Kingsley for several ideas and references used in this article.

2 Jones, 1964.

3 A notable exception is the volume *Hommes et richesses* 1989. See also the brief, but highly informative introduction (by Cécile Morrisson and Jean-Pierre Sodini) to Hodges and Whitehouse, 1996: 5–11.

4 Jones, 1964: 823 (the last four sentences of his chapter, and the only significant intrusion of archaeology into his work on the economy), referring to Tchalenko, 1953–8.

5 Field-surveys – Greece: summary of several surveys in Alcock, 1993: 33–92 (though with an emphasis on the earlier Roman period); Cyprus: see Chapter 6, pp. 109–111; Israel: Gibson, 1995; Jordan: most recently, Barker *et al.*, 1997. Standing remains – southern Turkey: e.g. Foss, 1994; Syria: Tchalenko, 1953–8; Tate, 1992; Jordan: e.g. Sartre, 1985; Israel (Negev): e.g. Segal, 1983. Excavated church-mosaics in Israel and Jordan – Ovadiah and Ovadiah, 1987; Piccirillo 1993. The most obvious gap in the archaeological record is the absence of recent extensive and systematic work from Egypt.

6 In modern Syria, Greece and Israel – the three regions where the best comparative material is currently available – rural settlements are much commoner from the late antique period than from early Roman times.

7 Cypriot red-slip ware: Chapter 6, pp. 113–114. LR1: Chapter 4, pp. 76–77, and Chapter 6, p. 113. LR4 & 5: Chapter 3, pp. 52–55.

8 Balkans: Cameron, Ward-Perkins and Whitby, 2000: 701–703, with further references.

9 Thomas, 1988.

10 Also for marble, a topic little covered in this volume; though see Chapter 6, p. 115 for marble imports into Cyprus. For a general discussion of the distribution of late antique Proconnesian products: Sodini, 1989.

11 Discussed in Cameron, Ward-Perkins and Whitby, 2000: 376–377.

12 See also Chapter 3, pp. 45–46, for archaeological and documentary evidence from Palestine of the specialised production of goods other than pottery. Particularly interesting, because the various species can be reliably provenanced, is the evidence for the distribution of fish overland, even over long distances.

13 It is, of course, theoretically possible that copper objects were produced only, or primarily, for export; but this is both intrinsically unlikely, and disproved by the finds within the Empire.

14 Contrast the more than 100 kiln sites documented in Spain's Guadalquivir valley (the production zone of early-imperial Dressel 20 amphorae): Chapter 4, p. 69.

15 This approach was pioneered by David Mattingly for Tripolitanian oil-production: Mattingly, 1988.

16 Settefinestre: Carandini *et al.*, 1985: 241–50. Tripolitania: Mattingly, 1988: 36–38; Oates, 1953: 97–101 (Henschir Sidi Hamdan); Cowper, 1897: 279–282 (Senam Semana).

17 Crawford, 1990.

18 For similar recent views, in favour of military supply as the prime reason for the distribution of many amphorae: Arthur, 1998; and Van Alfen, 1996: 210–213, where the early seventh century Yassi Ada shipwreck, with its cargo of 103 LR1 and 719 LR2 amphorae, has ceased to be a merchant ship and has become instead a supply ship for Heraclius' military campaigns.

19 *Vita S. Severini*, ed. R. Noll (Berlin 1963), cap.28 (English trans. L. Bieler, *Eugippius: the Life of Saint Severin* (Washington 1965), p. 83). The story tells of how Severinus miraculously provided oil for the poor of the city of Lauriacum, which was then difficult to obtain "because merchants had great difficulty in importing it". On the one hand, the story testifies to an interruption of regular supply; but, on the other hand, it shows that some oil still reached Noricum and that it was still regarded as a staple necessity. Needless to say, our source does not tell us whether the oil arrived overland from the head of the Adriatic, or (perhaps more likely) upriver from the Black Sea; nor does it tell us which kind of amphora it travelled in.

20 For Proconnesian: Sodini, 1989: 163–186.

21 E.g. Wickham, 1988: 190–2.

22 For examples of different views: Kennedy, 1985 (plague and other disasters); Foss, 1975 (Persians); Tchalenko, 1953–8, I: 435–438 (Arab invasions); Pentz, 1992 (no change, even into Arab times).

23 Brown 1971a. A very rough count of the entries in the recent Bowersock, Brown & Grabar (1999), found 169 that are specifically eastern, against 66 that are western.

24 The match is a close one, except perhaps for Greece, which seems to have shared the fifth and sixth century prosperity of the East, but (outside Athens) plays a minor role in the religious and intellectual history of the period.

25 Chapter 6, p. 114 provides one small but very concrete example of a close connection between economic and cultural sophistication. Literary texts reveal the contacts of Cypriot churchmen with Alexandria, Constantinople and elsewhere. These all-important cultural links were undoubtedly the result of Cyprus' central position on the shipping-routes of both late antique trade and the late antique State. Historians have in the past been very prepared to explore the economic foundations of religious experience (see, for instance, Brown 1971b, on the social and economic context that may have produced the Syrian Holy Man). But historical work of the last decade or so has rather shaken loose of functional anthropology, sociology, and any suspicion of economic determinism, and now tends implicitly (though not explicitly) to treat religious life as if it occurred in a material vacuum.

Bibliography

Arthur, P., 1998. 'Eastern Mediterranean Amphorae between 500 and 700: a View from Italy'. In L. Saguì (ed.) *Ceramica in Italia: VI-VII secolo. Atti del convegno in onore di John W. Hayes, Roma, 11–13 maggio 1995* (Firenze), 157–183.

Barker, G.W., Creighton, O.H., Gilbertson, D.D., Hunt, C.O., Mattingly, D.J., McClaren, S.J. and Thomas, D.C., 1997. 'The Wadi Feynan Project, Southern Jordan: a Preliminary Report on Geomorphology and Landscape Archaeology', *Levant* 29, 19–40.

Bowersock, G.W., Brown, P. and Grabar, O. (ed.), 1999. *Late Antiquity. A Guide to the Postclassical World* (Cambridge, Mass).

Brown, P.R.L., 1971a. *The World of Late Antiquity* (London).

Brown, P.R.L., 1971b. 'The Rise and Function of the Holy Man in Late Antiquity', *JRS* 61, 80–101. (Reprinted in Brown, P., 1982. *Society and the Holy in Late Antiquity* – London, 103–152).

Cameron, A., Ward-Perkins, B. and Whitby M. (ed.), 2000. *The Cambridge Ancient History* XIV (*Late Antiquity: Empire and Successors, A.D. 425–600*) (Cambridge).

Carandini, A. *et al.*, 1985. *Settefinestre. Una villa schiavistica nell'Etruria romana*, 3 vols. (Modena).

Cowper, H.S., 1897. *The Hill of the Graces* (London).

Crawford, J.S., 1990. *The Byzantine Shops at Sardis* (Cambridge, Mass.).

Foss, C., 1975. 'The Persians in Asia Minor and the End of Antiquity', *English Historical Review* 90, 721–747.

Foss, C., 1994. 'The Lycian Coast in the Byzantine age', *DOP* 48, 1–52.

Gibson, S., 1995. *Landscape Archaeology and Ancient Agricultural Field Systems in Palestine* (Doctor of Philosophy Thesis, University College, London).

Hodges, R. and Whitehouse, D., 1996. *Mahomet, Charlemagne et les origines de l'Europe* (Paris). (French edition of their *Mohammed, Charlemagne and the Origins of Europe*, London 1983.)

Hommes et richesses dans l'Empire byzantin, vol. I, (IVe-VIIe siècle), 1989 (Paris).

Jones, A.H.M., 1964. *The Later Roman Empire. A Social, Economic and Administrative Survey* (Basil Blackwell, Oxford).

Kennedy, H., 1985. 'The Last Century of Byzantine Syria: a Reinterpretation', *Byzantinische Forschungen* 10, 141–183.

Mattingly, D.J., 1988. 'Oil for Export? A Comparison of Libyan, Spanish and Tunisian Olive Oil Production in the Roman Empire', *JRA* 1, 33–56.

Oates, D., 1953. 'The Tripolitanian Gebel: Settlement of the Roman Period around Gasr ed-Dauun', *PBSR* 21, 81–117

Ovadiah, A. and Ovadiah, R., 1987. *Mosaic Pavements in Israel* (Rome).

Pentz, P., 1992. *The Invisible Conquest. The Ontogenesis of Sixth and Seventh Century Syria* (Copenhagen).

Piccirillo, M., 1993. *The Mosaics of Jordan* (Amman).

Sartre, M., 1985. *Bostra des origines à l'Islam* (Paris).

Segal, A., 1983. *The Byzantine City of Shivta (Esbeita), Negev Desert, Israel* (Oxford).

Sodini, J.-P., 1989. 'Le commerce des marbres à l'époque protobyzantine'. In *Hommes et Richesses dans l'Empire byzantin*, 163–186.

Tate, G., 1992. *Les Campagnes de la Syrie du nord du IIe au VIIe siècle. Un example d'expansion démographique et économique à la fin de l'Antiquité* (Paris).

Tchalenko, G., 1953–8. *Villages antiques de la Syrie du nord. Le massif du Bélus a l'époque romaine*, 3 vols. (Paris).

Thomas, C., 1988. 'The Context of Tintagel. A New Model for the Diffusion of Post-Roman Mediterranean Imports', *Cornish Archaeology* 27, 7–25.

Van Alfen, P.G., 1996. 'New Light on the 7th-c. Yassi Ada Shipwreck', *JRA* 9, 189–213.

Wickham, C., 1988. 'Marx, Sherlock Holmes and Late Roman Commerce', *JRS* 78, 183–193.